New Directions in Latino American Cultures

Series Editors
Licia Fiol-Matta
Latin American and Puerto Rican Studies
Lehman College
Bronx, New York, USA

José Quiroga
Emory University
Atlanta, Georgia, USA

The series will publish book-length studies, essay collections, and readers on sexualities and power, queer studies and class, feminisms and race, post-coloniality and nationalism, music, media, and literature. Traditional, transcultural, theoretically savvy, and politically sharp, this series will set the stage for new directions in the changing field. We will accept well-conceived, coherent book proposals, essay collections, and readers.

More information about this series at
http://www.springer.com/series/14745

Mabel Moraña

Arguedas / Vargas Llosa

Dilemmas and Assemblages

Translated by Andrew Ascherl

Mabel Moraña
Washington University in St. Louis
St. Louis, Missouri, USA

Translated by Andrew Ascherl

New Directions in Latino American Cultures
ISBN 978-1-137-57522-7   ISBN 978-1-137-57187-8   (eBook)
DOI 10.1057/978-1-137-57187-8

Library of Congress Control Number: 2016939270

© The Editor(s) (if applicable) and The Author(s) 2016
This work is subject to copyright. All rights are solely and exclusively licensed by the Publisher, whether the whole or part of the material is concerned, specifically the rights of translation, reprinting, reuse of illustrations, recitation, broadcasting, reproduction on microfilms or in any other physical way, and transmission or information storage and retrieval, electronic adaptation, computer software, or by similar or dissimilar methodology now known or hereafter developed.
The use of general descriptive names, registered names, trademarks, service marks, etc. in this publication does not imply, even in the absence of a specific statement, that such names are exempt from the relevant protective laws and regulations and therefore free for general use.
The publisher, the authors and the editors are safe to assume that the advice and information in this book are believed to be true and accurate at the date of publication. Neither the publisher nor the authors or the editors give a warranty, express or implied, with respect to the material contained herein or for any errors or omissions that may have been made.

Cover illustration © The Paper Street Design Company / Alamy Stock Photo

Printed on acid-free paper

This Palgrave Macmillan imprint is published by Springer Nature
The registered company is Nature America Inc. New York

Translator's Note

While most of the sources cited by the author are from Spanish editions (either originally or in translation), throughout the translation of this book I have used published English translations whenever they were available. When published English translations were used for quotations from works by the authors on whom this study focuses (José María Arguedas and Mario Vargas Llosa), the in-text citations refer first to the Spanish edition and then to the published English translation. All other translations of Spanish-language sources in this book are my own. I have also included a minimal number of brief translator's notes among the author's original endnotes. These appear in square brackets. I would like to express my gratitude to Mabel Moraña for the opportunity to work with her on this translation, as well as for her patience, kindness, generosity, and friendship.

Acknowledgments

This book emerged from an invitation from Sergio R. Franco, a professor at Temple University, to participate in a session dedicated to the work of José María Arguedas that took place at the 30th International Congress of the Latin American Studies Association in San Francisco in May 2012. The return to the work of Arguedas and Vargas Llosa from new theoretical perspectives motivated me to carry out, starting with this meeting, an extensive confrontation with both writers' work, above all with regard to their cultural and ideological origins. This book would not have been possible without the stimulus and great quantity of materials, information, and clues which Sergio generously brought to my attention during the process of drafting the manuscript. To him, then, goes all of my gratitude. I also thank Alex Eastman, for his bibliographic assistance and for the careful correction of drafts and page proofs. To Iberoamericana/Vervuert, and particularly to Simón Bernal, goes my thankful appreciation for their invaluable editorial care. My appreciation to Martha Canfield, director of the Centro Studi Jorge Eielson, in Florence, Italy, and to Alessio Minelli (photographer), for allowing me access to the reproduction of the beautiful painting that appears on the cover of the Spanish edition of this book.

Contents

1 Introduction — 1

2 Opening — 7

3 Arguedas and Vargas Llosa, or the Dilemmas of the Model Intellectual — 13

4 Archaism as Floating Signifier — 39

5 Language as a Battlefield (I): The Dilemma of the Sign — 69

6 Language as a Battlefield (II): The Narcissism of the Voice — 103

7 Toward a Poetics of Social Change: Truth, Modernity, and the National Subject in José María Arguedas — 129

8 Which Truth? Otherness and Melodrama in Vargas Llosa — 163

9 Endpoint? Death/The Nobel Prize   221

Works Cited   249

Index   269

CHAPTER 1

Introduction

In analyzing the work of Arguedas and Vargas Llosa, I have not attempted to address comprehensively the properly literary aspects of their texts but rather to interpret them as a cultural gesture and an ideological *performance* whose characteristics and meaning are inseparable from the historical, social, and political contexts that correspond to the distinct stages of their production as literature. At the same time, I have been attentive to the representational strategies that each author sets in motion in order to penetrate the intricate labyrinths of Andean culture and also, in Vargas Llosa's case, of the variety of settings over which the flight of his imagination and technique unfolds. Few authors from the same country and the same era are in fact more disparate than those with whom the following pages are concerned. At the same time, this disparity leads to significant intersections and even convergences that are worth analyzing as alternative paths by which one can approach the social and ideological problematic of our time.

My project has been to address both José María Arguedas's fragmented, unconcluded work and Mario Vargas Llosa's triumphant poetics starting from the questions that the most recent cultural theory allows us to formulate around issues such as the construction of subjectivity, the representation of affects, and the relations between aesthetics and ideology and the biopolitical dimension that it reveals, in a decisively influential way, in Latin American symbolic production. I have also elaborated on the relation between the weakened category of national culture and

© The Editor(s) (if applicable) and The Author(s) 2016
M. Moraña, *Arguedas / Vargas Llosa*,
DOI 10.1057/978-1-137-57187-8_1

the emergence of global frameworks, between culture and the market, and between language, identity, and representation. It has been essential for me to understand the mode in which anthropology and literary creation are intertwined in the poetic discursivity of both authors and the forms in which each one of them negotiates, in his own way, conflicts of class, ethnicity, and genre in the construction of fiction. My intent has been to pursue meticulously the transformations of both authors' work over the decades, facing the processes of social and political change in the Andean region and, more broadly, in Latin America, without neglecting to consider other phenomena that correspond to the greater context of Western culture: the decreasingly auratic dimension of contemporary literature, the notorious fluctuations of the function of the intellectual with respect to the state, the complex responses to modernization issuing from very diverse politico-ideological horizons, the transnational dynamics that intensified and reconfigured themselves after the end of the Cold War, the always-present intercultural conflict in postcolonial societies, and the symbolic dimension of these struggles which encounter in language their most arduous battlefield.

My objective has been to disentangle the specific forms that each of these writers produce in order to deal with the dilemmas of their time: tradition/modernity, Quechua/Spanish, local/global, socialism/(neo)liberalism, affect and desire/instrumental reason, Western epistemology/local knowledges, and identity/alterity. The emphasis of the present study could not help but fall back, again and again, on the negotiations, ambiguities, and conflicts that characterize the coexistence of diverse epistemologies in the same cultural context and the same era. In a broader sense, to put it in Deleuze and Guattari's terms, the question that motivates the present study can be summarized by asking what the relation is between the literary machine and the war machine, and the love machine and the revolution machine. For me, the principal meaning of the texts I analyze here is based on this relation, and although each reader can answer these questions for himself or herself, the following pages advance hypotheses that can potentially convert these issues into a collective practice.

The notion of the *dilemma* or *double bind* suggested by Gayatri Spivak in her most recent book, *An Aesthetic Education in the Era of Globalization* (2012), opens up theoretical paths that certainly have numerous predecessors in the Latin American critical context. The already copious literature on Arguedas and Vargas Llosa was instrumental to my approach to the literary and cultural textualities of both authors, as well as for my comprehension of their particular spaces of intellectual activity. However, from the perspective that I propose here, properly literary textuality is less relevant than the cultural texture that contains it. But if theoretical references—above all, postcolonial criticism—abound in this study, they are no more important than those which refer to the culture of the Andean region, to its tenacious and painful political, social, and cultural intrahistory, whose alternatives and significations I have only been able to trace here through modest and approximate explorations.

In the Spanish version of this book, two quotations were offered at the beginning of the text. The first is from Homi Bhabha, who asks:

> What was modernity for those who were part of its instrumentality or governmentality but, for reasons of race or gender or economic status, were excluded from its norms of rationality, or its prescriptions of progress? What contending and competing discourses of emancipation or equality, what forms of identity and agency, emerge from the "discontents" of modernity? (qtd. in Mitchell, "Translator Translated" 82)

The second passage is from Gilles Deleuze and Félix Guattari:

> As an assemblage, a book has only itself, in connection with other assemblages [...] We will never ask what a book means, as signified or signifier; we will not look for anything to understand in it. We will ask what it functions with, in connection with what other things it does or does not transmit intensities [...] A book itself is a little machine; what is the relation (also measurable) of this literary machine to a war machine, love machine, revolutionary machine, etc.—and an abstract machine that sweeps them along? We have been criticized for overquoting literary authors. But when one writes, the only question is which other machine the literary machine can be plugged into, must be plugged into in order to work. (*A Thousand Plateaus* 4)

In my opinion, these passages (which originally appeared as epigraphs) summarize key aspects of the study of the Peruvian cultural field on which this book focuses and provide a form of conceptual orientation for interpreting the subject matter. The first quotation, from Bhabha, problematizes the connections between modernity and rationality, between progress and legitimacy, and focuses on the hierarchies, exclusions, and discriminatory policies that from the beginning accompanied the implementation of modernity, particularly in peripheral societies. At the same time, Bhabha introjects the element of affect into the interpretation of modern protocols: the idea of "discontent," the frustration of desire, and the indifference of modernity toward need and inequality. The second passage, from Deleuze and Guattari, introduces, in turn, the notion of the book as a *literary machine* that connects with others for the production of meaning, a process that in no way develops without the articulation of multiple domains. The literary work is understood as a complex system of assemblages that is by nature always fluid, unfinished, and unstable. The essential operation is that of *plugging into*, of producing connections and circuits that "transmit intensities"—not definite meanings, but significant fluxes that constantly defy our expectations and redefine the horizons of rationality, emotion, and imagination. These are the premises that guide the present study, allowing the analysis of these two Peruvian authors to reveal a challenging platform for the exploration of the margins of modernity in Latin America and for the responses that emerge in order to contest the project of modernity from different aesthetic and ideological positions.

The suicide of José María Arguedas and the Nobel Prize bestowed on Mario Vargas Llosa constitute, both separately and in conjunction, a challenge to Latin American thought. The former marks an iconic, historical, and symbolic instance of the development of cultural resistance among the oppressed peoples of the continent since the Conquest and signals the inescapable necessity of political and cultural reflection on the themes of decolonization and the search for *other* forms of modernity for the heterogeneous societies of Latin America. The latter establishes a specific form of cultural and ideological leadership that recognizes in the market, in the integration of Latin America to the West, and in the articulation of the politics of neoliberalism new forms of intellectual triumphalism and cosmopolitanism from which Latin American *difference* is absorbed and resignified in the wide and foreign field of world literature. Together, these events expose the tensions, conflicts, and paradoxes that form the plot of the regional and continental history of Latin America, particularly since the Cuban Revolution. The coexistence of both events—mourning and recognition, tragedy and celebration—marks a crossroads that goes far beyond the field of literature; it also has to do with profound ethical and ideological choices, with very distinct forms of the development of subjectivity, and with the disparate meanings that emerge from both language and silence. Both events, the suicide and the Nobel Prize, themselves constitute a challenge to the country that was the birthplace of some of the most profound poetic, narrative, and essayistic works written in Spanish.

Disappearance and recognition thus present an unavoidable invitation to think the history of the modern nation, its unkept promises, its benefits, and its social cost.

I have always considered Peru to be a source of some of the principal landmarks of Latin American cultural history—from the early texts of Inca Garcilaso, Guamán Poma de Ayala, and Lunarejo, to the brilliant thought of José Carlos Mariátegui, Antonio Cornejo Polar, and Aníbal Quijano, through the fundamental contributions of Gustavo Gutiérrez and Alberto Flores Galindo. These landmarks allow us to read with clarity the persistent and difficult development of critical-theoretical categories and of socio-cultural analysis that, without abandoning dialog with political and philosophical thought from other latitudes or resorting to glorification and fundamentalism, are able to capture Latin American specificity. Although this is an undertaking that takes place in different ways in different regions of Latin America, in my opinion, no country offers, as does Peru, so many conceptual propositions and achievements or such a luxurious and profound panorama of poetic diversity. I have dedicated a good part of my academic effort over the years to the study of some of the authors mentioned above, and I remain convinced that Peru holds many of the keys to comprehending the thorny process leading to the decolonization of thought and the critical understanding of Latin American history. If this book contributes in any way to these objectives, it will have been worth both the effort devoted to its development and the risks that its proposals imply.

CHAPTER 2

Opening

In her recent book *An Aesthetic Education in the Era of Globalization* (2012), Gayatri Spivak elaborates with special emphasis on different aspects of the role of language and translation in the construction of identities, above all in relation to the migrant subject, which seems to be the most prominent and elusive inhabitant of postmodernity. Conceiving of identity, beyond all essentialism, as a fluctuating concept that is socially and politically negotiated and as a product that is designed to be exchanged and consumed (where use value and exchange value can be seen as two sides of the same coin of the symbolic product), Spivak weaves the different chapters of her book around the idea of the *double bind*[1] that defines the construction of subjectivity and the processes of representation in postcolonial settings. She understands "double bind" as the type of dilemma or disjunction in which two possible yet contrary directions of action or thought are situated. The individual subjected to the double bind thus remains imprisoned in an (il)logic that, based on language, simultaneously introduces an option or alternative while closing off the possibility of choosing. This double bind (without a doubt, a *no-win situation*[2]) is considered a form of control that does not involve outright coercion: a problematic conjuncture—an ethico-ideological trap—that, from a position of authority and power, submits the subject to an irresolvable conflict that generates anxiety and confusion, causing a fragmentation of his or her world, and dissociating the consciousness that perceives it.[3] Created as a theoretical tool for understanding the cognitive pathology that accompanies schizophrenia, the concept of the double bind is expanded here to the field of cultural theory and to the study of the dilemmas that particularly affect the postcolonial subject and the relations between dominant and dominated cultures.

The wide range of multicultural examples Spivak analyzes (almost all linked to European literature or to the literature of former European colonies) illuminates this conflict as inherent to the subaltern condition and to its symbolic production, arising either *in situ* or in transnationalized spaces. Such scenarios require careful analysis due to the changes that these displacements generate at a subjective and socio-cultural level. Undoubtedly, in spite of her constant references to Middle Eastern cultures, the author tries to present an analysis that is global in scope. Lamentably, Spivak seems not to know of the existence of José María Arguedas (1911–1969), a postcolonial, migrant, transcultural writer who would exemplarily illustrate her argument. Her references to Latin America or to *latinidad* are limited to a number of references to Guillermo Gómez Peña, one reference to Ernesto Cardenal by way of his poem about Marilyn Monroe, and some obligatory allusions to Aimé Cesaire and magical realism.

This attention to socio-cultural and politico-economic dilemmas is nothing new in Latin American debates. These topics have been the extensive focus of long-running debates about *criollo* consciousness and *mestizaje*. The latter discussions, which have taken place in various ways since the colonial period but which have intensified during the modern period, have more recently given way to the categories of transculturation (Ortiz/Rama), non-dialectical heterogeneity (Cornejo Polar), and cultural hybridity (García Canclini), which focus above all on the theme of intercultural struggles and identitarian dissociation in peripheral societies. However, the main difference between these critical categories (which seem to overlap with one another at times) lies in the way in which they conceive of the modes of development of socio-cultural conflict. While the notion of transculturation focuses mainly on movements from the center to the periphery and the cultural assimilation promoted by the processes of modernization in local cultures, the concept of hybridity aims at reconciling diverse qualities into a new form that would be distinct from those which gave rise to it.[4] The concept of non-dialectical heterogeneity, meanwhile, suggests the maintenance of the disruption that affects a social totality (such as that in the Andean region, for example) characterized by the tense coexistence of seemingly irreconcilable cultural systems. In this concept, the conflict between heterogeneous elements is not diluted in a final synthesis, nor are antagonisms dissolved in the liberal notion of *difference*. Rather, the oppositions that occur in contexts marked by cultural heterogeneity remain present, active, or latent, and are closely linked to relations of domination which regulate the forms and degrees of the negotiation of power and the effectivity of the resistance that this power generates. Antonio Cornejo Polar is probably the critic who most accurately identifies in the Latin American context the persistence of a double and unsynthesized register that extends to the realms of social experience as much as it does to issues of language (Spanish/pre-Hispanic languages), communicative technologies (orality/writing), and forms of literary expression at the level of both "high" and popular culture (novel/song, for example). These cultural tensions, which point to the economic inequalities and antagonisms inherited from colonialism, have resulted in *systems* that coexist in constant conflict within the same cultural sphere and temporality. As a *double bind*, this duality affects both intersubjective dynamics and the perception and interpretation of the world and life, resulting in a subject split by a conflict that encompasses all levels of identity construction, both individually and collectively.[5]

My intention here is not to provide a critical review of these categories (which is something I have done elsewhere), but rather to approach the idea of the *double bind* at the fraught intersection between the work of two prominent Peruvian writers: José María Arguedas and Mario Vargas Llosa.[6] The first, considered the intellectual hero and undisputed icon of cultural criticism, is one of the most representative figures of the dilemmas of interculturality in Latin America. He is likewise a symbol of failure and hope, of fragmentation, and of the struggle for the impossible overcoming of the polarities of race and class that span Latin American history. The second, a privileged inhabitant of the World Republic of Letters, situated at the heights of international recognition (the culmination of which was the Nobel Prize in Literature awarded to him in 2010), extends, however, across a less admirable spectrum, ranging from the leftist positions he held in the 1960s to his failed campaign for the Peruvian presidency in the 1990s.[7]

Both authors can be united and separated, on the one hand, by their respective conceptions of history (their particular mode of articulating the historical dimension in the fictional domain), and, on the other hand, by the demands and rituals of language. They are separated above all by the different responses that each one articulates with regard to the dilemma of postcoloniality in the Andean region and the ways in which both authors are inscribed within the context of Occidentalism. In this study I propose that it is precisely in positioning both writers in relation to capitalist modernity and at the linguistic level (which is to say, in the conception and uses of language, in the strategies and content of communication and literary expressivity) where one can resolve the dilemmas that traverse the entirety of their work, and moreover, the intellectual and ethico-ideological fields that each one represents and which constitute opposite extremes of the modern *spectrum*. I understand *spectrum* here in its double sense as both *specter* and as *scope* or *range of degrees* in order to allude to, in the first place, the ghostly—spectral, material and at the same time illusory, *ideological*—forms of modernity that haunt the Andean region, society, and imaginary, as a project of Westernization initiated during the colonial period and developed by the subsequent criollo republic. Secondly, *spectrum* also makes an allusion to the broad range of models and *intensities* that accompany the process of domination and resistance, of assimilation and differentiation that began in the 16th century and that both authors—each in his own register—re-present and revise in the context of modernity.

To understand the way in which this double spectrality is revised and revisited in the work of the authors discussed here (the modalities assumed by the ghost of an imagined modernity and the nuanced and unequal modes of application of that civilizing matrix in the Andean region), it is necessary to clarify the aesthetico-axiological platform that sustains their literary and cultural production and the way in which each author assumes the role of intellectual in his historical moment.

Notes

1. [In English in the original, as are all instances of this term in the present book.—Tr.]
2. [In English in the original.—Tr.]
3. The anthropologist Gregory Bateson elaborates the theory of the double bind as a tool for understanding schizophrenia, understood as a state of internalized confusion for the victim who feels subjected to dilemmas that do not present any satisfactory, rational resolution. This state perpetuates the feeling of cognitive division and the fragmentation of consciousness. As Gayatri Spivak indicates (as does Homi Bhabha in elaborating his idea of the "Third Space"), in *1984*, George Orwell describes "doublethink" as the type of "double thought" or double register which is necessary to function

in repressive societies. In Orwell's concept, however, an element of "bad faith" or hypocrisy obscures the use of this procedure, which Bhabha and Spivak conceive of (within their own theories) instead as a strategy of subaltern resistance. See, for example, the way in which Spivak explains her appropriation of the concept throughout *An Aesthetic Education* as well as Rutherford's interview with Bhabha, in which they discuss these issues.

4. These concepts have yielded diverse interpretations and critiques. Moreiras considers the notion of transculturation, for instance, to be an integrative formula that tends to dilute antagonisms. For example, in the 6th chapter of *The Exhaustion of Difference*, which is titled "The End of Magical Realism: José María Arguedas's Passionate Signifier," he says: "Transculturation is a war machine, feeding on cultural difference, whose principal function is the reduction of the possibility of radical cultural heterogeneity" (195–96). The function of hybridity, in turn, has resulted in the aforementioned concept of the "Third Space" developed by Homi Bhabha, which will be discussed later in the present study and which in many aspects is linked to the idea of the "double bind" reformulated by Spivak.

5. Cornejo Polar approaches the theme of the "migrant subject" from this perspective in which he radicalizes a conflict that concerns, in reality, the Andean subject in its totality. He refers to the "bifrontal and—if one wishes to exaggerate—schizophrenic narratives" of "migrant discourse" ("Non-Dialectical Heterogeneity" 118). See also, "Indigenismo and Heterogeneous Literatures: Their Double Sociocultural Statute," where Cornejo Polar more expansively discusses the concept of heterogeneity.

6. Related to these topics, see the studies dedicated to the work of Cornejo Polar, particularly to the theme of heterogeneity and transculturation in *Asedios a la heterogeneidad cultural*, edited by José Antonio Mazzotti and in *Antonio Cornejo Polar y los estudios latinoamericanos*, edited by Fiedhelm Schmidt-Welle, as well as the essays included in my books *Crítica impura* and *La escritura del límite*.

7. For different approaches to Vargas Llosa's ideological and literary fluctuations, see, for example, Degregori, Rowe, and Kokotovic. On Vargas Llosa's dissociation from the Cuban Revolution in response to the Padilla affair, see Kristal, "Política y crítica literaria," which includes details of the polemical exchanges between Vargas Llosa and Cuban authorities (Fidel Castro and Haydée Santamaría, among others), as well as of his prohibition from returning to Cuba and the international repercussions of this chain of events.

CHAPTER 3

Arguedas and Vargas Llosa, or the Dilemmas of the Model Intellectual

According to Enrique Lihn, "We are contemporaries of different histories."[1] Without a doubt, Arguedas and Vargas Llosa constitute two very different models of the modern intellectual, although the relation that each one maintains and elaborates with modernity is completely different from that of the other. Both writers' work represents a distinct version of social and cultural alterity in Peru, starting from a field of clearly differentiated values and representational strategies. Thus, we can ask ourselves, borrowing Spivak's words, what is "the self that runs the *other machine*," which is to say, the "self that causes the other" (100, emphasis added)? This is a question that orients us toward the construction of subjectivities based on elements of class and ethnicity, as well as on the inscription of the lettered subject [*el letrado*][2] in cultural institutionality (tradition, canonical record, educational apparatus, media, etc.), an inscription that both of the authors analyzed in this book utilize in a particular way.

In this sense, it is fair to say that both Arguedas and Vargas Llosa are conscious of their own paradigmatic value within national, regional, and Latin American culture, although each one inscribes his work and the intellectual profile that sustains it in the lettered world [*el mundo letrado*] according to his own social and ideological position. Arguedas, rooted in the persistent values of the dominated culture, can be defined by an adherence to indigenous traditions, myths, and idiosyncrasies, the struggle with language, and the reclamation of the margin as a space of resistance and epistemological privilege. This space articulates alternative knowledges, marginalized languages, and social practices marked by the sign of heroic victimization. In this sense, within both the Latin American imaginary and that of international Latin-Americanism, Arguedas occupies not only the place of utopian desire but also the more obscure site—the blind spot—of bourgeois guilt. He embodies in many senses the prototypical tormented writer who is one with his work and ends up sacrificing himself at the altar of literature. At the same time, he represents the alternative to—the negative image of—the organic intellectual whose success is based on his or her complicity with power. However, his work is by no means univalent, and it is torn [*se debate*] between the dominant lettered, criollo regime with respect to which Arguedas laboriously defines his own production and the marginalized, vernacular Quechua culture that fed his childhood experiences and nourished his adult sensibility.

Through a flawless lyricism in which experience is sublimated in discourse and pain is sublimated in poetry, Arguedas's work testifies to the crimes of colonialism and those of the criollo republic. The identification with the subaltern, the experience of migration, translingualism, biculturality, aesthetic experimentalism, heightened sensibility, vitalism, the experience of nature, the opening toward the mythic, the magical and the popular, the primacy given to the individual and the private, and the confessional and testimonial tone of his texts, all constitute in themselves a kind of cultural capital that stands at the axis of the fluctuating and at times *light*[3] panorama of postmodernity from which one can re-evaluate his writing. Many of his premises and declarations and many of the strategies he utilizes to direct his denunciation of marginalization and his vindication of the cultural value of the oppressed seem to have emerged as a sign of the theoretical and social problematic catalyzed, since the final decades of the twentieth century, by the breakdown of the redemptive promise of capitalist modernity understood as the gateway to a world of plenitude, progress, integration, and tolerance. The primary problems taken up by the agenda of cultural and postcolonial studies include the discrediting of the myth of the nation as a unified, homogeneous, and harmonious space (and its celebration, instead, as a place of intercultural hybridization); the emphasis on the theme of *difference* constructed as identity; the importance attributed to language and translation as areas for the negotiation of not only linguistic but also cultural meaning; the recognition of migration as one of the essential components for understanding our time; the relevance attributed to the construction of individual and collective subjectivity and to the theme of affect as a space of articulation between the public and private spheres; and the understanding of the biopolitical dimension and of the theme of race and ethnicity as the axes on which the mechanisms of social control and collective resistance turn. These new critical and theoretical approaches are instrumental for the study of a world in which the modern certainties that constituted the foundation of national imaginaries are collapsing. In large measure, the terms of this collapse were advanced by Arguedas, whose work prepared the field for the understanding of new spatial and temporal arrangements, for the construction of unprecedented forms of identity, and for the emergence of new modalities of knowledge production and intercultural dynamics. These transformations destabilize *the social* and empty *the political* of traditional meanings and familiar mechanisms. Understood as a symbolic *intervention* in capitalist modernity, Arguedas's works acquire, from this critical perspective, a transnationalized and transdisciplinary dimension that reinscribes his writing in the literary canon and even corrects previous readings of his texts which followed a more narrowly regionalist approach.[4]

At the other end of the spectrum, Vargas Llosa could in turn be described as paradigmatic of another form of the incorporation of the intellectual into the peripheral Latin American modernity. In Latin America, one can still read the traces of the lettered criollo who, since colonial times, has been sustained through the power of the word—both literary and political—as a device for personal legitimation and as a platform for public expression. Vargas Llosa's narrative work is grounded in the skillful use of literary language which characterized the exclusive and commercialized framework of the Boom and which early in his career propelled him to superstardom within the Andean literary canon. In fact, since the 1960s, his work has been defined as representative of Peruvian national culture and understood thereby as the ideal paradigm articulating the distinct socio-cultural systems that make up Peruvian society. At the same time, his work was presented as an exportable product through which the local was negotiated according to a universality determined as much by the transnationalization of symbolic capital as by the accelerated reintegration of the region into the cultural realm of Occidentalism. Thus, from the beginning of his literary career, Vargas Llosa has positioned himself in the very heart of the intellectual field that, in those years, was defined by the triumph of the Cuban Revolution and the political orientations that emerged from it. As an urban criollo intellectual intimately connected to the processes of both national and international cultural institutionalization, he soon became one of the most recognizable and charismatic Latin

American figures of his time. His works represent middle-class participation in market society and the promotion of the symbolic commodities it generates as marketable products available for mass consumption.[5]

However, Vargas Llosa's distancing of himself from the Latin American left in response to the "Padilla affair," as well as his criticisms of the Cuban regime more generally, created an irreparable fissure in the intellectual field that affected if not exactly the literary appreciation of his work then certainly the politico-ideological perception of his intellectual profile.[6] Although he continues to be recognized as one of the most brilliant and prolific writers in the Spanish language, accumulating awards and increasing his visibility to a planetary extent, the decomposition of Vargas Llosa's image would constitute for many an obvious and irreversible symptom of the tensions and conflicts that affected not only the literary system of the Boom but also the cultural project of "the new man." Linked to the principles of the Cuban Revolution, this latter project attempted to consolidate a viable alternative to "bourgeois humanism," moving away from the prototype of the elitist, Westernized intellectual that it represented.[7] Vargas Llosa's split with the Cuban regime (which can be traced back to the beginning of the 1970s, following his criticisms of Fidel Castro's government for its policies condemning ideological dissent in Cuba) gradually increased until it crystallized into a recalcitrant anti-leftism that culminated in his support for intransigently conservative governments such as that of Margaret Thatcher. Ultimately, his positions assumed an increasingly neoliberal politico-economic reorientation that favored the tyranny of capital and the dynamics of globalized markets over national interests.[8]

Misha Kokotovic offers a good overview of Vargas Llosa's rightward turn in the 1980s, a time which corresponded with the most active period of the Shining Path in Peru, and explains that the racism of criollo elites was revived in this context. Indeed, according to a fundamental tendency of hegemonic thought in Peru, the Shining Path's ideology is considered to be identical to barbarism, confirming the idea that the indigenous population (which was in reality the main victim of Andean political radicalization) constitutes "an obstacle to progress and the principal reason for Peru's backwardness" (Kokotovic, *La modernidad andina* 217).[9] Based on his increasingly pure individualism, now reinforced by an adherence to the ideology of the global market and an elitism that his growing literary fame helped to consolidate, Vargas Llosa situated himself in a neoliberal position that was as distant from the socialism he previously had passionately defended as it was from populism, which he considered a corrupted, demagogic, and regressive form of indigenism. It was with this cultural and ideological baggage that Vargas Llosa went about constructing everywhere his profile as a public intellectual in which he came to be obsessively occupied by the analysis of the dichotomy of *modernity* versus *barbarism*, both in his fiction and in Peruvian society in the 1980s. Vargas Llosa understood that it was precisely in this conjuncture (which he saw as an insurmountable obstacle), in this ethical, political, and cultural *double bind* that both the future of the Andean region and the destiny of his own cultural prominence were to be defined, this latter already having been impacted, although not diminished, by his estrangement from the left and by his identification with the most reactionary wing of contemporary politics.

In 1983, Vargas Llosa chaired an investigative commission (appointed by President Fernando Belaúnde Terry) to investigate the murder of eight journalists in Uchuraccay, the seat of the Iquicha indigenous communities in the department of Ayacucho.[10] The commission's work, as well as Vargas Llosa's own ideas following these events, both in the official report and in his later fictional texts, reveals the insistence of prejudicial, stereotypical, and discriminatory ways in which Vargas Llosa conceived of Andean ethnico-cultural heterogeneity. This manifested itself particularly in the way he portrayed the situation of indigenous communities, their long history of marginalization and state aggression, and the tragic consequences of their resistance to the hegemonic power of the criollo nation.

The commission chaired by Vargas Llosa recognized that among the causes that would have led the villagers of Uchuraccay, who confused the journalists with members of the Shining Path, to decide to kill them in an act of self-defense should also be counted the abuses that the indigenous population was subjected to by both Shining Path "*terrucos*"[11] and the Peruvian Armed Forces. The interaction of forces from very different ideological, social, and political positions created a very complex narrative of responsibility, guilt, and victimization around these events. Reliably analyzed by anthropologists, political scientists, and cultural critics, the events of Uchuraccay reveal the existence of an intricate discursive web that ultimately points to the Peruvian state's incompetence and disengagement regarding structural violence in Peru as well as the situation of indigenous communities in a society that is constitutively blind to the epistemologies and concrete needs of the latter as a segment of society that forms part of the national project.[12] In an excellent article titled "Alien to Modernity: The Rationalization of Discrimination" (2006), dedicated to analyzing the purpose of the Uchuraccay investigative commission, Jean Franco comments on, among other issues, the role that Vargas Llosa took on, assuming the position of rationality and common sense in relation to a world that he presents as an anachronistic and chaotic space marked by violence and magical-religious tendencies that would, because of its irrationality, come into conflict with the dominant models of thought in the criollo nation. As Franco notes, the way the report characterizes the distinct social groups involved in the events of Uchuraccay is telling. The representation of the journalists (the language used to describe them, the reconstruction of their actions while they approached Ayacucho, the anecdotes presented to the reader) strongly contrast with the report's obscure and grudging references to the indigenous population of the region. While the former are treated with respect, as representatives of criollo reason threatened by barbarism, the Indians (the collective character of the Uchuraccay tragedy that reappears, e.g., in Vargas Llosa's *Lituma en los Andes* [*Death in the Andes*], *El hablador* [*The Storyteller*], and other works) are represented as primitive, driven by instinct, and unable to control their actions or completely understand their consequences (Franco, "Alien to Modernity" 6–8). Thus, Vargas Llosa establishes two narratives that correspond to the parallel and isolated social strata of Andean society, which he organizes according to a preexisting hierarchy of qualities and rights connected to the pyramid of power and its cultural codes.

Franco notes: "As the Truth Commission pointed out, Vargas Llosa's interpretation of events conformed to a paradigm that essentialized cultural differences and constructed an image of a totally isolated and primitive community outside of citizenship" ("Alien to Modernity" 11). Franco also notes that Vargas Llosa's intervention in the events of Uchuraccay, both in his investigative conduct and in the report and articles that he produced about these events ("Sangre y mugre de Uchuraccay," e.g.), causes one to wonder about the roots of violence in Peru and the nature and scope of the system of justice in a multilingual society. At the same time, it also raises suspicions about the ethical status of literature and the authoritarian nature of the *lettered city*. In the social context in which the events of Uchuraccay occurred, where the indigenous population (a majority of whom are exclusively Quechua speakers) had already been cornered by marginalization and the violence unleashed on the region by the Shining Path and state forces, criollo institutions fail to encompass the tremendous diversity of the often contradictory social layers that those events simultaneously hide and reveal. It is undoubtedly the dominant epistemology, the resources of the hegemonic language, and the technology of writing and of enlightenment rationality that emerge victoriously in the simulacrum that is the application of social justice in multicultural societies. In these environments, the majority of the indigenous population does not actively participate in political life, is not considered part of civil society, and has little to no control over the apparatuses which investigate and represent the *truth* that always seems to reside in a space which excludes victims.

The culturalist strategy of contriving inequality as *difference* and relegating the consequences of exclusion and social injustice to the intangible realm of *alterity* stands in the way of focusing on the deep and structural problematic of race and class which affects postcolonial societies and which has haunted the torturous process of modernization for centuries. Always interpreted in relational terms—the Indian as the negative of citizenship, a status controlled by the privileged sectors of Peruvian society—the social articulation of race and class points (at least when it refers to the indigenous sector) to the identification of a residue, a track or trace of the ancient pre-Hispanic cultures that continue to disappear as history marches on. However, even during the process of disappearance, these cultures are seen as an impediment to the drives of progress and the projects of imposing a Europeanized—or North-Americanized—modernity which excludes otherness. The rights of the indigenous population are not understood as *natural*, but rather as *endowed* through reluctant processes of negotiation, concession, or restitution that always point to the hierarchical position from which some ground is strategically ceded in the unfinished struggle for total control of the most dispossessed sectors.

As a writer, Vargas Llosa converts into a literary theme the still-burning embers of ancient cultures without perceiving them as part of contemporary society.[13] In his political and literary treatment of this segment of Peruvian society, Vargas Llosa always makes evident the gap that exists between the epistemologies, practices, and values of marginal groups and the criollo or mestizo sectors that have been able to integrate themselves into the national project. As a conservative intellectual, Vargas Llosa fills this gap with paternalism, disdain, or condescension as he sees fit. Incapable of perceiving a popular, alternative, and heterogeneous modernity that would be able to include difference in a participatory or egalitarian way, the intellectual model that Vargas Llosa embodies confronts indigenous culture as someone visiting archeological ruins, trying to extract an aesthetic yield from something that is at the same time a testimony of what once was and what is ceasing to be, something that exists almost because of its absence, offering the spectacle of its progressive and inevitable disappearance.

In his analysis of the events of Uchuraccay and of the role played by the commission chaired by Vargas Llosa, anthropologist Enrique Mayer has referred to "the missing voices" in the process of the revelation of popular testimonies about the murder of the journalists, particularly the voices of the villagers. Their accounts were always mediated by translators, interpreters, and experts in different academic disciplines and transmitted in an elliptical form, in third person, and in indirect discourse, as if behind the representational strategies of alterity a concrete (id)entity capable of representing itself did not exist (Mayer 490). Vargas Llosa records clipped words, confusing expressions, and silences from the other, without reproducing any complete phrase in an attempt to be faithful to the speaker's thought. This fragmentation indicates not only the speaker's supposed rational deficiency but also his or her existence beyond the limits of the cultural and axiological system of the nation-state: the *other* as the specter of an unattainable citizenship, an anonymous member of a people that lives at the margin of history, as Hegel prophesied about America. With a condescension that constitutes more a cultural gesture than a recognition of the materiality and exigencies of the dominated culture and the underlying causes of the events that sink their roots into the systemic inequality of Peru and its official state policies, the indigenous population is considered simultaneously guilty and exempt from all responsibility. They are the anomalous subject of a regime that places them both inside and outside a legal order that encompasses them without representing them.

One of the forms of address the villagers used toward the members of the investigative commission, according to Vargas Llosa's account, was "*Señor Gobierno*" ["Mister Government"], a prosopopoeia that assumes an insurmountable interpersonal distance and a symptomatic identification between intellectual and institution, knowledge and authority, insofar as both share, from the perspective of the dominated, an identical form of participation in the discourses, protocols, and privileges of hegemonic power. Thus, Vargas Llosa produces a narrative of Uchuraccay that appeals to rhetorical manipulation, lexical selection, and the ability of the writer to construct a potential version of events that accommodates the stereotypes which abound in the collective imagination and which insinuate themselves into Peru's institutional order. As Manuel Scorza notes, the annihilation that accompanies the history of indigenous people is understood almost as a natural event. This history always glosses over the massacre of indigenous people as if it were simply one of the four seasons of the year. The principle invoked by Vargas Llosa according to which literature must "lie knowingly" (which is the reason why he always carefully investigates the contexts that frame his fiction) circles like a specter around the textuality and texture of the never adequately clarified events of Uchuraccay. The problem of truth is the specter that haunts not only the writing that narrates these events but the consciousness and social guilt that they generate.[14]

Literature and politics converge constantly in Vargas Llosa's work, not just as cultural and ideological practices but also as spaces of performativity and personal projection that converge on the public stage, mutually feeding off one another. In 1984, the Peruvian writer sustained a polemic with Mario Benedetti about issues linked to ideology and the role of the Latin American intellectual in the context of the transformations that were taking place throughout the continent during that decade.[15] In this polemic, Vargas Llosa refers to the intellectual "as a factor of political underdevelopment in our countries" and as the cause of the "ideological obscurantism" that remains alive in the region. His criticisms of intellectuals who continue to demonstrate their commitment to the Cuban Revolution point to the previously mentioned process of using language as a device for self-legitimation. His criticisms also take aim at these intellectuals' attempts to maintain the field of culture not just as a space for competition in cultural production but also as a realm of power struggles that have a direct impact on the commodification of symbolic products.[16] The attacks that Vargas Llosa directed toward writers of the stature of Alejo Carpentier and Pablo Neruda, for example, illustrate a strategy for the distribution of recognition or criticism in which Vargas Llosa assigned himself to the place of equanimity and ideological freedom that would stand in contrast to the political positions of those who have been "conditioned" by ideology and act, according to the Peruvian writer, as if they were socialist robots. It is not difficult to perceive in Vargas Llosa's attacks a paradoxically defensive attitude that over-argues his positions and diminishes (classifies, reduces, and devalues) anyone in an opposing position as a way of consolidating cultural power.

In spite of the lightweight and conventional way in which Vargas Llosa confronts the understanding of *the social*, he seems to have a clear consciousness of the existence and operation of what Pierre Bourdieu calls *social subspaces* (i.e., the artistic, the political) inasmuch as they are fields that have their own hierarchies and develop their own power struggles within the broad network of relations that constitute civil society. Hence his intention to place himself in both spheres and control the logics that define them: their behaviors, the places they have in common, and the values that drive them. Likewise, Vargas Llosa does not seem unable to recognize the relative autonomy of the *cultural field* within which social agents, through their dispositions and habits, develop social strategies and carry out power struggles, connecting themselves in distinct ways to prevailing forms of domination and resistance. It is in this context that his condemnation of the "cut-rate intellectual" [*"intelectual barato"*] appears, referring to intellectuals who are prone to ideological fanaticism. In the 1980s, Vargas Llosa identified this notion with Marxist tendencies that he considered to be dogmatic and doctrinaire, a characterization that calls to mind religious persecution.[17] Following his usual strategy of assigning virtues and defects, his characterization of the "cut-rate intellectual" is supported by the idea of the degradation of Western culture which Vargas Llosa would develop throughout his career as a call-to-arms in response to the perceived loss of Western values and the growing feebleness of "high" culture, which is under threat from democratization. In "El intelectual barato,"[18] Vargas Llosa chronicles the progressive disappearance of the traditional and romantic role of the thinker, artist, or cultural professional. In this conception, the intellectual is seen as a cultural hero, a bastion of knowledge, and a defender of civic values:

> the belief, or rather the myth, existed that intellectuality constituted something like the moral reserve of the nation. It was thought that this small, helpless body, which heroically survived in an environment where artistic endeavor, research, and thought not only were not supported but often harassed by power, was kept uncontaminated from the decadence and corruption that had been practically undermining society as a whole: administration, justice, institutions, political parties, the armed forces, unions, and universities. ("El intelectual barato" 332)

This vision of the intellectual as "the keeper of values which in other spheres [...] had disappeared" concealed, according to the writer, his true marginalization from public affairs. "The truth was," Vargas Llosa indicates, "that the intellectual had not been given a seat at the table of power because, with rare exceptions, he was not tolerated there" (ibid. 333). "The appetite for power" that Vargas Llosa identifies in Peruvian intellectuals who participated in the process of the expropriation of newspapers carried out by socialist General Juan Velasco Alvarado in 1974 is the characteristic feature of those whom the writer calls "cut-rate intellectuals."[19] In a complementary classification, Vargas Llosa also criticizes those who fall within the rubric of the "progressive intellectual," which is to say those who are active in revolutionary parties, hold anti-imperialist convictions, and defend the nationalized economy but at the same time take advantage of the privileges available from ties to developed countries from which they extract benefits and perks, thereby casting aside their political convictions. Vargas Llosa places himself in a presumably uncontaminated and superior position from which he pontificates on ideological themes, assigning to himself the role of defender of ethical values.

Vargas Llosa approaches the theme of the intellectual from a (melo)dramatic, literary perspective, as if he were dealing with any of the other categories he uses as inspiration for his fictional worlds. Thus, although enthroned in the mechanisms of power, or at least always wary of reaching that juncture, Vargas Llosa perceives the ideal intellectual as a rebel, a supposed self-designated leader of a constant and generalized resistance against the status quo. In this sense, José Miguel Oviedo estimates that it is the figure of transgression that principally attracts Vargas Llosa, and this can be seen in the way he represents soldiers and intellectuals in his work. In this sense, Vargas Llosa's novels establish a subtle critique of heroism, starting from those socio-cultural subsystems and the violations of hierarchical ordering that they inspire. However, as Oviedo observes, these "traitors" are always destroyed or reabsorbed by the system that they want to subvert. In this framework:

> the great figure who embraces and integrates all those violators of the general norm, the most incorrigible, combative, and contradictory character is the intellectual who, within Vargas Llosa's personal ideology, is always defined as marginal, like a sniper and perhaps like an undesirable who has lost all rights in society. (Oviedo, "Tema del traidor y del héroe" 149)

The "distribution of symbolic capital" is one of the principal roles which high-profile intellectuals assign to themselves. As a paradigmatic superstar writer, Vargas Llosa claimed this prominent position for himself precisely during one of the most productive (and therefore most competitive) periods of international attention to Latin American literature (and Latin American culture in general), a flourishing which lent itself to innumerable interpretations, exegeses, and critiques by Peruvian intellectuals.[20]

Indictments, classifications, verdicts, pronouncements, critiques, and controversies about the most varied themes of culture and politics create a verbal panoply which reveals the arrogance and the individualism of one who passes judgment and disseminates opinions, placing himself above others who become the object of his commentaries. Regarding the practice of literature, insofar as it is an exchangeable commodity in the global market, Vargas Llosa has struggled to maintain an organizing role for himself within the intellectual and ideological fields. From his perspective, these fields possess a symbolic potential that could have been compromised in some measure due to his estrangement from the left. His understanding of the cultural field as a *field of force* compels him to insist on the role of literature since its connection to dominant social projects defines its modes and degrees of symbolic dissemination and actual influence in society.

In the polemic with Mario Benedetti mentioned above, Vargas Llosa reaffirms the idea of literature as an almost indiscriminate form of *subversion*, which is to say, as a practice of individualism that perpetuates the romantic idea of the non-conformist, rebellious intellectual against the status quo, whatever the political definition of this status quo or its efficacy for organizing civil society may be. He indicates, for example, in his study of *Tirant lo Blanc*, that:

> A novel is something more than an objective document; it is above all a subjective testimony of the reasons that lead whoever wrote it to become a creator, a *radical rebel*. And this subjective testimony always consists in a personal addiction to the world, in an insidious correction of reality, in a transformation of life. (Vargas Llosa, *Carta de batalla por Tirant lo Blanc* 86)

As we can see, Vargas Llosa's vision of the novelist has to do with the projection of an *I* that assumes itself as an indispensable part of reality, which is to say, as a subjectivity that should leave its imprint on society based on an attitude more than on a concrete message, a public gesture that seems to matter more than the content it carries. In many cases, Vargas Llosa's own intellectual *performance*[21] seems to adapt itself too specifically to those principles and to empty itself of real substance, making evident, as Benedetti notes, a frivolity and an eagerness for public recognition that exceeds the importance and the foundations of the opinions being expressed. This rhetoric, riddled with commonplaces about the mission of the intellectual and the role of literature (which Vargas Llosa has elaborated on at length for more than five decades), at times overshadows his literary work.

Beginning in 1987, Vargas Llosa threw himself completely into politics and launched a campaign for the presidency of Peru. The principles that informed his new public endeavor were the same as those that we have been discussing up to this point. This rightward-turning intellectual's profile, faithful to the most orthodox versions of economic neoliberalism and the conservative politics that accompany it at the socio-cultural level, was bolstered by his modernizing obsession against barbarism and the "Africanization" of Peru (Degregori, "El aprendiz de brujo" 73). As Jean Franco has pointed out, the identification of archaism and violence as "indigenous" qualities, an argument that had long justified racial discrimination among the dominant sectors of Peruvian society, became for Vargas Llosa a true "political philosophy." At the macro level, the neoliberal program was now augmented by derivative ideas that sought to energize the electorate by emphasizing individual responsibility and the wealth of opportunities offered by the globalized economy: any nation can advance along the path of progress if they know how to compete at the international level, the same way any citizen can incorporate himself into the world of business. For Vargas Llosa, political, social, and economic exclusion is a personal choice that has little to do with objective conditions and institutional responsibilities.

Vargas Llosa's political program recuperated old clichés of conservative politics which emerged like larvae around specific themes, such as Alan García's project of nationalizing the banks, which Vargas Llosa considered a "dictatorial threat." This would be the catalyst for Vargas Llosa's political career—a career characterized as an example of "aristocratic liberalism" (Degregori, "El aprendiz de brujo" 94) and which would culminate in 1990 with Alberto Fujimori's electoral triumph.[22]

Carlos Iván Degregori has highlighted the complete marginalization of the theme of ethnicity in Vargas Llosa's political and aesthetic agenda as an indication of a discriminatory conservatism based on "the mercantilism of skin," a concept the Peruvian anthropologist defines as

> that benefit enjoyed even today by criollos in Peru, where having white or light-colored skin still grants one the good fortune of "differential rent," which one gains simply by showing one's face. Or not even that. Sometimes it is enough to speak Spanish (and speak it well, with a particular accent)

over the telephone to make it effective, because it is an advantage of ethnicity and culture rather than race. ("El aprendiz de brujo" 87–88)

What Degregori is trying to define here, apart from an unblemished residue of coloniality in the unequal and peripheral modernity of the Andean region, is an oligarchic feature that is internalized and manipulated by the criollo intellectual (in this case, Vargas Llosa) in whom the psycho-social tendencies of his class manifest themselves and are taken to the extreme from his particular position in the elite literary and political world of Peru. From this position, the opinions he expresses disseminate and perpetuate a reactionary ideology that is projected over distinct cultural and political fields.

Mirko Lauer has defined Vargas Llosa as an "imaginary liberal" who, having rejected ostensibly leftist positions that were fashionable in the 1960s, ran a predictable path that led to the conservative platform on which his presidential candidacy rested decades later. Interpreting this trajectory, Lauer highlights above all Vargas Llosa's tireless search for a "social and political identification of class" based on which he assumed his place as the "liberal critical consciousness" of Peru, which was, according to Lauer, a paradoxical pursuit for someone who, as a leader of that ideology, should have rather aspired to act ethically beyond the divisions of class and political parties ("El liberal imaginario" 100–101). According to Lauer, Vargas Llosa's marketing and promotion of his own work was organized around his desire for maximum visibility and public influence. The social and political responsibilities that Vargas Llosa took on, such as serving as president of the Pen Club or as chair of the commission charged with investigating the events in Uchuraccay, for example, reveal his desire to cover the greatest possible spectrum of positions and roles at both a national and international level, reflecting a level of activity that would help to consolidate his celebrity and result in an increase in the popularity and consumption of his literature. But apart from this desire for omnipresence, what stands out for Lauer is the inconsistent and deferential practice that accompanied Vargas Llosa's emergence as a cultural civil servant. This practice was especially characterized by a "double standard" that Vargas Llosa applied to the interpretation of the plural and multiple reality of his time, opposing modernity to primitivism, and criollo society to indigenous society, as if he were referring to a really existing romantic struggle between good and evil which did not need to be debated or discussed.

Thus, the shift from leftism to Thatcherism evident in Vargas Llosa's ideological trajectory could be summarized as a Manichean tendency completely opposed to the necessary impartiality and political and social sensitivity that one would expect to be required of a member of the Commission for Truth and Reconciliation which investigated the Uchuraccay murders and the war between the Shining Path and the Peruvian Armed Forces in the 1980s.[23] Degregori explains Vargas Llosa's involvement in these commissions as a consequence of a "political marketing"[24] effort that not only makes politics into a spectacle but in so doing also disseminates a flattening and simplistic perspective on social reality in which both socio-cultural complexity and ideological density are diluted. As Degregori argues:

> converting the market into a unique principle of order and uniformity, [the members of Movimiento Libertad] imagine a flat, level country where the only differences are those that exist between rich and poor: they underestimate both the country's politics and its ethnic and cultural complexity. ("El aprendiz de brujo" 84)

Compared with the central role Vargas Llosa played during the global rise to popularity of Latin American writers in the 1960s, Arguedas (who in 1958, on the cusp of the Boom, published *Los ríos profundos* [*Deep Rivers*, 1978]), despite his growing visibility, was always located at the margin of that select group of writers, probably owing to the fact that he was widely considered to be a writer of "indigenous literature" and in this sense connected to the localism of his predecessors. Perceived as an author who was inclined toward ethnographic documentarism and the production of fictitious worlds related to folklore and *costumbrismo*, and considered by some to be the bearer of a destructive and melancholic vision of indigenous history, Arguedas's work circulated through different channels than those traversed by his contemporaries and enjoyed a more delayed recognition at the national and international levels—a recognition which was undoubtedly based on very different factors from those that would contribute to the enshrinement of the most famous writers of the Boom. Indeed, the relation that Arguedas's texts established between literature and anthropology seemed to follow a direction that was completely foreign to the experimentalism of authors like García Márquez, Fuentes, Cortázar, and Vargas Llosa himself, who ventured down the open roads of the *nouveau roman* and made use of cinematic techniques and popular culture when they were not taking refuge in the imagery of magical realism.

In 1963, Vargas Llosa won the Premio Biblioteca Seix Barral for *La ciudad y los perros* [*The Time of the Hero* (1968)], a novel that would eventually come to be seen as one of the original sources of the Boom for its combination of intimacy and social criticism, particularly for its treatment of the corrupt culture of the military.[25] Close on the heels of this first novel and the stories published a few years earlier under the title *Los Jefes* (1959),[26] Vargas Llosa's subsequent works firmly established him as the first author from the region who managed to transcend the limitations of the local and achieve a universality that allowed him to write about themes related to Andean culture that, while representing the uniqueness of Peruvian society, its conflicts, and its imaginaries, was also able (based on a controlled and attractive exoticism) to make itself accessible and appealing to readers in other parts of the world. Already from this early stage of his career, there was every indication that Vargas Llosa had found a foolproof way to conquer the transnationalized space of literature and to go on to become part of a canon that would transcend the dreaded limits of provincialism and the mediocrity of national culture that he fervently denounced on so many occasions.

A comparative reading of Arguedas and Vargas Llosa—less as textual analysis than as a way to explore the cultural practices of both authors—could very well be extended to other aspects of each author's work, including the construction of fictional worlds, the uses of language, and the total intellectual, aesthetic, and ideological project that is inscribed in their literature. Perhaps most seductive about this approach to reading is the possibility of exploring the processes by which these authors consolidated a paradigmatic quality of the 1960s and the decades that followed. This was an era rife with ideological polarization and widely varying positions with regard to the role of art and literature and the cultural and political relations within the turbulent and marginal societies of Latin America. It was characterized by a climate of unstable international tension, armed conflicts, resistance movements, and accelerated population growth. Indeed, to the politico-ideological repercussions of the events of May 1968 in France, the massacre at Tlatelolco in Mexico City in the same year, and the advance of pre-dictatorial repression in the Southern Cone in the late 1960s and early 1970s, one can add the economic downturn that occurred throughout Latin America in those years. These factors hastened the decline of models of social analysis that had served to conceptualize collective experience since Romanticism and that Boom literature would recycle due to its liberal foundations.[27] Various critics (Hernán Vidal and

Jean Franco, among others) have analyzed the relations between ideology and fiction as well as the new avenues that literature proposes for the elaboration of historical memory at the continental level.

The confrontation of positions regarding the relation between literature and society became a burning question when national liberation movements and Latin American dictatorships intensified, provoking a polarizing climate which in the realm of culture tended toward two possible outcomes: an attachment to local circumstances, or conversely, a defense of the cosmopolitan or simply that which has been reterritorialized. This is to say that a dilemma emerged in which the national, regional, and/or autochthonous were pitted against the foreign, modernizing, and transnational—to say nothing of the entire gamut of possible relations between both outcomes. In this sense, the Arguedas/Vargas Llosa relation recalls the polemic that Arguedas maintained with Cortázar between 1967 and 1969, during which the Argentine writer, who defined himself as "a moral being," contrasted the "planetary vision" that he supported (which was facilitated by the distance of exile) to the narrow "national mission" he ascribed to other writers, like Arguedas, based on their rootedness in "homeland values."[28] Vargas Llosa referred to Arguedas as a "cultural ecologist" (*La utopía arcaica* 29) because of his desire to preserve indigenous culture from modernizing depredation. We will see later that a very different attitude characterized Vargas Llosa's position regarding the theme of the autochthonous and the links between literature and anthropology in terms of both culture and methodology.

The primary dilemma of the era, posed between the exigencies of national rootedness and the search for universality, was not new in Latin America, where telluric rootedness and cosmopolitan drives had for centuries constituted two sides of the same coin of the project of modernization. If the transculturating drive had developed as a formula for a possible form of overcoming the restrictions imposed by regionalism, the *double bind* implicit in the dynamic of transculturation left even more to the discovery of the foundational conflicts that emerged from the systemic violence of postcolonial societies. For Cortázar, for instance, Arguedas's localist orientation was uncomfortably close to the dangers of fundamentalism and to a possible exaltation of nationalism that, according to the Argentine writer, could end up reviving the experience of fascism and was neither exempt from parochialism nor from the exoticization of the local, those self-celebratory impulses driven by liberalism (internationalization, free-trade, progressivism, etc.). In his polemic with Arguedas, the author of *Rayuela* opposed totalization to fragmentism, territoriality to transnationalization:

> Tellurism [...] is profoundly foreign to me because it is narrow, parochial, I would even say crude: I can understand it and admire it in those who cannot manage, for whatever reason, a totalizing vision of culture and history and who concentrate all of their talent in "local" tasks, but it seems to me a prelude to the worst developments of negative nationalism when it becomes the credo of writers who, almost always for reasons of cultural deficiency, persist in extolling the virtues of the homeland against any other values: my nation against the world, my race (because it all comes down to this) against all other races. [This process] can drift into such an exaltation of the self that, through a logical backlash, the path of the most senseless contempt is opened up to everything else. And then we already know what happens, what did happen until 1945, and what can happen again. (Cortázar, "Carta abierta" 8)

Vargas Llosa, who Cortázar mentions in this polemic to legitimate his own perspectives with the support of the celebrated figure of the Peruvian writer, would align himself directly with Cortázar's position, deeming that the Argentine writer's arguments would win the day. Vargas Llosa always perceived Arguedas as a permanent and elusive adversary who, by his mere existence, threatened not only his own work's critical prestige but also the very ethical, aesthetic, and ideological principles that supported it.

In response to these changes in the role of the intellectual and in the relation between literature and the state in the twentieth century, Jean Franco has identified among the writers from the end of the 1950s and the beginning of the 1960s two major paradigms which come together in that well-known and most traditional figure of the author: the *chronicler/storyteller* and the *superstar writer* who opts for mass-market cultural production. Each of these types are characterized by diverse narrative techniques that utilize memory, historical material, and individual and collective experience differently in the construction of fiction and the processing of meanings that symbolically represent a given social context. Franco connects these distinct narrative projects with the uneven development of Latin America and with the consequent differentiation achieved by literacy projects and the spread of, at first, lettered culture, and secondly mass culture throughout the region. According to Franco:

The dilemma of the novels of the early sixties is that they project a model of enterprise which is limited to the individual and his lifespan (the masculine possessive adjective is also significant). The novelist comes along to rescue from oblivion not "real" people but energies, desire, and dreams which have been swept aside in the backlash of history. But they are energies, desires, and dreams which still accrue to individuals. In this sense, it is an ideology of individual enterprise which is put into play even though the novels are not coextensive with ideology. ("Narrator, Author, Superstar" 156–57)

According to Franco, this "individual, essentially discontinuous, and fragmented project" comes out of the void left by the failure of dependent capitalism and the disappearance of communities that only reappear in a spectral way in popular culture and in imaginary representations of non-urban societies, now that cities constitute the natural environment of rationalized bourgeois life. The superstar writer develops in a realm situated beyond the limits of national culture: the space that is now dominated by images and that hurls the writer into the "society of the spectacle." From this realm the collective is reconfigured, now conceived in terms of mass society, ever more distant from national communities. The Arguedas/Vargas Llosa relation (and the polemic between Arguedas and Cortázar, which replicated the terms of the literary *double bind* of the 1960s) can be understood on the basis of the dualism Franco notes, which refers at the bottom to two rather different positions for the intellectual who lives on the margins of modernity and feels attracted to (or repelled by, as the case may be) the cultural and economic core of centralized capitalism.[29]

If Arguedas is always "Haunted by the specter of anachronism" (Franco, *The Decline and Fall* 161), Vargas Llosa's work—either due to the selection of certain issues directly related to the phenomenon of mass culture (*Tía Julia y el escribidor* [*Aunt Julia and the Scriptwriter*], e.g.) or because of the treatment of other topics, like primitivism (*El hablador*), violence (*Lituma en los Andes, La historia de Mayta* [*The Real Life of Alejandro Mayta*]), political corruption (*Conversación en la Catedral* [*Conversation in the Cathedral*]), or the tension between civilization and barbarism (*La guerra del fin del mundo* [*The War of the End of the World*])—designates him as a comfortable inhabitant of modernity, which he approaches from fluctuating and acquiescent ideological and political positions. While the storyteller develops a literature established in affectivity and in empathy with a world surrounded by the process of modernization, the superstar writer crosses extensive registers which exclude (or minimize or degrade) the representation of the indigenous world in which archaism, primitivism, and barbarism tend to superimpose themselves as synonyms for backwardness, ignorance, and irrationality. Vargas Llosa's well-known defense of neoliberalism and his adherence to Western modernity dismisses out of hand indigenous cultures and populations as residues of colonialism, as recalcitrantly anachronistic, and as unassimilable to the project of the criollo republic. Facing the *ethos* of capitalist modernity and national institutionality as the basis of the Peruvian nation, Vargas Llosa emerged as an organic intellectual of a nationalist project that he himself hoped to lead from within the state apparatus. For his part, Arguedas maintained (despite basing himself in Lima and working as a bureaucrat and educator in diverse cultural organizations) an alternative position that established him above all within progressive circles both inside and outside of Peru.[30]

Postcolonial thought will serve to further strengthen Arguedas's reception through the relation that can be established between his work, the forms of subjectivity that he represents, and the themes of subalternity, multiculturalism, migration, and social movements, all of which have occupied the critical and theoretical agendas of the humanities and social sciences since the end of the Cold War. In this context, the Arguedas/Vargas Llosa duality exemplifies the ethical and aesthetic *double bind* that has been imposed on the history of the region since it became intertwined with that of the West. Indeed, both authors, especially when they are analyzed as two sides of the same coin of a still-unsolved dilemma of Andean society, represent, on the one hand, the inescapable stance against colonialism and the forms of domination enshrined within the criollo republic and, on the other hand, the demands imposed by the processes of Westernization that drive growth and an accelerated cosmopolitanization of societies that are peripheral to "high" capitalism during the second half of the twentieth century and up to the present day in the twenty-first century.

Notes

1. This verse, from Enrique Lihn's poem "Ay Infelice" (*Al bello aparecer de este lucero*, 31), was recuperated by Cornejo Polar in his article "Para una teoría literaria hispanoamericana," in the context of a discussion about multilingualism and "multihistory" in Latin America. Cornejo Polar refers to "a history made of many times and rhythms, something like a multihistory that advances time as much as it plunges it, cumulatively, into a single moment."

As Enrique Lihn says in a memorable verse," he adds, "we Latin Americans 'are contemporaries of different histories'" ("Para una teoría literaria hispanoamericana" 11).
2. [The term "*letrado*" ("lettered" in English) refers to the elite, educated class of cultural, intellectual, political, and social gatekeepers who have traditionally imposed hegemonic order in Latin America since the colonial period. The foundational text on the concept of the *letrado* is, of course, Angel Rama's *La ciudad letrada* (published in English as *The Lettered City*, trans. John Charles Chasteen, Durham: Duke University Press, 1996.—Tr.)
3. [In English in the original.—Tr.]
4. This orientation is none other than that which encourages the criticisms of *Todas las sangres* made by anthropologists, sociologists, and historians who found in the work an inaccurate, if not outright mistaken, portrait of Peruvian reality. See in this respect the concepts expressed by Arguedas and other intellectuals in ¿*He vivido en vano?* as well as in the book collecting the debates of the First Meeting of Peruvian Narrators.
5. According to Hernán Vidal's well-known analysis, "The appearance of the [Boom's] most representative works coincides at its peak and in its impact with the consumerist orientation of the most advanced Latin American economies from the mid-1950s to the late sixties" (67).
6. The "Padilla affair" refers to the series of events that began with the imprisonment in Havana of the Cuban writer Heberto Padilla, who, in 1966, won that country's Julián del Casal National Poetry Award for the book *Fuera del juego*. The decision of the jury (made up of, among others, José Lezama Lima and Peruvian writer César Calvo) raised protests in the Union of Cuban Writers because the book was considered counterrevolutionary in official circles. In March 1971, Padilla, who was at that time a professor at the University of Havana, was detained and imprisoned for reading poems from his book *Provocaciones* at a recital. From prison, he wrote a letter (which is believed to have been coerced) in which he claimed to repent for his counter-Revolutionary positions. This led to a series of international protests and reactions from intellectuals who expressed their disagreement with the Revolution's methods, which some characterized as a form of cultural Stalinism. In one famous letter, such internationally recognized intellectuals as Octavio Paz, Julio Cortázar, Simone de Beauvoir, Susan Sontag, Jean-Paul Sartre, Marguerite Duras, Jaime Gil de Biedma, Alberto Moravia, Pier Paolo Pasolini, Alain Renais, Juan Rulfo, Carlos Fuentes, Carlos Monsiváis, José Revueltas, Mario Vargas Llosa, and others denounced the persecution of Padilla and, more generally, the ideological censorship carried out in Cuba. This conflict was followed by a series of actions in which the Cuban government revised its cultural policy, summarized in the slogans, "Art is a revolutionary weapon" and "With the Revolution, everything;

against the Revolution, nothing." As a result of these international efforts, Padilla left Cuba as an exile and settled in the USA, where he worked as a teacher until his death in 2000. The "Letter to Fidel Castro" is reproduced in *Contra viento y marea* I (166–68). See also Vargas Llosa's own "Un francotirador tranquilo" (*Contra viento y marea* I 101–212), written in October 1974. In this article, commenting on Jorge Edwards' book *Persona non grata* (1973), Vargas Llosa aired his own perspectives on the Cuban government and recorded his gradual disillusionment with socialism. On Vargas Llosa's relation to the Padilla affair, see Kristal, *Temptation of the Word*, Chap. 3.

7. For Vargas Llosa's take on this ideological issue, in addition to the copious existing literature on the theme, see his statements in the interview he gave to Alfredo Barrenechea.
8. Vargas Llosa refers on multiple occasions to Margaret Thatcher's persona and governmental style. In his "Elogio de la dama de hierro" ["In praise of the Iron Lady"], for example, he expresses his unabashed admiration for the energy with which Thatcher carried out privatization and the implementation of meritocracy, measures that resulted in the strengthening of global capitalism. He conveys to Thatcher his "unreserved admiration, that reverence that is nothing short of filial that I have not felt for any other living politician, but which I have felt, in contrast, for many intellectuals and artists (like Popper, Faulkner, or Borges)." Vargas Llosa has claimed that the government of "the Iron Lady" was "probably the most fecund revolution that has taken place in Europe in this century and one that had even more contagious effects in the rest of the world. A revolution without bullets or deaths, without flamboyant speeches or operatic meetings, accomplished with votes and laws, with the strictest respect for democratic institutions, and, because of this, unable to arouse the enthusiasm or even the comprehension of the intelligentsia, that class which manufactures mythologies and dispenses revolutionary auras" ("Elogio de la dama de hierro" 11).
9. Kokotovic notes, as do other critics, the change that Vargas Llosa manifested in that period of ideological shifting, in which he reevaluated the work of Sartre and Camus (a point that will be alluded to later in this study), determining that he now had more in common with the moderate thought of the second thinker, whose ideas allowed him to reaffirm his adherence to individualism, to confirm the importance of money as the basis of capitalist modernity, and to comprehend both the primacy of the market and the theme of liberty understood as a right that does not necessarily involve social justice. Vargas Llosa himself worked on the ideas of the philosopher and sociologist Karl Poppper, the economist Friedrich von Hayek, and the political scientist Isaiah Berlin, for example, to whom he dedicated admiring articles collected in *Contra viento y marea* I.

10. As chair of this commission, Vargas Llosa collaborated with legal scholars, anthropologists, journalists, lawyers, psychoanalysts, linguists, and photographers. For more on this commission, see Enrique Mayer's article "Peru in Deep Trouble" as well as Jean Franco's "Alien to Modernity." The commission's final report was drafted in 1983. See Vargas Llosa, *Informe de la comisión investigadora*.
11. [*Terruco* is a Peruvian slang term meaning "terrorist."—Tr.]
12. On the subject of Uchuraccay and the Shining Path, one can consult, among other sources, Alberto Flores Galindo, *Buscando un inca*; Enrique Mayer, "Peru in Deep Trouble"; Nelson Manrique, *El tiempo del miedo*; Carlos Iván Degregori, *Qué difícil es ser dios*; Misha Kokotovic, *La modernidad andina*, Chap. 5; and Mirko Lauer, *El sitio de la literatura*.
13. The representation of the relation between archaism and violence associated with the theme of indigeneity was frequently a part of Boom literature, such as "Chac Mool" by Carlos Fuentes, "La noche boca arriba" ["The Night Face-Up"] by Julio Cortázar, and so on. (see Franco, "Alien to Modernity" 12).
14. On these problems linked to the theme of truth and the definition of the concepts of victim and aggressor, see Moraña, "El ojo que llora."
15. The polemic was initiated with an interview Vargas Llosa gave to the journalist Valeno Riva, which was published in the Italian magazine *Panorama* on 2 January 1984 with the title, supposedly suggested by the editors, of "Corrupt and Content," as a pejorative allusion to Latin American intellectuals who served in the ranks of socialism. The previous exchange between Benedetti and Vargas Llosa appeared in *El País* between April and June of the same year.
16. Mirko Lauer comments on this polemic in *El sitio de la literatura*, 106.
17. Rowe has emphasized this by referring to the condemnatory tone with which Vargas Llosa confronted the critical reception of his aesthetic-ideological positions, defining it as a polemical tone that tends to disqualify one's adversaries instead of refuting their ideas.
18. [The text cited here, from 1974, shares its title with Chap. 14 of Vargas Llosa's later 1993 memoir, *El pez en el agua*, which was translated the following year as *A Fish in the Water*. Although the two texts deal with the same theme, they differ substantially. The translation here of the phrase *intelectual barato* as "cut-rate intellectual" follows Helen Lane's translation of the title from the text published in *El pez en el agua*.—Tr.]
19. On these "cut-rate intellectuals" see also Larsen, "Mario Vargas Llosa: The Realist as Neoliberal" (*Determinations* 142) and Sergio R. Franco, "The Recovered Childhood."
20. Pierre Bourdieu defines symbolic capital as "any property (any form of capital whether physical, economic, cultural or social) when it is perceived

by social agents endowed with categories of perception which cause them to know it and to recognize it, to give it value." Vargas Llosa is clearly conscious of the importance of cultural power and of the close ties between the cultural field and the political field and for this reason attempts to interweave them and link them since "the state, which possesses the means of imposition and inculcation of the durable principles of vision and division that conform to its own structure, is the site par excellence of the concentration and exercise of symbolic power" (Bourdieu 47).

21. [In English in the original.—Tr.]
22. Degregori refers to Vargas Llosa bringing up the idea of the *pituco*, which in Peru and other Latin American countries is used to refer to "criollos who, in addition to being wealthy, combine transnational and aristocratic elements in their behavior. Admiration for and familiarity with the first world, mixed with the old arrogance and overbearingness toward the lower classes, especially those of Andean origin [...] To be *pituco* is one way of being a pretentious snob" ("El aprendiz de brujo" 97).
23. In a similar capacity, Vargas Llosa was also involved in other Truth Commissions, for example, in Chile. See Moraña, "El ojo que llora."
24. [In English in the original.—Tr.]
25. Vargas Llosa distinguished himself as one of the most prolific and diverse writers of the Boom. According to some assessments, his work is characterized by a grasp of the grand narratives that traverse history and by an attempt to organize through literature the chaos of the real—in contrast to the literature of García Márquez, for example, who focused rather on more enclosed anecdotes and on the configuration of organically constituted worlds. For his part, Fuentes offered a more historicist, diachronic, and metaphorically represented version, while Cortázar was a cerebral storyteller seduced by the ludic dimension of the real. See, for example, Raymond Williams, Chap. 2.
26. [English translations of the six stories collected in *Los Jefes* were published along with a translation of Vargas Llosa's second collection of short stories, *Los cachorros* (1967) in *The Cubs and Other Stories*, trans. Gregory Kolovakos and Ronald Christ, New York: Harper and Row, 1979. –Tr.]
27. Hernán Vidal defines the utopian myth as "the romantic conception of national histories as a peregrination between two poles, barbarism and American degradation, that began with European civilization and was transferred to the Americas" (51). In a complementary way, the utopian myth supposes that "the American *socius* will arrive at a utopian state through a radical break with the past" (53).
28. Regarding this topic, see Moraña, "Territorialidad y forasterismo: la polémica Arguedas/Cortázar revisitada."

29. In the 1970s, Jean Franco and Hernán Vidal wrote critical evaluations that emphasized the rupture of utopian thought as proof of the weakness of the liberal project and studied the repercussions of these processes in literature. See, for example, Franco's "The Crisis of the Liberal Imagination and the Utopia of Writing," and Vidal's *Literatura hispanoamericana e ideología liberal*, in which he analyzes the relations between liberalism, dependence, and romantic aesthetics as the coexistence of diverse rationalities that frame the literary projects of the Boom.
30. The positions Arguedas occupied include chief of the Instituto de Estudios Etnológicos del Museo de la Cultura (Institute of Ethnological Studies of the Museum of Culture) and secretary of the Comité Interamericano de Folklore (Inter-American Committee of Folklore), beginning in the 1950s. In 1956, President Odría nominated him as Minister of Culture, a post which Arguedas declined. In 1963, he was named director of the Casa de la Cultura del Perú, a position Arguedas occupied until his retirement in 1966. As an educator, he taught courses in ethnology and in social sciences at the University of San Marcos. He also taught Quechua in the Agrarian University of Molina, where he ended up committing suicide on 28 November 1969.

CHAPTER 4

Archaism as Floating Signifier

Of all the ideologemes that circulate around the two authors who are the object of the present study, the notion of *archaism* is undoubtedly one of the most polemical and most frequently used. This term is utilized liberally in the literary and cultural criticism that focuses on these writers' work, and it also persistently appears in their own writing about the perspectives they each hold on Andean culture and its complex dialog with modernity. Indeed, both writers define themselves on the relation they each have to national culture as well as on the positions that they maintain with respect to cultural politics, the preservation of aboriginal patrimony, and the ways and degree to which indigenous communities should be integrated into the public sphere. Arguably, one could say it is from the representational axis of indigenous cultures where the work of Arguedas and Vargas Llosa emerged and developed, in each case with a different specter haunting the process of the production of meaning. In Arguedas's work, this specter extends outward, taking as its origin the vital experience that began during his childhood, in which he had direct contact with Quechua culture. From the first, foundational stages of socialization, complemented later by a Westernized education that allowed him to comprehend and further develop his communitarian roots, Arguedas was able to channel, translate, and interpret the essence of subaltern culture, integrating it into the dominant culture through diverse strategies. In this way, he was able to reinscribe experience in discourse and subjectivity in writing.

For his part, Vargas Llosa proceeds by cautiously and reluctantly approaching the edges of criollo culture: examining the substance of local alterity from an external and privileged position that always permits him to represent the drama of Peruvian interculturality *from outside and above it*. The conflicts of class, race, and gender therefore appear in his work as shifting geological layers from whose realignments the problematic (which is to say, incomplete and perhaps doomed) modernity of the Andean region emerges, fragmented and provisional.

While Vargas Llosa documents the vicissitudes of the modern project as the melodramatic turning point promising some form of historical redemption, Arguedas pauses to bear witness to the social cost of these processes, the failures and perversions of capitalist modernity. He poetically discerns and explores the possibility of *other* forms of being modern, forms that are capable of preserving and developing alternative paths that, without excluding *the modern*, refunctionalize it, converting it into *one* of the civilizing matrices of the contemporary era, mitigating in some measure its authoritarian and exclusionary universalism. For Arguedas, *archaism* is synonymous with cultural legacy, tradition, and historical sedimentation, while for Vargas Llosa it means delay, primitivist residue, and an atavistic remnant that obstructs progress and persists as an anachronism in contemporary societies.[1] For the former, the quality of the archaic is similar to *the authentic* or *the legitimate*, providing a basis for a genuine cultural archeology; for the latter, "archaic" is a term of condescension which allows him to disqualify anything *outside* of capitalist modernity without having to evaluate the substance of that which is rejected, without perceiving in the ruins the soul of the object.[2]

Hence, in the Arguedian context, framed by the hope of emancipation and social justice, the notion of archaism is always linked to utopia, to the search for a conceptual space that would permit the elaboration of the pre-Hispanic legacy. This utopian space would constitute a fundamental part of the inalienable collective identity of the indigenous and project toward a future framed by the inescapable promises and perversions of modernity. Utopia is thus a non-place, simultaneously the projection of a dream and the symbolic recuperation of that which was lost.

In his study of Andean utopia, Flores Galindo defines the concept of utopia in its classical sense (and in the way it functions within the thought of the Andean region) precisely as an identitarian procedure in which memory and historical imagination are articulated. As he points out, utopia is, in the first place, a kind of mythologization of the past. An attempt to locate the ideal city, the impossible kingdom of happiness neither in the future nor outside of the temporal or spatial frame, but rather in history itself, in a past collective experience that is thought to be both recoverable and just—the idealization of the Inca empire, [which implies] navigating against the current to overcome both dependence and fragmentation [and] to find in the reconstruction of the past the solution to the problems of identity. (*Buscando un inca* 22)

For Vargas Llosa, on the other hand, this utopia is defined by the promises of neoliberalism and the free market as instances of individual realization and the surmounting of the failures and contradictions inherited from colonialism and deepened by the criollo republic. In the new stage of capitalist transformation, in which new connections with peripheral areas and new agreements for exploiting and acquiring the wealth of former colonies are established, the lettered subject [*el letrado*] projects himself as the mediator between this reconfigured ideology of progress and the remnants of the pre-Hispanic world.

From this perspective, which is firmly established in the idea of the intellectual as a savior who preaches the good news of modernizing redemption, Vargas Llosa consistently characterizes Arguedas as the representative of a demagogic and sentimentalized project, defined romantically around a chiaroscuro of pain and lyricism, exaltation and melancholia, where poetry and autobiography mutually contaminate and sustain one another. In Vargas Llosa's assessment, Arguedas's work emerges as an ideologically impure literature, floating and ambiguous. It appears as a literature that appeals to *other* forms of rationality which presuppose an epistemological subject radically resistant to dominant models and irreducible to the requirements of an ideal European modernity. For Vargas Llosa, Arguedian emotionality is a subterfuge, a language game that breaks a silence which is almost inherent to Andean identity such as it has been defined and administered by the ideological apparatuses of the criollo republic. He finds here a point of contention with the narrative work of his rival, whom he never ceases either to admire or to denigrate. In short, Arguedas is Vargas Llosa's nemesis. If the latter author represents *hubris* (the arrogant, messianic consciousness that incarnates and disseminates the ideals of bourgeois humanism), the former represents the spirit of retribution: an echo of the extinguished voices who come back from the dead and who understand, as Spivak suggests, that the subaltern does not *really* speak if there is no one to hear and understand her words, that literature exists only if it is received and incorporated into the social imaginary of the epoch, which is to say, only if it is a cultural intervention and not just creation made with words.

The references that Vargas Llosa makes to both Arguedas himself and his work are constant and practically obsessive, as are his continuous allusions to the themes of archaism, primitivism, and barbarism. The book he dedicated to the author of *Los ríos profundos* bears as its title precisely *Arguedas: la utopía arcaica y las ficciones del indigenismo* (1996) (Arguedas: the archaic utopia and the fictions of indigenism) and has as its primary purpose the identification of elements within Arguedas's life and work that would reduce him to a writer still susceptible to magical thinking and seduced by myth, incapable of overcoming a subjective, victimized, and conservative vision of history and of Peruvian culture.[3] The title suggests that Arguedas's work harbors an idyllic thought tinted with unreality and anachronism. It also points to the fact that indigenism, as a movement and as a strategy of representation, refers to a *truth* that can be falsified and denaturalized by approaches that deform its original meaning. But where does this truth reside, and what strategies can be used to undermine it? Does it have an essential, hidden character linked to the positionality of the subaltern and his or her epistemological privilege? Does it require a precise site of enunciation, whether epistemic, geocultural, or ideological? What are its material supports, its forms of manifestation, its degrees and levels of signification? What norms are mobilized to summon it and to symbolically represent it?

Hernán Vidal identifies in Boom literature three principal myths that originate from within the Romantic aesthetic: (1) the Adamic myth—the erasure of the colonial past and the establishment of a new order in capitalist modernity; (2) the Dionysian myth—the manifestation of barbaric instincts; and (3) the utopian myth—the search for an alternative to the dominant social project. These three myths occasionally manifested themselves in the dynamic of the Andean social drama of the 1960s. As actors in this drama, Arguedas and Vargas Llosa constituted opposing ways of conceiving *the national* as the space/time of a contradictory modernity in which divergent histories are simultaneously lived.[4] In this sense, *La utopía arcaica* constitutes a discursive stage for these three perspectives, dramatizing the conflicts and disagreements between them as well as the relations between the representations of them, impressing upon them different articulations that result from their ideological and ethical positions.

In this book, in which the Arguedas/Vargas Llosa relation is explicitly constructed through a critical-biographical textuality, two aspects are fundamental. The first relevant element is the way this discourse is contextualized. The second is the position of enunciation from which the author characterizes his subject—who is simultaneously Vargas Llosa's adversary, a character in the narrative he is constructing, and a representative figure of the positions that he is interested in addressing and refuting. In this way, the objective information that Vargas Llosa deploys is counterbalanced by the process of subjectivization the text reveals. Thus, Vargas Llosa's critical voice and the materials he organizes all reveal more about the author of the text than about the object of his biographical study.

With regard to historical context, it is important to remember that at the time the book was published, Vargas Llosa was firmly established in the literary field both at the national and international levels. By then he had published more than 12 novels and had received numerous literary awards of major international significance (e.g., the Premio Biblioteca Breve for *La ciudad y los perros* in 1963, and both the Premio Rómulo Gallegos and the Premio Nacional de Novela en Perú for *La casa verde* in 1967). Vargas Llosa had also been inducted as a member of the Academia Peruana de la Lengua in 1977 and of the Academia Española in 1994, and he was awarded with the Legion of Honor by the French government in 1985. Many of his most important essays of literary criticism, including texts about *Tirant lo Blanc*, García Márquez, Flaubert, Sartre, and Camus among others, had been published in previous years, and as a result, Vargas Llosa's knowledge of the field of culture was already well established. Multiple essays dedicated to demonstrating his knowledge of the process of literary composition (*La verdad de las mentiras* [1990], e.g.) further guaranteed his position as a critic, including his political memoir, *El pez en el agua* (1993) [*A Fish in the Water* (1994)] (a book that tells the story of his political career as if it were that of a triumphant candidate revealing the secret of his electoral success). Taking all this into consideration, by 1996, when *La utopía arcaica* was published, Vargas Llosa had already achieved a level of fame that supported his profile as an intellectual to the same degree that his narrative technique supported his literature. He also enjoyed a level of credibility that, in some measure and without really even trying, was put to the test in this book, which was dedicated to the only Peruvian author he could challenge by presenting a different interpretation of social conflict in Peru and the political options that this conflict made available. In this sense, Arguedas represented a type of moral conscience—a form of social guilt—that Vargas Llosa's real and fictitious worlds had been able to dismiss from his literary and political imaginary although not displace completely from the Peruvian ideological and cultural horizon—at least not from those segments of society that were more aware of the problems of marginality and social injustice in the Andean region.

Furthermore, with respect to historical context one should not forget that the late 1990s, when *La utopía arcaica* was published, correspond to the ideological and cultural climate that followed the fall of the Berlin Wall and the end of the Cold War. While the consequences and the significance of the defeat of state socialism were being dealt with and the *weak thought* of postmodernism was rapidly spreading throughout the Western world, the rumblings of the Boom were giving way to much more fragmentary and ideologically inconsistent aesthetic proposals than those which had characterized the decades immediately following the Cuban Revolution. A perspective was opening up in which literature would undergo a process of decentralization before the rapid advances of a world saturated by mass media and characterized by technological invasion, the resources of audiovisual communication, and the growth of the market as a space of competition for the globalized consumption of real and symbolic products. The intellectual field, previously framed by the ethico-ideological project of the Left, suddenly appeared as disoriented and rambling, a condition which fueled the advance of opportunistic postures that no one had dared to express publicly in previous years.

The ideologeme of archaism—around which Vargas Llosa organized his critique of Arguedas and against which he implicitly constructed as antithesis the perspective of modern and enlightened thought (which Vargas Llosa defined as his own discursive position)—sounded in this context like an indefensible anachronism. If in previous decades (such Mariátegui's era) the use of this concept had formed part of an emancipatory project connected to the themes of social justice, anticolonialism, and the construction of a heterodox socialism adapted to the conditions and needs of Latin America, within the new ideological and cultural horizon at the end of the twentieth century, such aims were identified with the idea of the failure of the Left and would acquire a *démodé* or even retrograde connotation insofar as they seemed to suggest a return to the past and an unwavering resistance to the progress crucial to establishing capitalist modernity.

With the Shining Path having been dismantled in the previous decade and with 27 years having gone by since Arguedas's death, in a climate of the rampant growth of neoliberalism (in which Vargas Llosa's political ambitions had been crushed), *La utopía arcaica* constituted an exasperated concession to the cruel gods—not of poetry but of intellectual obsession and unadulterated individualism. These gods thus represented an updated *form of being* in Peru, with a well-defined ethico-ideological conception of culture, with an *ethos* ultimately capable of destabilizing through its mere existence the precarious equilibrium of the social and political forces of a region plagued by inequality and injustice.

La utopía arcaica does not spare any rhetorical or ideological resource in its eagerness to advance the thesis of the complete loss of validity of the emancipatory utopia of Andean collectivism and socialist revolution. These latter two ideals are identified with both Arguedas himself and his work and are put to work as a link between the archaism/modernity duality that informs Vargas Llosa's critical text. To this outmoded form of utopian thought (from which Vargas Llosa ostensibly derives Arguedas's "racism," "anachronism," and "irrationalism") the Nobel Prize winner opposes the modern utopia of salvation through progress, where the market comes to occupy the place of faith in a desacralized world.[5] This utopia, consistent with the principles of neoliberalism, derives from the full realization of Enlightenment rationality and points to equalizing forms of social experience and democratized access to consumer goods. With a condescending style (when not openly denigrating Arguedas's work), Vargas Llosa's critical point of view is supported by an antiquated autobiographical fallacy that supposes it can derive the characteristics of an author's work from his or her life choices. Thus, he uses the extant information about Arguedas's unfortunate childhood, and even the circumstances and repercussions of his suicide, to relegate the author of *Todas las sangres* to a "privileged and pathetic" time. Even though, in order to retain some credibility, Vargas Llosa's critique allows for some praise, recognizing certain qualities and influences from Arguedas in his own work (something which he had already acknowledged in earlier texts and speeches), there is no doubt that *La utopía arcaica* constitutes, as others have already argued, "an elegant tombstone with which to bury José María Arguedas" (Castro), who nevertheless remains alive within Vargas Llosa as an open wound that is ultimately impossible to ignore.[6]

Suffice it to say that the interpretation that Vargas Llosa superimposes onto Arguedas and his work exaggerates some aspects while minimizing others in order to benefit the linear argument that *La utopía arcaica* deploys in its construction of its biographical subject. Although

Arguedas's work clearly demonstrates an understanding of the inevitability of modernity and the necessity of rationally articulating the traditional components of Peruvian society which are particularly prominent in indigenous communities, this understanding obtains no relevance in *La utopía arcaica*. Instead, in Vargas Llosa's critique the interpretive balance leans more toward denouncing Arguedas as an anachronism. Vargas Llosa ascribes to the writer from Andahuaylas a resistance to modernity, which is presented simply as one of the many backward features characteristic of the indigenous population. This anachronistic tendency is used to explain Arguedas's supposed deficiencies of technique—which is to say the supposed absence of the same literary devices that have been recognized and praised in Vargas Llosa's own literature. Thus, even in recognizing Arguedas's literary merits, Vargas Llosa characterizes his work as hampered by an irreducible form of primitivism that prevents it from reaching the heights attained by Juan Rulfo or Miguel Ángel Asturias (to mention just two other writers representative of transculturation) and which causes Arguedas to remain a lower-order writer within the hierarchies established by his critic and compatriot:

> Arguedas was a great primitive writer; he never came to be modern in the sense Rulfo did, although he also wrote about the rural world. He came close with *Los ríos profundos*, where, thanks to a sensibility and intuition that made up for his lack of familiarity with the great formal innovations (in the use of language, in point of view, in the organization of time and space) that narrative has achieved since Marcel Proust, Franz Kafka, Joyce, and Faulkner, he came to construct a story with the autonomy and internal coherence that are essential features of modern narrative. But, instead of staying on this course, in his future fiction he slid backward, formally speaking, to the more conventional and rudimentary techniques of realism and naturalism, which in large measure frustrated his most ambitious novelistic project: *Todas las sangres*. (Vargas Llosa, *La utopía arcaica* 198)

Even "the desperate final attempt to be 'modern'" represented by *El zorro de arriba y el zorro de abajo* (1971) [*The Fox from Up Above and the Fox from Down Below* (2000)] ended up being, according to Vargas Llosa, a frustrated effort in which experimentation with different forms of discourses, languages, and cosmovisions failed to assemble successfully all the perspectives that make up the novel, namely, "fantasy, memory, testimony, and action" (*La utopía arcaica* 198). For Vargas Llosa, the book is "choppy and plaintive," "crippled and uneven," a discourse delivered from the edge of the abyss, a limit-experience that is only considered legitimate because the author's death tragically authorizes it from the metaliterary realm and will thereby always and forever frame its reading.

In order to dismiss Ángel Rama's critical admiration, Vargas Llosa even disputes the authenticity of the cultural content Arguedas used. As he points out, "that which Arguedas 'transculturated' from Quechua to Spanish was not a preexisting reality but was in large measure invented by him, a subjectivized, biased, historical experience, recreated based on his own desires, visions, and fantasies: a literary fabrication." In the same way, Arguedas's translations of stories and songs from Quechua "are translations only in appearance; in fact, they are creations shaped out of the clay of someone else's raw material" (Vargas Llosa, *La utopía arcaica* 157–58).

Because of both its critical disposition and the historical, cultural, and political moment in which it was published, *La utopía arcaica* was intended as a knockout punch to one of Vargas Llosa's literary competitors and ideological opponents, but above all to a way of conceiving literary phenomena and of conceptualizing the political struggle that still contained an ideological potential capable of reactivating hidden forces and forms of consciousness that were repressed in the Andean region. And in so doing, the floating notion of archaism was absorbed into the concepts of barbarism, primitivism, and tellurism, as one can see in Vargas Llosa's elaboration of the above-mentioned polemic between Arguedas and Cortázar.

Vargas Llosa himself identifies in Arguedas the *double bind* that implies, within a vision that wants to be progressive and utopian, the desire to conserve the premodern legacy. This is, Vargas Llosa argues, a "terrible dilemma" that is difficult to articulate, both for the modernizing project of the criollo elite and for the egalitarian society prefigured by socialist thought. This makes Arguedas a lost, marginal figure due to his own exceptionality, a romantic possessor of a form of thought that is unattainable in any of the ideological registers of his time, a kind of ideological pariah, a loner.

In the accurately titled section "The Dilemma of a Cultural Conservative," Vargas Llosa notes that Arguedas, who recognized the underdeveloped and marginal situation of the indigenous population and struggled for the improvement of their living conditions, clung to the culture of the past and its legacy, including magical thinking, which is technically incompatible with Marxist theory. Vindicating the principles of a Marxist orthodoxy in which he did not believe, Vargas Llosa insists on emphasizing Arguedas's inconsistency, referring to the latter's respect for the magical (which Arguedas himself pointed out he had never detached himself from) as "Arguedas's drama," in which the author of *Todas las sangres* failed to choose between socialism and irrationalism: "In sum, it was," Vargas Llosa says, "the 'archaic,' 'barbaric' character of Indian reality—the traditional and what it had digested of Western culture—that Arguedas loved and with which he felt profound solidarity..." (*La utopía arcaica* 30–31).

This *double bind* that would trap Arguedas at the intersection between premodernity and the utopia of progress for indigenous populations, between conservatism and socialism, is conceptualized by an author who, in his superstar status, sees himself as equally distant from both positions, occupying a place of not just social but epistemological privilege with regard to his lettered adversary in particular and to his contemporaries in general. According to Vargas Llosa, Arguedas's inability to resolve satisfactorily the dilemma between archaism and modernity provoked the "failure" of many of his literary endeavors—*Todas las sangres*, for example, a novel that Vargas Llosa does not hesitate to describe as "simultaneously his greatest defeat and the most ambitious [work] he ever wrote" (*La utopía arcaica* 31). Vargas Llosa describes this novel (to which he also alludes in his Nobel Prize acceptance speech, acknowledging that the concept expressed by its title is the best way he knows of to define Peru) in the pettiest possible way, critiquing Arguedas as an example of "the sacrifice of sensibility at the altar of ideology." Vargas Llosa is referring here to the effort that Arguedas had undertaken in order to "adapt his behavior to the image of him that progressives had fabricated" (*La utopía arcaica* 31).[7]

Based on the above, and beyond the alternatives assumed by this opposition between the two authors, it is clear that the theme of archaism has a continued and pressing relevance in the Andean region, where colonialism survives, established within modernity at all levels of social life.[8] Hence, the revision of history and judgments about colonialism are recurring, polemical themes in the region. Kokotovic has traced Vargas Llosa's ideological evolution, comparing, on one hand, the positions he expresses in two essays about the Conquest: "El nacimiento del Perú" (1986) and the expanded version of this text published in English as "Questions of Conquest: What Columbus Wrought and What He Did Not" (1990), and on the other hand, the novel *El hablador* (1987) [*The Storyteller* (1989)], published at the beginning of his presidential campaign. As Kokotovic indicates, in these texts, Vargas Llosa expounds on two ideological lines that guided his electoral campaign: his defense of private enterprise (the free market) as the only possible path for modernization for his country and his idea about the incompatibility of modernity and cultural heterogeneity (particularly for the survival of indigenous cultures) in modern Peru. According to these ideological lines, the complete lack of both individual initiative and the capacity for independent decision-making in indigenous communities, as well as the strength and persistence of "archaic and aboriginal" cultural traits, would have been the determining factors, first, of the defeat pre-Hispanic cultures suffered at the hands of the Spanish, and in subsequent centuries of the inability of Andean society to fully accomplish the process of modernization. Faced with the reality of what he calls *cultural apartheid*, Vargas Llosa confirms the failure of any potential attempt to assimilate the indigenous to criollo society. In "Questions of Conquest" the author says: "Perhaps there is no realistic way to integrate our societies other than by asking the Indians to pay [the] price [of that integration]," a price which Vargas Llosa describes in detail: "renunciation of their culture, their language; their beliefs, their traditions and customs, and the adoption of the culture of their ancient masters." And, he adds: "If forced to choose between the preservation of Indian cultures and their complete assimilation, with great sadness I would choose modernization of the Indian population, because there are priorities; and the first priority is, of course, to fight hunger and misery."

Vargas Llosa poses in the following terms the *double bind*, which according to him torments the criollo consciousness with regard to surviving indigenous cultures:

> It is tragic to destroy what is still living, still a driving cultural possibility, even if it is archaic; but I am afraid we shall have to make a choice. For I know of no case in which it has been possible to have both things at the same time, except in those countries in which two different cultures have evolved more or less simultaneously. But where there is such an economic and social gap, modernization is possible only with the sacrifice of the Indian cultures. ("Questions of Conquest")

Vargas Llosa attributes the qualities of primitivism, isolation, and lack of communication to indigenous peoples at the end of the twentieth century. He proposes that the indigenous cultures already slaughtered by the Conquest must now be sacrificed, or better yet, must sacrifice themselves in order to adapt to criollo modernity. As Kokotovic points out, for Vargas

Llosa, "indigenous peoples need to abandon their collective identity in order to become the abstract individuals of liberal theory" ("Mario Vargas Llosa" 449). By opposing an exclusionary, authoritarian, and elitist conception of modernity to an equally restrictive notion of indigenous culture as a form of sociality that is recalcitrantly resistant to change and integration, Vargas Llosa poses an irresolvable dilemma—a *double bind*.[9] However, the considerations that form his argument are not limited to passing judgment on the innate character of pre-Hispanic cultures; rather, they extend even to the constitution of criollo society itself from independence onward. Based on the initial weakness of aboriginal populations that were so easily defeated by the "infinitesimally small bands of Spanish adventurers," he points out how "a chronically 'underdeveloped' world that has, for the most part, remained incapable of realizing its goals and visions" was engendered (Vargas Llosa, "Questions of Conquest"). Incorporating central concepts from developmentalism and from the Alliance for Progress (which were both rampant ideologies throughout Latin America in the 1960s), Vargas Llosa's discourse transfers principles of social integration and economic progress (such as these were perceived from the privileged and exclusive perspective of the criollo elite with aspirations of political leadership) to the realm of culture and to his interpretation of the Peruvian cultural field. However, in the same movement (and as the counterpart of the same message he would convert into the ideological core of his candidacy for the Peruvian presidency) he represents in every possible way his fear of and anxiety about the marginalized social groups that surround and haunt him, like specters of the real nation threatening the possible nation. The Dionysian myth that Hernán Vidal speaks of (the overflowing of primitivism) looms over both the liberal utopia of progress and the Adamic pretensions of erasing the remnants of colonialism and creating a new beginning for Andean history.[10]

From a cultural(ist) perspective, Vargas Llosa is related to the pre-Hispanic legacy through his literature (as well as through the political fiction that surrounded his presidential candidacy) by avoiding a thorough elaboration and real contact with modern indigenous culture, as if the term "modern indigenous" constituted an oxymoron that the writer could not bear to consider.[11] His dismissal of Arguedas's cultural politics has to do with this dilemma posed by the multitemporal existence of indigenous culture: an element of the past, a component of the present, and a challenge from the future—a historical continuity that Vargas Llosa fragments and disarticulates as if he were dealing with narrative plans for his fictitious world. William Rowe recalls that in the critical edition of Miguel Angel Asturias's *Hombres de maíz* (1949) [*Men of Maize* (1975)], Vargas Llosa "recognizes the richness of indigenous culture, but only insofar as it belongs to the past. Because on the other hand he circumscribes it within the categories of the 'primitive mentality' and Jungian archetypes incapable of constructing a contemporary rationality" ("Vargas Llosa y el lugar de enunciación autoritario" 72–73).

Analyzing *El hablador*, Doris Sommer observes that the novel begins with a "double take": a reaction of surprise that causes the narrator to feel alienation and shock when some primitive artifacts and photographs displayed in a store window in Florence take him back to the Peruvian jungle and a time when he believed he had escaped the troubled national reality that, in spite of the distance, had beleaguered him during his stay in Europe. In Levinasian terms, the Other, who is inescapable, persistently demands recognition. *El hablador* is thus, according to Sommer, "a sustained performance of simultaneity. Primitive Peru is, admittedly, outside of the narrator named Vargas Llosa. But it holds him, along with us, hostage in its gaze" ("About-Face" 95).

The problem is not simply accepting the existence of the Other but running the risk of identifying so deeply with the Other that the borders of the self begin to blur, leading to an experience of such absolute alterity that it jeopardizes the possibility of interculturality as a path toward mutual understanding and social justice.[12] In any case, the simultaneity Sommer refers to does not (con)fuse the terms of the identity/alterity duality but rather dramatizes them even more forcefully.

Sommer identifies the dilemma that runs throughout the novel and Vargas Llosa's narrative and essayistic work in general. As Sommer notes, following Enrique Mayer, Arguedas had served as an inspiration to Vargas Llosa in the composition of the character of Saúl Zuratas, who embodies in *El hablador* the figure of the romantic and traditionalist anthropologist who struggles for the preservation of primitivism in the face of modernizing projects. Zuratas, in turn, articulates the same "dichotomous and inflexible" thought (Sommer, "About-Face" 100) that Vargas Llosa himself uses in his political program, tracing a curious journey, starting from and returning to the iconic figure of Arguedas, unexpectedly uniting the extremes of the Andean ideological spectrum.

In this sense, Jean Franco has noted that Vargas Llosa's perspective reinforces the thesis of two Perus: one archaic and violent and the other open to modern values—a vision that essentializes cultural differences and constructs an image of a primitive indigenous community resistant to social change that existed outside the limits of citizenship ("Alien to Modernity" 11). Thus, it appears as an "Andeanism" that would be similar to the "Orientalism" theorized by Edward Said insofar as it is a stereotyped and romanticized ideology of *cultural* types that do not coincide with the complex and radically heterogeneous social and cultural reality of the region.

In one of the sharpest analyses of *El hablador* ever written, Sara Castro-Klarén explores the proximity between literature and anthropology, interpreting it, at least in some respects, as a problematization of the ethnographic model that is the basis of regionalism and the urban/rural, center/periphery, writing/orality oppositions that sustain it. Starting from an overcoming of the subject/object dichotomy proper to regionalist narrative, *El hablador* dramatizes the dialogic relation between two voices: a narrative function that unfolds in an alternation of speakers within the novel that may be "real," or may be presented only as an assemblage intended to definitively destabilize the presence/absence of the subject. The voices of the "Western" narrator and of the "storyteller" who recreates and reformulates the protocols of orality are inscribed, in turn, within the inescapable frame of power relations that determine the position and projection of each enunciation. Westernization and primitivism, modernity and archaism, criollo identity and indigenous alterity are presented as though they can be perceived, strictly speaking, as antagonistic spaces; they admit of relatively fluid dynamics and symbolic hybridization, and above all they lead to the blurring of epistemological and representational boundaries that sustain the binary relation. In a way that recalls the strategies proposed by Lévi-Strauss in *Tristes Tropiques* (1955), *El hablador* orients itself from the center to the periphery. In effect, starting from the "hard" core of the lettered city, reinforced by the classical enclave of Florence and by erudite references to Western culture throughout the text, the narration extends to the most remote margins of the occident, where the lost world of the Machiguengas agonizes in a space/time that can only be recuperated and represented symbolically. In the world that extends beyond the Western logic of discourse and knowledge, identity is diluted and recycled as part of a life cycle that is subject to its own rules and dynamics. The figure of Tasurinchi is one example. Tasurinchi is one and all, the place that the community occupies and the form that it assumes, the missing link between nature and culture, between the self and the other, which leads the never-ceasing march without which life would stop, overcome by lack and fear. Tasurinchi is to a great extent that which provides the material that the speaker organizes, building a bridge between temporalities, languages, territories, and forms of consciousness. Vargas Llosa causes the proliferation of the mediations between observer and observed, between the world that has the privilege of power/knowledge and the dominated universe, the unattainable object of desire (Castro-Klarén, "Monuments and Scribes" 52). What is at stake in the always-failed attempt to represent the space-time of archaism and the primitive is the insurmountable alterity of the Other, its presence emerging in the instant in which the self is abandoned and in which the certainties that sustain modern rationality are dissolved. Faced with the difficulties of making the Other intelligible through discourse and the risk of converting it into a symbolic product, Lévi-Strauss poses (as Castro-Klarén astutely shows) the dilemma of knowledge, lived as guilt and anxiety. The anthropologist, placed in front of a reality that is turning to ashes, admits to being a prisoner of a double weakness: on the one hand, that which he observes afflicts and perturbs him; on the other hand, that which he does not see torments him like an accusation.[13] According to Castro-Klarén:

> It is this double infirmity of the impossible subject-object relation in ethnography that Vargas Llosa drives to its own absurd limits in the solipsistic discourse of Zuratas-Mascarita-Tasurinchi-Vargas Llosa. With a very important local political twist, *El hablador* will make use of such double infirmity in order to propose the idea that the naked storyteller and, by extension, Indians in Peru, are but the invention of ethnography. ("Monuments and Scribes" 46)

From this perspective, the paradigmatic Amazonian population comes to represent the emblematic place of the Tahuantinsuyo such as it was reconstructed by archeology and ethnographic discourse. Metonymically, the Machiguengas are the pre-Hispanic past and the totality of the indigenous world: an object produced by discourse tailored to the desires of the dominant cultures which project on that construct the guilt of colonialism, as well as the desires of the criollo republic, which ends up annihilating what remains of cultural alterity in the name of progress and modernity. In this sense, *The Storyteller* is, according to Castro-Kláren, a projectile fired at the immobile corpse of indigenism: the challenge to a system of representation in which Western power/knowledge makes evident the definitive incommensurability of the Other, its inaccessible, unfathomable being, which exists only as *residue and ruin*, and as a testimony to everything it lacks.

El hablador thus dramatizes the interstice, the intermediality, the crack that in postcolonial societies inevitably divides the existential territories of different cultures which coexist as the scraps of a badly assembled collage within the modern nation. The novel also dramatizes the place of discourse: its connective action that keeps diminishing insofar as it moves from communities held together by myth, daily practices, and the need to resist to the forms of being that are disintegrated by the action of progress and by the crushing weight of Western grand narratives. Thus, in *El hablador*, discourse is multifaceted and undoubtedly intriguing (restless, delirious) in its Kafkaesque ability to transform itself and at the same time remain sign, signal, symbol, emblem, replica, and ventriloquism, passing from originary chaos to organicity, from the supplicating, repeating, fragmentary, and poetic rhythms of myth to novelistic polyphony, from sermons and prophecies to daily speech, from the language of dreams to the memory of literature, the discourse of the media, and the parrot's cacophonous chattering that reproduces the voice of the Other in an irrational echo.[14] In the final analysis, however, this Babelic proliferation is encompassed—and therefore organized—by the dominant language, integrated through the resources of the lettered city into dominant discourses which domesticate its primitivism. The reader of *El hablador* gets the impression that the novel's thesis consists of emphasizing precisely the existence of the innumerable contents of a world that is parallel to criollo society. These contents, which reveal other forms of experience and knowledge of the world, are, naturally, uncontainable and thus endowed with a spectrality that relentlessly haunts modernity.

As a discursive formation, *El hablador* enshrines in the heart of the story *the narrative function* redoubled as a game of mirrors in which masks multiply as metaphors of the subterfuges of identity, which in turn only exists as an ingenuous belief in the unicity of the self which occupies a position in relation to otherness. The novel establishes the simulacrum as a literary device representative of the identities that participate in the postcolonial drama. Nationalism is inseparable from the guilt of social exclusion and the nostalgia that is produced by the constant experience of loss. This manifests itself, for example, in the fragmentation of the narrative voice and in the alternation between different spaces and times (Florence, the Amazon jungle, the lettered city, the atemporality of myth, the nomadism of constant exodus, the continuous present of the modern nation). Not coincidentally, Zuratas is assigned the status of *Jew*, which is inevitably associated with the themes of wandering, alterity, and the horrors of extermination. Guilt and nostalgia are also expressed through the instability of the place of enunciation and the unstable equilibrium that sustains individual and collective subjectivity, whether real or fictitiously constructed.[15] Simulacrum and postcoloniality thus turn out to be two sides of the same coin that represents the symbolic exchange between cultures in societies fractured by imperial domination and the criollo republic.

Castro-Kláren has called attention to the aspect of *divertimento* in Vargas Llosa's text by noting, in her study of politics and poetics in *El hablador*, how the novel can be read as a taking of position with respect to the discursive formations of ethnography and indigenism:

> The portrayal of the Machiguenga's cultural story can now be regarded as a *divertimento* that charmingly breaks into the development of the central theme: the interpretation of cultures. In other words, this reading of the politics of the novel renders Tasurinchi as the "*gracioso*," a self-deprecating alter ego, in the tragedy played by the acknowledged hero, the novelist, and the antagonist, *indigenista* ethnographers. (Castro-Kláren, "Monuments and Scribes" 47)

Castro-Kláren cites one of the dialogs between the main narrator of the novel and Saúl Zuratas, before their experience in the Amazon:

> "You're an Indigenist to the nth degree, Mascarita," I teased him. "Just like the ones in the thirties. Like Dr. Luis Valcárcel when he was young, wanting all the colonial churches and convents demolished because they represented Anti-Peru. Or should we bring back the Tahuantinsuyo? Human sacrifice, quipus, trepanation with stone knives? It's a laugh that Peru's last Indigenist turns out to be Jewish, Mascarita." (Vargas Llosa, *The Storyteller* 99 [*El hablador* 98, qtd. in Castro-Kláren 48])

As Bhabha notes, the mimic (in the case of *El hablador*, that of the kaleidoscopic construction of Zuratas/Mascarita/Tasurinchi/Vargas Llosa, the parrot, the central discourses—the Bible, Kafka—replicated in the anomalous context of the postcolonial periphery) is a countercultural device of appropriation of dominant knowledges whose meanings are transformed and reshaped in the language of the dominated. In the above quote from *The Storyteller*, mimicry and irony (parody) destabilize the position of savior taken up by Zuratas, identifying it with an already disparaged indigenist ventriloquism. In it, the lettered subject [*el letrado*] pulls the strings of the ethnico-cultural construct from the platform of the criollo nation. From this perspective, the figure of the storyteller (and his to a certain extent minstrel-like or rhapsodic practice) loses density: the storyteller is like a talking parrot; his discourse is the repetition of a bygone, archaic utopia that has been discarded by modern history.[16]

As has been noted elsewhere, the condition of Vargas Llosa's storyteller differs notably from the Benjaminian image of the *Erzähler* [Storyteller], which can be seen on different levels in Zuratas' discursive practice. Instead of communicating direct experience, the memory of personal experiences accumulated as knowledge that comes from life itself, Vargas Llosa's storyteller transmits erudite and educated references recycled through orality. This is communicated through the subterfuge of the copy in the form of a story that is in reality a pastiche, a simulacrum, and a farcical reproduction to an unspoiled, pristine audience that is understood as original, primordial, and authentic.[17]

In this way, the articulation of literature and anthropology that Arguedas and Vargas Llosa accomplish—their stances toward the archaic and their definitions of that category itself, to which both authors attribute quite different values—undoubtedly constitutes one of the points of contention in the comparative study of the work of these prominent Peruvian writers. In this sense, it is the production of distance between the narrative perspective (the *ideological* place of enunciation) and the represented world that frames one of the levels of differentiation between these two narrative projects. Another level has to do with the very notion of nationality and national culture which encompasses nothing less than the valorization of the modernizing project and the horizon of expectations in which each one of the positions being analyzed here is inscribed.

Obviously, however, one should not fall into the trap of essentialism that leads to reducing or stereotyping the complex aesthetic-ideological profile of these two authors. For example, it would be naive and imprecise simply to identify Arguedas with the "pure" and uncontaminated space of the native, as if his principal merit were the representation of a form of testimony or faithful documentation of the rescue and transfer of indigenous substance to the artificial and carnivalesque world of literature. At the level of cultural practice (although undoubtedly in a way that reflects his own ideological and disciplinary register), Arguedas forms part of the *lettered city* not only because of the quality of his literary production but also because of his anthropological work and his trajectory as an educator and cultural administrator. At the level of language (the most *primary and foundational level of culture*, at least in the sense we are pursuing it here), the drama of biculturality is exposed as an agonizing and permanent struggle to achieve the expression of marginal themes and issues to the dominant culture without "losing one's soul," which is to say, while maintaining one's fidelity to *difference*, a touchstone of postcolonial identity as represented by Arguedas. The question is: through what means is this *difference* represented? Additionally, how does one negotiate the distance between Peruvian reality and the world represented in fiction and in ethnographic discourse so that these knowledges and representations can be used as a way to overcome the colonialist roots from which they derive and as analytic and interpretive tools for emancipatory practice?[18] Arguedas wrote neither Indianist nor indigenous or properly indigenist literature, because the epic story of interculturality that his work represents transcends those domains, gathering itself together in a place of co-belonging and co-legitimacy similar only to that of Inca Garcilaso who, in an incorporative but non-dialectical movement, oscillates between opposing cultural registers.[19] Arguedas's work does not dramatize the heterogeneity of a literary product made by an intellectual whose background is radically different from the represented world, as may be the case with Clorinda Matto de Turner's *Aves sin nido* (1889) [*Birds Without a Nest* (1904/1995)], in which it is precisely the external quality of the perspective from which indigenous culture is observed that is communicated with the greatest eloquence. Rather, Arguedas's literature poses another conflict: that of the tense coexistence of diverse and even antagonistic epistemic protocols within the same subject. In Rowe's words, the authors that concern us here expose two divergent approaches to the modernizing project: "Mario Vargas Llosa's modernization is homogenizing. José María Arguedas's is multi-temporal: his literary work moves between the modern and the non-modern and simultaneously deals with semiotic forms from both worlds" ("A propósito de *La utopía arcaica*"). Rowe coincides here with Cornejo Polar ("Hipotesis").

Lived as a struggle between diverging worldviews as well as between discordant ethico-ideological positions, this epistemological duality manifests itself as an irresolvable conflict that extends to the processes of the production of knowledge and symbolic representation. This redoubling, or co-belonging, supports arguments against Arguedas by giving a foothold to critiques of his lack of consistency or his "confusion" of registers and rationalities. Sebastián Salazar Bondy, for example, locates the dilemma between dominant epistemology and alternative epistemology, connected to local knowledges and traditions that have been buried and marginalized by modernity. He notes in this regard: "I find that José María Arguedas has double vision with regard to Peru, he exhibits a double doctrine, and he demonstrates a double conception of Peru which is somewhat contradictory, although he does not consciously believe it to be so" (Arguedas, et al., ¿He vivido en vano? 25–26).

This double vision is expressed in the magical and almost pantheist conception of nature that Arguedas develops out of Quechua culture and which coexists with his Western, rational, and scientific university education. This double perspective provokes a zone of exchange and cognitive contamination in which divergent perspectives make communication difficult: "I find two conceptions of the world, and I see that, sociologically, the novel [*Todas las sangres*] is not a useful document unless the line of separation between these two worlds is very carefully, very methodically established—a task which I believe is impossible to accomplish" (ibid. 22–23).

Victim of the inequality and marginalization caused first by colonialist domination and second by the domination of the criollo republic, Arguedas vicariously expresses through his characters, his plots, and his narrative language—but also through his direct personal references—a divided, contradictory, alienated subjectivity, a "non-dialectical heterogeneity" in which the extremes not only touch one another but also are intricately intertwined in clashing and fraught imaginaries. His texts thus reveal forms of collective consciousness in which the processes of social (self-)recognition do not betray a unified image of identity but rather one that is kaleidoscopic, unstable, and constantly negotiated between the realms of power and resistance.[20]

The Arguedian world poses challenges, insofar as both bicultural belonging and bilingualism appear as the coexistence of magical elements within a socialist utopia, in which notions like *pachacuti* (cataclysm, earthquake) and revolution can be articulated and coexist in order to produce a politico-cosmological explanation of the social world (including its catastrophes and transformations). To these challenges, one can add the question of discipline in Arguedas's work. In this way, attacks on the theme of archaism and its contemporary forms of representation emerge from diverse but complementary perspectives. Subordinated to the limit-areas of knowledge, namely, anthropology and literature, Arguedas's work redefines the frontiers of both, demonstrating that the conventionalism of methodological divisions and representational devices (by which literary writing and ethnography are evaluated) corresponds to forms of cognition which differ from those of the Andean world, in which nature, customs, poetry, history, magic, and politics tend to intermingle in holistic visions in which each element mutually depends on the others that make up the totality of culture.

William Rowe has studied, among other topics, the convergences between literature and anthropology at the linguistic level in Arguedas's work and has observed that, while in the world of fiction the political element (class stratification and struggle) tends to predominate and antagonistically relate itself to magical thinking, anthropological language is much more culturalist in style and concentrated in the representation of ethical aspects.[21] According to Rowe, Arguedas's universe runs through a progression that autonomizes the Quechua world. Novels like *El Sexto* (1961), in which social stratification is crudely represented, are inclined toward a world of passions and the intersubjective relations that in whispered tones evoke society in toto. Gabriel, the protagonist and narrator of this prison novel, is torn between the world of the Andean sierra and the world of the coast where criollo culture reigns. This division demonstrates the conflicts inherent to a cultural co-belonging that affects him as much as the ideological division between *apristas*[22] and communists that he tries to escape by prioritizing affective and cultural considerations instead. In the same way, anthropological studies like those Arguedas produced on the city of Puquio lend less importance to economic factors than they do to cultural factors, demonstrating *mestizaje* as a metaphor of possible integration.[23] A similar movement toward the cultural is apparent in his studies of migration that later crystallized in the fictitious world of *El zorro de arriba y el zorro de abajo*. Arguedas likely understood that it was important for his fictional representation of the indigenous world to refrain from excessively superimposing a dominant epistemology (whether it was liberalism or Marxism) over the conceptualization of the dominated culture, and instead to allow the indigenous world to proceed in accordance with its own cultural and epistemological parameters. While political thought is a privilege of modernity (at least as it is understood within a criollo culture based on European matrices), indigenous society maintains an attachment to cultural legacies in which belief (religion, myth, superstition, imagination, etc.) plays a fundamental role. This coexistence of different and conflicting epistemologies in Arguedas's work uniquely transfers and combines categories belonging to different cultural perspectives, converting his literature into a veritable laboratory of symbolic experimentation which emphasizes, among the multiplicity of elements represented in it, the importance of the ethnic as both a principal form of domination and, as Aníbal Quijano has put it, "social classification." According to Quijano's definition:

> Coloniality is one of the constitutive and specific elements of the global pattern of capitalist power. It is founded on the imposition of a racial/ethnic classification of the population of the world as the cornerstone of that pattern of power, and it operates in each of the plans, spheres, and dimensions—material and subjective—of daily social existence and social scale. ("Colonialidad del poder" 342)[24]

Processes also develop within Arguedas's project of cultural representation that cover a broad spectrum of intensities and degrees. Melisa Moore has emphasized, for example, that the work on identities and paradigms emerging from the concept of *mestizaje* constitute a "discourse of archetypes" which, however, do not obscure the ethnic variety constitutive of the mestizo sector or the amount of nuances between the *cholo* and the Indian, which are in turn subject to a series of variants based on region, class, gender, and so on. In this sense, Moore points out that Arguedas's work focuses more on the necessity of representing heterogeneity than on presenting fixed categories at both the ethnographic and literary levels:

> Between the *cholo* Cisneros and the *ex-Indian* Rendón, for example, there is a world of differences, especially in that which refers to acculturation. Arguedas' objective in elaborating a model of *mestizaje* that is neither acculturated nor asymmetric, that is not determined by subordination, and is based on what he observed in the Mantaro region, becomes evident in *Todas las sangres*. (*En la encrucijada* 97)

For her part, Priscilla Archibald, in her book *Imagining Modernity in the Andes* (2011), has emphasized Arguedas's intellectual flexibility, which allows us to understand the discontinuity of his literary style, from the most ethnological devices of his books which are inclined toward the visual (*Yawar fiesta*) or toward expository lyricism (*Los ríos profundos*), to the much more dislocated and "postmodern" techniques of *El zorro de arriba*. Thus, while the social object and the aesthetico-ideological objective remain constant and consistent throughout the entirety of Arguedas's work, the symbolic representation varies, and it explores and adapts itself to distinct registers of feeling and intelligibility in the process of imagining a modernity *with* the Indian. Flores Galindo has highlighted the journey traced by Arguedas's work with regard to geocultural spaces: from the rustic and "Arcadian" (Escobar) setting of *Agua* to the capital of the province in *Yawar fiesta*, and from there to Abancay, the provincial capital in *Los ríos profundos*, to arriving at the representation of Peru in general in *Todas las sangres* and the final retreat into the port of Chimbote in the *Zorros*. As for Arguedas's representation of social classes, the route extends from the poorer sectors to the upper classes (*Dos ensayos* 14–15). In the same sense, Cornejo Polar perceives, as Flores Galindo reminds us, the expansion of the settings and the range of characters in Arguedas's work that, from the initial Indian/cacique duality, goes on to include oligarchs, landowners, and industrialists in later works (*Los universos narrativos*). A similar development appears with regard to language, since Arguedas's literature traverses multiple stages of idiomatic "purity" and "contamination," covering a spectrum that spans from the texts in Quechua (accompanied by glossaries or footnotes) to linguistic interpolations or hybridizations, bilingual versions, or writing produced in the "artificial Quechua" of *Yawar fiesta* and in the unblemished Spanish—the "clean saying"—of *Los ríos profundos*. Alberto Escobar summarizes this transition as the process that goes from the translinguistic paradigm to the diglossic paradigm (*Arguedas o la utopía* 138).[25]

Finally, framing the relation of the sierra to the coast, Arguedas's work follows an itinerary that describes the process of the spread of capitalism in the Andes and in rural areas: the growth of the domestic market, the expansion of the means of communication, and the economic fluctuations that took place approximately between 1940 and 1970 (Flores Galindo, *Dos ensayos* 15). But undoubtedly the most significant process from the point of view of the Arguedian world is the desire for representation, no longer of an archaic and obsolete world, but rather of the effects that modernity causes in cultures that have been conquered by colonialism. One of the most notorious aspects highlighted by Flores Galindo is the gradual weakening of Quechua-speaking society which occurred parallel to the advance of Spanish as the language of literacy, to the detriment of indigenous languages and dialects. This consequently led to a transformation of the educational system in the 1960s—a transformation that derived from the modalities taken over by the capitalist system and from the processes of industrialization and mechanization that characterize it. The impact that these changes produced in Andean culture, changes which seem to extend and increase on a daily basis, is considered one of the factors that contributed to the final break of Arguedian sensibility. Hence, the *Zorros*, in which the author narrativizes the imminence of his own death, has been considered the text that marks the peak moment of a struggle that, insofar as it was intensely personalized, is also key to understanding the collective process of decomposition of the Andean world that continues to be undermined by an irrational and discriminatory modernity.

José Guillermo Nugent analyzes what he calls the "conflict of sensibilities" in Arguedas's posthumous novel based on the study of the two paradigmatic settings that organize the narrative: the market and the cemetery in Chimbote, which he considers to be "opposing spaces of modernity." Connected to these spatial matrices, a global process of the construction of meaning develops, resulting in a tense oscillation that transmits the idea of fragmentation and a dissociative intensity that is paralleled by the narrator's interior state. Not coincidentally, the Arguedian saga culminates in a self-destructive act that confirms social loss and its personal repercussions. It is in this sense that Alberto Moreiras interprets Arguedas's suicide as the end of transculturation, an end that survives insofar as it provides evidence that there cannot be a truly effective reconciliation between modernity and indigenous cultures without a subjugation—a radical subalternization—of the dominated cultures.[26] The allegorical density of the *Zorros* thus extends not only to all levels of Andean culture but also to Latin America in its entirety as a postcolonial space, a seat of civilizing, conflictive collisions that advanced capitalism ultimately confirmed through the implementation of economic developmentalism in the second half of the twentieth century. In the *Zorros*, the "boilings" [*"hervores"*] (narrative unities) represent the brutal devastation of indigenous cultures by transnationalized capital, the maelstrom of feelings, languages, and epistemes that intertwine in a process that leads to the degradation of the human and of the real and figurative death of the author. The subjective world of affectivity and desire thus traverse this epic tale of capitalist dehumanization. The port is a space in which the private and the public collide with a symbolic violence that exceeds actual violence. The impact of social conflict reaches beyond the limits of fiction, reversing the terms of traditional geopolitics. *El zorro de arriba y el zorro de abajo* thus represents the symbolic inversion of the known world. Now, the coast is devastated by the Andes, Quechua colonizes the spaces of Spanish, mythical animals occupy the stage on which life itself desists, cannibalizing the author and sacrificing him at the altar of literature and history.

NOTES

1. Contrasting the work of both writers, Cornejo Polar points out that while Arguedas thematizes "the phenomena of social destructuration," Vargas Llosa "closely follows the process of modernization of Peruvian society" (*La novela peruana* 252–53).
2. When Arguedas uses the concepts of *the barbaric* or *the primitive* he generally does so to characterize the social antagonisms of class and race that traverse the Andean society. See, for example, Arguedas's prologue to the 1954 edition of *Diamantes y pedernales* (which also includes the stories originally published in his 1935 collection, *Agua*).
3. As Rodrigo Montoya indicates, "*La utopía arcaica* is the fruit of a lengthy work presented and discussed at different points throughout seminars at Cambridge University (1977–78), Florida International University (1991), Harvard University (1992), and Georgetown University (1994). Two of the chapters of this book reproduce texts Vargas Llosa previously published on Arguedas's novels *El Sexto* and *Los ríos profundos*. Vargas Llosa revised and corrected the new versions of both texts, but in the case of the essay on *El Sexto* he eliminated and added several entire paragraphs" ("Rodrigo Montoya critica *La Utopía Arcaica*").
4. Vidal bases this theorization on the matrix of liberalism as the ideological platform that has sustained Latin America's cultural edifice since the nineteenth century. Cornejo Polar deviates slightly from this perspective, understanding liberalism instead as having been employed belatedly in the Andean region and which only ever achieved tepid support owing to the coexistence of neocolonial structures that hybridized the process during which the Church, for example, continued to exercise its influence, in contrast to what occurred in other regions. Hence, Romanticism was also much more diluted in Andean countries, firmly planting itself in that region rather in a *costumbrista* style that allowed for the survival of regional elements within the unequal process of modernization. This is what Cornejo Polar refers to as the "contradictory simultaneity" in which diverse and even contradictory rationalities and temporalities coincide and in which the sacred and the profane inhabit the same space. Regarding this idea, see Cornejo Polar, "La literatura hispanoamericana del siglo XIX," and also Sanjinés, who comes closer to Vidal and Cornejo Polar's readings of the Andean case.
5. Regarding Arguedas's "racism," Vargas Llosa points out that his work, particularly *El Sexto*, carries out a "schematic and no doubt premeditated distribution" of attributes that assigns conflicting qualities to coastal and mountain societies. In *El Sexto* "everything that is depraved, foul, and vile in prison is from the coast [...] In contrast, the generous and noble spirits are either from the mountains, like Alejandro Cámac and Mok'ontullo, or at

least a provincial from Piura like Policarpo Herrera…" And, he adds: "…this unconscious topographical and ethnic Manicheanism Arguedas takes up from the most radical variant of indigeneist ideology is one of the key points of the *added elements* in the novel, one of the properties of the fictitious world that distinguish it and make it independent from the real world" (*La utopía arcaica* 215). Along with the proof of the *added element*, which is not foreign to Vargas Llosa's own novelistic work, should be included a profound study of the causes that influenced the emergence of ethnico-cultural models and behaviors and their prolongation within the modernity that Vargas Llosa defends with so much effort, as if he were free of similar aberrations.

6. See also Montoya, "Rodrigo Montoya critiques *La utopía arcaica.*"
7. Vargas Llosa's criticisms of Arguedas's ideological position, undoubtedly what seemed to him to be one of his compatriot's most vulnerable aspects and based on which he hoped to discredit the latter's literary accomplishments, becomes a leitmotif throughout *La utopía arcaica* and other texts focusing on Arguedas. In the same way, the themes of archaism and barbarism constitute an obsession that dominates Vargas Llosa's thought. Thus, he attributes to Arguedas himself the same anachronistic quality that he attributes to his work. He says, for example, "Arguedas's literary generation was the last in Latin America to adopt from the beginning to the end of its trajectory a vision of literature in which the social prevailed over the artistic and, in a certain sense, determined it and for which it was hardly less than inconceivable that a writer would disassociate their work from a revolutionary attitude—or at least a certain mimicry thereof" (*La utopía arcaica* 17). In other instances, he accuses Arguedas of ideological opportunism: "Although he never joined the Communist Party, and in spite of his differences with the line the latter adopted with regard to the question of the Indian, Arguedas was, like the majority of Peruvian intellectuals of that time, in the same neighborhood—the typical progressive intellectual, collaborating in sentiment and in rhetoric, who safeguarded a certain independence and avoided committing himself to anything…" (*La utopía arcaica* 155). Paradoxically, Vargas Llosa's critiques coincide here with those that the Shining Path leveled at Arguedas, whom the insurgents did not in any way consider a "fellow traveler," to use Vargas Llosa's expression. In 1989, the Shining Path newspaper *El Diario* published a vehement attack on Arguedas which critiqued his "whiny magical nationalism," characterized him as a partisan of North American anthropology, and condemned his "sly-as-a-fox indiophilia" [*indiofilia zorra*] in a clear reference to his posthumous novel.
8. As Cornejo Polar notes, Andean modernity, within which colonialism continues to survive, functions on the basis of this fractured social reality, as if "the *patria* had been founded in the cleavage of a great historical contradiction, at

the clear-cut intersection of an archaic world unable to imagine itself at the margin of divine transcendence and a modern world determined to accept responsibility for itself as a human production" ("La literatura hispanoamericana del siglo XIX" 17).
9. According to Kokotovic, by posing modernization and cultural preservation as mutually exclusive terms in the Andean region, Vargas Llosa props himself up on his own definition of Western modernity as the only one possible and on his own particular conception of indigenous peoples as frozen in the space/time of an invariable historical and social condition that inevitably situates them at the margins of (and even against) social change and cultural interaction.
10. Analyzing Melanie Klein's contributions to the social sciences, particularly their applicability to the study of certain characteristics of Andean society, Gonzalo Portocarrero recognizes that "[the] definition of the archaic and its (non)place in Peru today are at the center of a polemic that runs throughout Peruvian society." Referring to the authors that concern us here, the Peruvian sociologist notes the following, in a way that coincides with the analysis proposed in the present study: "Vargas Llosa assimilates the archaic to that which has neither sense nor utility but which is preserved by pure inertia. Therefore, in order to modernize, Peru would have to purge itself of that non-Western encumbrance: the Quechua, communitarian aspiration, resentment toward success. To normalize itself according to a developmental pattern recognized as universally valid. On the other hand, however, Arguedas thinks that the 'archaic' is an inheritance that we must not renounce because it represents the foundation of our historic originality. Within that which he calls 'the archaic' would be the seeds of a modernity that would overcome colonialism, that would allow Peru to reconcile itself with its own history. One often remembers that 'archaic' comes from *archē*, which simultaneously signifies beginning and foundation. This etymological reminder implies that renunciation is not only undesirable but also impossible [...] In short, at the same time that Vargas Llosa postulates the modernizing compulsion in Arguedas, he insinuates the possibility of a reparation. Nevertheless, as has been indicated, reparation is an uncommon attitude in a country where, even today, paranoid schizophrenia reigns" (Portocarrero, "Melanie Klein desde Peru").
11. When referring to Vargas Llosa's direct contact with indigenous culture, one should mention his travels to the Amazon jungle—the first upon returning from his first trip to Paris at the end of the 1950s, accompanied by the Mexican anthropologist Juan Comas and others, and the second in 1964. During these trips, he recorded aspects of the Aguaruna, Shakra, and Huambisa cultures, gathering information that supported the composition of *La casa verde* and other novels that represented life in the jungle and, in a

broader sense, the experience of cultural otherness. These experiences would be utilized in Vargas Llosa's elaboration of his conception of the primitivism/modernity duality. He wrote an article about his first voyage to the Amazon that was published in the journal *Cultura Peruana* entitled "Crónica de un viaje a la selva." See also Vargas Llosa's *La historia secreta de una novela*.

12. Sommer cites here the objections that Dussel makes to Levinas regarding the experience of the Other, which is to say, the degrees and repercussions of the ethical commitment ("About-Face" 95).

13. The relations between anthropology and literature as well as aspects of the crisis of ethnographic discourse are analyzed in Moraña, "Borges y yo: Primera reflexión sobre *El etnógrafo*."

14. On ventriloquism in *The Storyteller*, see also Castro Urioste, who analyzes the novel as a "discourse of the Conquest."

15. For an exploration of the indeterminacy of narrative function in *The Storyteller*, see, among others, Faverón Patriau, who notes that "the principle of indeterminacy would indicate, to put it abstractly, that the fictional history that Vargas Llosa has designed is constituted on the pillar of permanent doubt about the source of the storyteller's discourse" (461).

16. On the role of the parrot in *El hablador*, see Standish.

17. Standish suggests that *El hablador* is tacitly in dialogue with two Borges texts, "Brodie's Report" and "Pierre Menard, Author of the *Quixote*," where the themes of identity/alterity, original/copy, truth/speech are exhaustively addressed.

18. In Arguedas, the theme of anthropology is fundamental, as is its connection with North American ethnography and its position regarding the representation of non-dominant cultures which, if not explicitly connected to it, is at least infused with the problematic of anthropological discourse. For a general summary of the interpretive directions that follow the critique of Arguedas, see Rowe, "Arguedas y los críticos," and Sergio R. Franco, "Diez líneas de fuerza."

19. For Rowe, "Mario Vargas Llosa's work is effectively indigenist or non-indigenist (*Lituma en los Andes*) or a parody of indigenism (*La historia de Mayta*)" ("A propósito de *La utopía arcaica*"). On indigenism in Arguedas's work, see Huamán, Chap. 1.

20. For Alberto Moreiras, this duplicity transmits the idea of a decisive rejection of all possible conciliation between antagonistic cultures: "Arguedas's demon is the uncanny will to speak two languages, to live in two cultures, to feel with two souls: a double demon, a demon of doubling, perhaps happy but also mischievous [...] In his affirmation of doubledness, Arguedas makes manifest his forceful rejection of the ideology of cultural conciliation, indeed stating his final conviction that, at the cultural level, there can be no conciliation without forced subordination" (*The Exhaustion of Difference* 196).

21. Rowe has addressed the theme of culturalism, which is essential in Arguedas's corpus and also of fundamental importance for understanding the development of anthropology in the historical and cultural context from the 1940s onward. He emphasizes above all that, far from being about a problematic that is concerned with the development of the discipline of ethnography, the orientation of anthropological discourse registers profound ideological tensions: firstly, regarding the importance of the category of *class* for the understanding of social conflict, and secondly, with regard to the notion of culture itself as a space of representation and struggle that can never reach a political dimension that remains limited to the consideration of superstructural factors. Rowe mentions, for example, the opposition between the views of Juan Ossio and Rodrigo Montoya regarding the importance of the element of ethnicity, which in many cases comes to obscure the economic realm and the problematics that extend from it (inequality, exploitation, marginalization of the indigenous population, etc.), reducing the problem to racial questions. From there, Rowe explores the relation between magic and politics, especially the subversive value of the former, a topic that would on its own deserve a more extensive analysis in contemporary studies, starting from the basis established by Rowe himself. See his essay, "El novelista y el antropólogo frente al lenguaje."
22. [*Aprista* denotes a member of the Alianza Popular Revolucionaria Americana (American Popular Revolutionary Alliance), or APRA, a center-left political party in Peru.—Tr.]
23. See, for example, the article Arguedas produced under the title "Puquio: una cultura en proceso de cambio," published in the *Revista del Museo Nacional* in 1956, as well as other studies collected in the volume *José María Arguedas: Formación de una cultura nacional indoamericana*, edited by Ángel Rama.
24. Arguedas's work and Aníbal Quijano's sociological analysis, principally his concepts of social classification, coloniality, eurocentrism, and the ethnic factor as a challenge to capitalist developmentalism have so much in common that it seems paradoxical that Quijano was one of the intellectuals who made such strong objections to Arguedas at the roundtable on *Todas las sangres* in 1969 (the interventions of which were published in ¿*He vivido en vano?*). The criticisms directed at Arguedas for his totalizing desire to represent the complexity of Peruvian society through fiction had a profound effect on the writer. Quijano reproached Arguedas especially for not having communicated in his novels the evolution of the racial question in Peru, which, according to Quijano, Arguedas understood as excessively bogged down by premodern forms of social existence. Arguedas's vision, according to Quijano, offered an overly simplified and anachronistic representation of the caste structure that had extensively developed in the region since the colonial era,

merging in the present with the stratification of classes. Quijano also criticized the role of the working class and even certain uses of language and the raw material of personal experience in Arguedas's fictitious worlds. Quijano clarified, however, the importance he recognized Arguedas's novel had within the context of Andean literature: "*Todas las sangres*," he said, "is, to me, one of the most important narrative enterprises about Peruvian society ever undertaken. From the writer's point of view, it constitutes an extraordinary progression in relation to his previous novelistic work, for its construction, for its use of literary devices, and above all, for the vastness and complexity of the written material, in spite of the linguistic vacillations, the weakness of the characters and environments that correspond to social conditions that the author has not sufficiently studied, the simplification of situations and conflicts in the service of preconceived ideas" ("De Aníbal Quijano to José M. Oviedo: En torno a un diálogo" 73). "Isn't it true, my critic friend," Quijano continues, addressing Oviedo, "that the weakest and most vaguely constructed settings and characters [in *Todas las sangres*] almost all belong to the world of high society and high finance, which Arguedas has not studied in depth? Is it not true that the economic conflicts and mechanisms that appear in the novel are portrayed in a rather simplified manner and do not add, for all that, anything noteworthy to the literary value of the story? Is it not true that the workers' group is obscurely presented, to the same extent that the novelist imagines a strictly indigenous possibility of modifying the social situation of the peasantry? Is it not true that Rendón Willka, a character with whom Arguedas claims to identify insofar as he is in a position to face the problems of the indigenous peasantry, appears with a revealing linguistic and psychological incongruity, sometimes speaking perfect Spanish and other times an elementary and faltering Spanish, exhibiting the behavior of a mestizo mutt [*cholo ladino*] and visionary at the beginning, to end up progressively buckling under the dense atmosphere of the mysticism and irrationality that surrounds the world of don Bruno? Can one not suspect that, insofar as the author identifies with the character, he demonstrates the incongruity and vacillations of his own position toward the alternatives open to Willka's conduct? And the idealization of the indigenous world, the faithful expression of Arguedas's permanent emotional adherence to his early experience—does it in any way vigor or verisimilitude to the literary development of the indigenous group in the novel?" (76).

25. In this regard, see Alberto Escobar and Luis Alberto Ratto, among others. Estelle Tarica provides another interpretation of Arguedas's trajectory toward Spanish, pointing out that his choice of this language would implicate the intention to move away from alienation and a quest for communicative transparency.

26. See Moreiras, *The Exhaustion of Difference* 204–207.

CHAPTER 5

Language as a Battlefield (I): The Dilemma of the Sign

At an early point in *El zorro de arriba y el zorro de abajo*, one of the titular foxes declares, "Well, then, the word must shatter the world" (*El zorro de arriba* 49/*The Fox from Up Above and the Fox from Down Below* 52). And indeed, Arguedas's literature developed between the poles of linguistic struggle (that "truly infernal fight with language" to which Arguedas refers) and the final silence imposed by death. That is to say, it developed in the space that opens up the *performance* of language that projects both the multiple resonances of the sign and the echo of the absent word. In this sense, Arguedian diglossia acquires an iconic dimension: it signals the moment when *difference* ruptures and exceeds the imaginaries of modernity.[1] The linguistic performativity that Vargas Llosa detected in Arguedas and subsequently criticized as simply a syntactic, phonetic, or orthographic aberration comes out of a centuries-long struggle between distinct communicative regimes—which is to say, between different epistemologies. The *mise en abyme* of this diglossic communication constitutes, in this sense, an exposé of the epistemological conflict that exists in the Andean region and which lies at the very heart of the coloniality that survives within modernity. Arguedas's work thus represents a form of hand-to-hand combat between speech and language, between discourse and voice, between the communicative property of language and its denotative capacity, and between expressivity and intelligibility. In Arguedas's writing, the subaltern speaks—but what is she really saying? What language does she use? What codes does the subaltern circulate, and how does she interpellate us

© The Editor(s) (if applicable) and The Author(s) 2016
M. Moraña, *Arguedas / Vargas Llosa*,
DOI 10.1057/978-1-137-57187-8_5

by using them? What sociolects does she activate? What does she demand of our *hearing*, without which speech would resemble silence?

The use of language in Arguedas's work mobilizes something more than the rationality and conventionality of the linguistic register: it mobilizes desire and memory, affectivity and historical imagination—which is to say, it mobilizes utopia.[2] Arguedas's *saying* [*decir*] supposes the creation of a space of intimacy with the reader—a reader who receives and interprets the resonances of orality, which arrives like a specter through the mediations of the written word. But the message is not bogged down in these intricate negotiations between linguistic norms which finally come together in the *language game* (Wittgenstein's *Sprachspiel*) that, in Arguedas's case, consists of the proliferation of hybridities, impurities, and contaminations.[3] Submitted to a process of de-familiarization and de-instrumentalization that delays the transmission of meanings, the message renounces the transparency of the sign, wagering instead on opacity. In this opacity, language calls attention to itself, establishing a dynamic of revelation and concealment, a dynamic of offering and withholding of meanings that mimics the macabre, biopolitical dance of capitalist modernity that oscillates between progress and marginalization, between the promise of social well-being and the annihilation of life itself.

Arguedas's literary language functions, within this context, as a metacommunicational operation that consists in the same unfolding of the sign that becomes a signal, a graphic and symbolic indicator of an *interruption* in the flow of linguistic registers and in dominant rationality, of an *intervention*—that is to say, of an intention to reformulate the cultural and social conflict from new premises—and of an *interpellation* of the reader. This unfolding occurs on multiple levels: (1) it is the *recipient* of the text (the active receiver of a frequently broken, fragmentary semantics which must be reassembled in order to capture the evanescent senses that direct writing); (2) it is the *listener* of the resonances evoked by languages that appear as strange systems, as "*misturas*"[4] that are at once both lyrical and anomalous, verbal and musical, subjugated to and disruptive of an "order" that is established along with colonialism and that persists as coloniality; and (3) it is the *spectator* of an unusual carnivalization of the signs that affect the instance of artistic reception by introducing elements that create confusion, alienation, and incertitude. This *demonstrative* level of Arguedas's writing is produced from a representational ostentation of that otherness whose textual presence problematizes the very bases of the social and communicative contracts (with this latter understood as the search for an exchange of opinions, information, and emotions that is founded on a common repertoire of signs and signals). What is interesting in Arguedas is that, as in Inca Garcilaso de la Vega and any other subject with a clear consciousness of his or her bi- or multiculturality, otherness is an explicit and openly constitutive part of *id*-entity, an element of alterity that forms and sustains the self, a form of exteriority that has been so internalized that it becomes one with the being in which it resides and which it defines in its ontic and cultural selfhood. This folding and refolding of language in speech dramatizes the process of the production of meaning: it exposes and curtails sense, it reveals and conceals, and it converts the literary text into an artifact, a collage, and a simulacrum, which is to say, into an *artifice* which challenges well-known forms of recognition and representation.

Faced with the *double bind* of postcoloniality in which the subject is torn between the models of the oppressor and the ancestral legacy of local cultures, between integration and resistance, Arguedas represents the most difficult and harrowing option—that of an intermediary, *in-between*[5] subject-position that, without renouncing the space opened by modernity, takes over these proposals on its own terms and according to its own system of values.

From the position of an *avant la lettre* postmodernity (which began when the certainties of modernity failed to take hold either socially or politically and thus collapsed), the Arguedian voice, from its impurity, inaugurated a *Third Space* of resistance and co-belonging, a new place of enunciation from which it could negotiate unexpected forms of meaning that were more than the sum of their original parts. Beyond all risk of exoticization or fundamentalism, the politics of the Third Space eludes polarization and essentialism. It is a refined form of hybridity that does not exclude but rather productively incorporates contradiction and ambiguity and that "ensures that the meaning and symbols of culture have no primordial unity or fixity; that even the same signs can be appropriated, translated, rehistoricized, and read anew" (Bhabha 37).[6]

Arguedas's linguistic and cultural drama is manifested in all the stages of his literary trajectory, which by no means followed a linear path. Rather, it took the form of a rhizomatic search for sense that explored distinct composite formulations and diverse languages. In the section of *Writing Across Cultures: Narrative Transculturation in Latin America* (2012)[7] dedicated to *Deep Rivers*, Ángel Rama highlights the struggle that Arguedas waged with language, a struggle which, according to Rama, was essentially no different from that waged by regionalist writers such as Rómulo Gallegos,

José Eustasio Rivera, or Mariano Azuela—a struggle that consisted in finding a "veristic" form of speech for characters from the lower classes (164–65). For Rama, in many texts Arguedas takes on the task—which Rama calls an interlinguistic *dilemma* (*double bind*)—of translating Quechua syntax into Spanish, managing to represent the dominated language in the form of a rudimentary Spanish, incorporating poorly conjugated verbs, the overuse of gerunds, and the elimination of articles and reflexive verb forms, as if he were dealing with "an artificial language such as the priestly tongue common in sacred texts," which confers a ritualistic tone to the speech of characters who represent indigenous cultures (*Writing Across Cultures* 166). Thus, *difference* becomes the principal frame of cultural identity at the cultural level, and the linguistic sign becomes a signal that constantly points to the structures of domination and to the difficult survival of subaltern culture within modernity.[8] Arguedas would thus function as "a contact agent between different cultures" (ibid. 68), creating a thought and an aesthetic that operate as a hinge between two worlds, two cultural systems, two traditions, and two epistemologies. Cornejo polar defines him as "a *modern fox* who carries out that intercommunicative mission on his own" ("Un ensayo sobre los *Zorros*" 300). Thus, already in his earliest texts, Arguedas's work destabilizes the criollo archive and the canonical register, intervening in it with a literature that is simultaneously intellectual action, testimony, and cultural *performance*.

As Alberto Escobar correctly noted in his exhaustive study of Arguedas's literary language, the composition of the stories in *Agua* (1935), in which the Indian/*misti* conflict is presented, was carried out as an investigation which developed "in the footsteps of orality" (*Arguedas o la utopia de la lengua* 107). For Lienhard, this elaboration of language follows the lineage opened up three centuries earlier by Guamán Poma, thus creating a transhistorical continuity in the Andean communicative project (*La voz y su huella* 197–99). In this initial stage of Arguedas's development as a writer, the primary objective was to amalgamate Quechua and Spanish and make them come together as a hybrid language able to transmit the spirit of the dominated culture and, at the same time, metaphorize its marginalization and resistance, its lyricism and its subaltern postcoloniality in a world subject to the hegemony of language and ancient, colonizing imaginaries. The stories in *Agua* (a book which exists in various editions) explore, above all on the formal level, the possibilities of translingualism and the diverse regional variants of Spanish.[9] At the level of the representation of the social, these stories present the irresolvable conflict between antagonistic social sectors which belong to irreconcilable economic and cultural realities in which the Indian occupies the most neglected position. It is also interesting, however, to observe the means by which Arguedas seeks to paratextually compensate for the marginalization of Quechua by adding footnotes, explanations of vocabulary, parenthetical translations, or glossaries at the end of the main text. He thus gives clear evidence of the peripheral and residual location of Quechua culture and its permanent precarity within Peruvian national culture at the same time that he draws attention to the unifying will of a writer who utilizes the space of literature as a symbolic laboratory for exploring the dynamics of interculturality. *Agua* exposes the symbolic nomadism of indigenous culture, placing elements that have been excluded by criollo culture on the margins of both literary canonicity and the text of the stories themselves. Thus, the stories dramatize the struggle for representational power and the dislocation of enunciative positions and cultural hierarchies that literature aggregates and recomposes in its own register.[10] Escobar summarizes the search for a literary language during those years:

> Arguedas was not seeking to create a variety of languages but rather a literary tool. He sought to alter or interpenetrate one code into another and in this way infuse an invigorating breath of fresh air into the literary language of his time, which (as was characteristic of the first wave of indigenism) was as foreign to him as the rhetoric of modernism. ("Relectura de Arguedas" n.p.)

But this process (which Luis Alberto Ratto calls "imbibing"—a process in which Spanish absorbs the Quechua which threatens to saturate writing entirely) is in Ratto's estimation a device, superimposed on the dominant language and with the same opacity incorporated into literary discourse, which fails to transmit any of the original nature of the represented world or the spirit of its culture. Focusing on the composition of *Yawar fiesta*, which was published in 1941 and which analyzes the relation between Indians and *mistis* and the intersections between emotionality and authority, as well as the conflicts between tradition and non-native culture, Arguedas raises the necessity of choosing between the authenticity of the dominated language and the desire to make oneself intelligible in the dominant culture. He is primarily concerned with the problematic of miscegenation [*mestización*] and the interference between cultural power and politico-economic power in an irremediably fragmented world. Perhaps it is precisely because of the irresolvable nature of the social conflict that the novel confronts that all of the procedures Arguedas experimented with turn out to be ultimately unsatisfactory.[11] His portrayal in Spanish of the people of Puquio seemed even to Arguedas himself to be a false solution to the problem of representation, in spite of the lyricism he achieved in his descriptions of the landscape and the impressions it makes on those who contemplate it. Although the chapters he read to his friends were received enthusiastically, Arguedas expressed his personal frustration:

> Under a false language, the world is shown to be invented, without substance; a typical "literary" world in which the word has consumed the work. (*Obras completas* 195–96)
> For five years I struggled to tear apart Quechua expressions and to convert literary Spanish into a unique instrument. I wrote the first chapters of the novel many times and always returned to the point of departure: the laborious and agonizing solution of bilingualism. (ibid. 197)

In the article titled "Entre el kechwa y el castellano, la angustia del mestizo" (1939) ["Between Quechua and Spanish" (1980)], Arguedas refers precisely to that moment of maximum socio-cultural tension and major creative frustration in which the *double bind* between necessity and legitimacy seems irresolvable:

> [if] we speak in a pure Spanish, we say nothing of the landscape nor of our interior world; because the mestizo still has not been able to claim Spanish as his language, and Quechua is still his authentic medium of expression. But if we write in Quechua we make literature narrow and condemned to oblivion. (qtd. in Escobar, *Arguedas o la utopía* 76/"Between Quechua and Spanish" 15)[12]

Thus, he opts for a combination of signs and sounds, meanings and connotations that make his literary texts an apparatus of intercultural articulation which seems to have had its most felicitous expression in "Warma Kuyay," the final story of *Agua*.[13]

In this way, at least for a time, Arguedas believed he had resolved the dilemma of language for his characters on the basis of *poesis*—the *double bind* created by the confrontation between hegemonic and subaltern language, communication and expressivity, sign and symbol, modernity and tradition, domination and resistance—and drawing from experimentalism since, as Escobar summarizes, "the co-presence of both languages and a composite bilingualism is the characterizing feature of the mestizo linguistic system" (*Arguedas o la utopía* 81). The "mixture" [*"mistura"*] that characterizes the narrative of this period thus emerges as a response to "the death throes of Spanish," a language which, as Arguedas points out, is steadily dying "as spirit and as a pure and sacred language" as it is colonized by Quechua.[14]

In the creation of this fictitious, imagined Quechua, Arguedas—the migrant, the translator—creates a new agreement for the reception of the text: as in an act of counter-conquest, he definitively changes a genre (the novel) which belongs to the civilizing project of the Eurocentric bourgeoisie and which colonizes the language of the colonizer, permeating its rhetoric, intervening in it with the ambivalent mixture of the sign.[15] The reader receives this literary act as a metaphor of the tenacity of the dominated and of the difference [*alternatividad*] of his or her culture. As Bhabha has pointed out:

> the importance of hybridity is not to be able to trace two original moments from which the third emerges, rather hybridity to me is the "third space" which enables other positions to emerge. This third space displaces the histories that constitute it, and sets up new structures of authority. (Rutherford 211)

The space of language is thus that which allows for the articulation of new forms of cultural authority, new intersectorial dynamics, and new forms of relating the past of subaltern cultures to the present. Arguedas subtly "disorders" language to adapt the communicative instrument to a vastly impure world. He strengthens language by rarefying it, installing in its conventional register that *Third Space* in which the displacements of spelling, phonetics, and meaning are situated, and in which impurity is the most expressive quality and the most powerful connotative mechanism.

Nevertheless, this tactic would soon appear to Arguedas to be excessively artificial and, in some forms, grotesque. Arguedas recalled in the 1950s, after gaining the benefit of hindsight on his earlier texts:

> I solved the problem [of indigenous languages] by making them into a special kind of Spanish that afterwards was deployed with horrible exaggeration in other works. But Indians do not speak that kind of Spanish, not with Spanish speakers and much less among themselves! It is a fiction. Indians speak Quechua. In all of the southern and central highlands, with the exception of a few cities, the main language spoken is Quechua. It is therefore

false and horrendous to portray Indians speaking in the Spanish of Quechua servants who have become used to living in the capital. ("Prólogo" in *Diamantes y pedernales* 10)

Arguedas understood that the creation of the new language he developed as a symbolic convergence of two worlds and as an innovative and necessary device that formed part of "the struggle over form" that he was carrying out nevertheless constituted a construct that was too foreign to the reality of the cultures that uneasily coexist in the Andean region. His proposed "special kind of Spanish" that Indians used neither among themselves nor to communicate with Spanish speakers was revealed as an artifice that, in its singular and utopian hybridity, lacked any poetic or social credibility. Indeed, through that process of "trans-codification" (Escobar) the spectrality of Quechua was always present, projecting its shadow over the framework of the *lettered city* [*la ciudad letrada*]. Arguedas intuited that, crafted in this way, as a symbolic register subject to an inverse transculturation in which the dominated language colonized the dominant language, the language that his characters were using was artificial, a pastiche, a simulacrum. Understood from within our contemporary vocabulary, these terms all refer to the aestheticist paraphernalia of postmodernity, a perspective which would find in Arguedas one of its most unexpected and involuntary champions.

In this historical context, Arguedas's "special kind of Spanish" is a form of *mimicry*—ideological, cultural, idiomatic—which, as Bhabha describes, is above all, "the sign of a double articulation," or in Spivak's terms, the unequivocal indication of a dilemma and an ambivalence, which is to say, of an interstitial, ambiguous, and disturbing position with regard to the dominant rational order. In the post- or neocolonial contexts, mimicry of the oppressed threatens the precarious stability of the *national*. It is an operation that decentralizes and counters the hegemony of the discourse of power, transferring the gaze toward the constitutive impurity of the communicative system and its restrictive and disciplinary regime: "The discourse of mimicry is constructed around an ambivalence; in order to be effective, mimicry must continually produce its slippage, its excess, its difference" (Bhabha, *The Location of Culture* 86).

Arguedas is aware that he is straddling the limit (theorized by Bhabha) between mimicry and mockery, along the border of excess, of carnivalization, and simulacrum. He seems to sense that postcolonial mimicry can only retain that "double vision" which informs it and which has its origin in the Janus-faced quality of the colonial criollo. Mimicry dramatizes the subject's "partial presence", suggesting that its absent and unrepresentable side resides between the lines of the visible, in a *being-there* that is at once impertinent and inaccessible, conspicuous and invisible. Bhabha emphasizes the undeniable fact that the representation of *difference* is basically a problem of authority and power and not simply the display of the desire of the Other and of its strategies of resistance to being *appropriated* (*signified*) by the oppressor (*The Location of Culture* 89). In this way, the recourse to mimicry can only be understood as a strategy that emerges in response to colonial domination, hence the constant need for *authorization* and recognition that marks the performative trajectory of the colonized subject. The mimicry that informs the creation of Arguedas's *third language/Third Space*, established as a "metonymy of presence," that not only *writes* (of) *mestizaje* but executes it, *inscribes* it as a *working hypothesis* in the textual body of the modern nation in order to disturb its textuality—its texture—and display its inherent contradictions.

Arguedas's next novel took a different approach. As Arguedas himself signaled at the end of the prologue to *Diamantes y pedernales*, the composition of *Los ríos profundos* seemed to indicate that "the process had concluded." This refers to the struggle between hybridity and universality, to the dilemma of the author who, without "losing his soul," did not want his literature to be alienated either from urban, upper-class readers in Lima or from the Latin American context in which the international rise of the exportable literature of the Boom had just begun. At the time, Arguedas's solution was to establish "Spanish as a legitimate means of expression in the Peruvian world of the Andes" ("Prólogo," in *Diamantes y pedernales* 10). He came to the conclusion that, in all its cultural authenticity and undeniable lyricism, Quechua was a language that lacked "instrumental" value since in the bicultural world the dominated language does not function as a tool of dissemination but rather as a means to repress elements that are already marginalized in themselves. Moreover, he realized that an attachment to local language means remaining within limited parameters. Having arrived at this point in his creative process, a point at which he adopted outright bilingualism, the anxiety that tormented him seemed to dissipate. The man who defined himself as a "modern Quechua" when accepting the Inca Garcilaso prize—an award that, significantly, united two iconic figures of transculturated Andean cultures—interpreted biculturality as a double path to accessing the real that enriched the writer's cognitive and communicative possibilities. Arguedas was now a "happy devil" [*"demonio feliz"*] who seemed to have at least temporarily avoided neocolonial guilt about subaltern cultures. He understood adopting the language of the oppressor as a strategic device that did not imply acculturation but rather a negotiation between different registers that modernity had linked together in its power structures. In my estimation, Arguedas's choice here, at this stage of his creative process, implies a tuning of the instrument of representation with the aim of attracting a reluctant readership to respond to the challenges of the local in an era of accelerated globalization. It is interesting to note, nevertheless, that Arguedas continued to use Quechua in his poetry, which is indicative of his conception of the differences between literary genres, their relation to the market, and their capacity to express the sentiments and the episteme of indigenous culture. Thus, Quechua remained within an intimate register for Arguedas, as something to be reserved, to be revealed only in measured doses, like an instance of exceptionality that has its own forms of codification and its own spaces of intersubjective circulation.

In *Los ríos profundos*, a novel that Arguedas considered his most complete work, the lyricism of the narrative is intertwined with magical elements and an anthropological and ideological approach to the world it depicts. Set in Abancay, the work sets up an ethnic multiplicity that is linked to the processes of *mestizaje* and the tensions that traverse it. In this novel, *mistis* invade social space and take over the ecclesiastical, political, military, and administrative structures of the city, perpetuating the forms of domination based in the control of land and material goods, the possession of which is disputed, creating divisions and conflicts at all levels of society. The *mistis* thus do not constitute a uniform social group but rather one that is in upheaval, full of vices and excesses, a segment of society in the process of change within a social structure that inevitably continues to transform, following the alternatives offered by the economic process. This novel expresses the desire to take on, in a more complete way than Arguedas had in previous novels, the fascinating and conflict-ridden universe of Andean heterogeneity without remaining prisoner to stereotypical representations of categories or behaviors. Instead, the narrative privileges the variable and at times paradoxical condition of the characters: Antero, the Markask'a ("the Marked One"), a student interested in indigenous culture, transforms himself into a *misti* and takes on the attributes and interests of that world and the behaviors required by those interests, moving away from his former nature:

He no longer looked like a schoolboy [...] He could have been dressed in riding clothes, with those leather-patched pants, carrying a whip in his hand and wearing a wide-brimmed straw hat on his head. He had the look of a small landowner, generous, full of ambition, and loved by his Indians. Where was the happy, skillful champion *zumbayllu* spinner of the school? His eyes that had watched the dance of the *zumbayllu*, mingling his soul with the dancing toy, now stared like those of a rapist, of a grown cub impatient to begin its life of freedom. (*Los ríos profundos* 119/*Deep Rivers* 107)

Oblivious now to the magic emanations of the spinning top, the appearance of the new *misti* reveals aggression and ambition: he is a lost soul who has passed over to the other side. At the same time, the character of Añuco, who comes from a disgraced family from the land-owning oligarchy, loses every penny he once had due to his behavior, thus radically changing his social status. Father Linares, guided by his beliefs, moves between the different worlds as if he were dealing with inevitable, divinely mandated divisions that cannot be questioned and within which religion operates as one more form of complicity and subjugation. The character of Ernesto, who is of *misti* origin but belongs emotionally to Quechua culture, fluctuates without any clear direction between both worlds without which the process of miscegenation [*mestización*] would not earn him an acceptable place in the stratified socio-cultural reality the novel portrays. Clergymen and landowners, mestizos and Indians, non-natives and *mistis*, indigenous servants and laborers [*pongos*], tenant farmers [*colonos*], communal landowners [*comuneros*], migrants, and natives of Abancay, all create a fluctuating relief of ambiguous conditions and problematic identities, submerged in deep rivers of mixed blood and confused sentiments beneath the weight of ancestral hierarchies.

The representation of the *cholo*, for example, points to an ambiguous segment of society which is fascinated by the benefits of social power and in conflict with the basis of its own social identity. Additionally, intermediary characters, like the *chicha* vendors led by Doña Felipa, lend an important dynamism to the narrative through the portrayal of the daily interactions of various sectors of society. Likewise, the character of Brother Miguel allows the reader to explore the theme of discrimination toward Blacks and therefore the existence of other less-frequently analyzed forms of ethnico-cultural marginality in the Andean region. Different forms of alienation abound in the plural universe of *Los ríos profundos*, pointing to the inescapable and prolific effect of dominant power over all levels of the subalternity that sustain it.

In this attempt at an all-encompassing and diversified representation, the interlinguistic relation is resolved through that which Estelle Tarica has called "a poetics of translation" (15).[16] The rapprochement between subaltern language and the Spanish text is accomplished through the indefatigable and creative search for equivalent meanings and epistemologies between diverse codes. Tarica perceives a symbolic convergence between the intelligible, the "cleanness" of the uncontaminated linguistic register, and Spanish as the language of literature, and, following Gustavo Gutiérrez, interprets the "cleanness" of Arguedas's language during this period in opposition to the "alienation" that was symbolized by the linguistic *mistura* of the stories in *Agua*, for example. Supposedly, according to this line of thinking, Arguedas would have assimilated the linguistic hybridity of that period to the alienation of the literary subject and the world he inhabits. Therefore, in *Deep Rivers* one should be able to see a thorough attempt to overcome that condition, making it so that the indigenous characters express themselves in the language of the Other. On the contrary, I believe that the move from *mistura* to "clean" language in this period of Arguedas's career represents instead a moment of communicative negotiation that explores the pole of interlocution from a new perspective. It is no longer just the place of enunciation that must be manipulated in literature but also the place of the recipient, eliminating the pretext of language, its opacity, and its tangled interaction with Spanish, proposing instead the transparency of the sign and its communicative clarity. Thus, the transmission of the message is privileged over the cultural gesture of the sign exposed in its contaminated and ambiguous duality. I do not believe, as Tarica points out, that Arguedas wanted to distance himself from linguistic *mistura* because it was perceived as an inextricable index of an "indigenous Spanish" [*"castellano indio"*], tangled and abstruse, but rather because he felt that translation more effectively revealed the diverse and even antagonistic nature of the cultural systems that make up the Andean region and their unequal and forced coexistence.[17] Attentive to the transformations that modernity continued to impose, Arguedas tried to redefine the Andean subject as a social agent and as a subject of history, attempting to situate the vicissitudes of the indigenous and the mestizo neither at the margins nor in the para-texts of the criollo canon, but rather in the central spaces of contemporary discourse.

Far from converging in the symbolic, face-to-face articulation of the texts, the codes of Quechua and Spanish dramatize their contradictory position within national culture, making clear through the artificiality of translation the always fruitless effort to get to the heart of otherness, to get to the profundity of its word and the irreducibility of its silences. I think that Arguedas felt it necessary to leave open to discovery the traps of hybridity as a utopia of convergence, as an ideological form of harmonic miscegenation [*mestización*] at the level of culture. In this sense, *Los ríos profundos* proposes rather to emphasize the void that exists between the oppressor and the oppressed, between Spanish and Quechua, between criollo and Indian, with an eye toward creating no longer an impure language that provisionally and artificially articulates two completely different codes but rather language as the metaphorization of a distance that should be assumed and elaborated as such, not as cultural *difference* but as economic, political, and cultural *antagonism*. Regarding hybridity in the sense we have been getting at here, Bhabha says:

> The pact of interpretation is never simply an act of communication between the I and the You designated in the statement. The production of meaning requires that these two places be mobilized in the passage through a Third Space, which represents both the general conditions of language and the specific implication of the utterance in a performative and institutional strategy of which it cannot in itself be conscious. What this unconscious relation introduces is an ambivalence in the act of interpretation. (*The Location of Culture* 36)

The "act of communication between the I and the You" out of which the interpretive pact Bhabha alludes to emerges has a special importance in Arguedas's work. The autobiographical perspective is precisely that which motivates that *Third Space* of cultural convergence in which the linguistic aspect is hardly the most visible part of the emotional frigidity in which the deep layers of Andean history and culture are submerged. Arguedas's bilingualism and biculturality, his condition as nomadic intellectual traveling between different geocultural, linguistic, and ideological locations, between divergent disciplinary protocols, and between diverse historico-cultural temporalities and regimes of rationality and affectivity situate him at the very heart of the postcolonial problematic and its anticolonial agenda. The place of enunciation and the *performance* of language that in Arguedas's work accompanies the determination of that symbolic *locus* are dramatically linked to remote moments of personal and intimate individual experience, extending themselves to the point that they encompass "the saga of the mestizo" (Rama, *Writing Across Cultures* 119–132) in a totalizing and arborescent way. This is the social, ideological, and identitarian instance that, in the period Rama calls the third indigenism (which began after Mariátegui and Valcárcel), redefines the forms of belonging to national culture and, from an eminently culturalist perspective, explores the terms and limits of Peruvianness, including both its unfathomable essentialisms and its politico-ideological derivations.[18]

Mesticidad—to use Rama's term—exists solely as an in-betweenness and is shot through with ambiguity and ambivalence. It is a space of intervention as much as a space of negotiation, the constitutive hybridity of which already in itself operates as an apparatus of un-authorization [*desautorización*] of the power and its discourses of legitimation:

> Hybridity is a problematic of colonial representation and individuation that reverses the effects of the colonialist disavowal, so that other "denied" knowledges enter upon the dominant discourse and estrange the basis of its authority—its rules of recognition. (Bhabha, *The Location of Culture* 114)

This intermediality is the operative space of translation, the process of the relocation, and transport of meanings that never cancel out the distance between communicative codes and epistemological spaces but rather dramatize it and make it evident, exposing it to the carnivalized background that comprise interculturality. Translation exposes above all that which is unrepresentable in the communicative *Third Space*, as well as the limits of the operations that it puts into practice in order to encompass and appropriate the significations it hosts.

The product of a long period of gestation, Arguedas's fourth novel, *El Sexto*, thematizes the experience of prison, taking into consideration the problems of class, race, sexuality, and language within the panopticon of the prison in which Arguedas himself was held during 11 months of detention (from November 1937 until October 1938).[19] A grim, eschatological, and at times grotesque novel, *El Sexto* departs notoriously from Arguedas's previous narrative program and only foreshadows, through the vortex of elements that motivate it, the chaotic space of *El zorro de arriba y el zorro de abajo*. Nevertheless, the autobiographical link that refers to the author's experience of the spaces and dynamics that he would later elaborate in the novel is, as in other texts by Arguedas, one of the common denominators that lends an organic quality to his literary project. The story of *El Sexto* is situated within a microcosm that accentuates contrasting elements and radicalizes different positions. Lyricism is a predictable and effective form of escape, and takes place in Gabriel's memory, establishing it in an idealized and almost pastoral world of songs and regional landscapes. Affectivity, memory, and desire create a tortuous narrative route that nonetheless leaves room for reflection and even for freedom— of thought, of expression—for those who now find themselves relieved of the impositions of the outside world and its regulations. At the level of language, the novel proliferates regional dialects, devices of phonetic representation, the reproduction of idiolects that compose a Babelic universe, mimicry, and farcical parody of the cultural and linguistic diversity of the Andean world—all of which is seen from the perspective of Gabriel, the narrator-witness who organizes the story. As Vargas Llosa says of the novel:

> At bottom, the book has been constructed of dialogues; the descriptive part is less important than the oral. [...] In *El Sexto*, with only one exception, those who speak are not Indians but inhabitants of Lima, highlanders who normally express themselves in Spanish, and people from other coastal areas. Arguedas tries to reproduce regional and social dialects—the Spanish of *piuranos*, of highlanders, of mixed African and indigenous [*zambos*], of more-or-less educated criollos—through phonetic writing, in the manner of *costumbrista* literature. And although he gets it right at times (for example, with the character of Cámac), at other times he fails and relies on idiosyncrasy and parody. This is evident when *zambos* or Don Policarpo speak; the use of slang expressions, deformations of roughly translated words, without artistic reconstruction, achieve an effect contrary to that which they intend (this was the capital crime of *costumbrismo*): they seem artificial, as if they were speaking with nasal or falsetto voices. In any case, even with these limitations, because of his rich use of emotion, deft use of contrast, and flashes of poetry, the book, like everything Arguedas wrote, leaves an impression of beauty and life. (*La utopía arcaica* 232)

In this way, the cultural *difference* that resides within *El Sexto* has to do with the palimpsest of class and race in the Andes, with their infinite variables and intricate local connections, with their minute and constant alterations of cultural, linguistic, and even ideological norms that occur in "the real world" and that the hermetic and fictionalized universe of the prison demonizes and subverts. The range of characters that the novel presents traverses a stark and violent spectrum that does not want for nuances or degrees of perversion and suffering. The pianist, a former music student, is raped by a group of prisoners and loses his mind until his fellow inmates murder him to steal his clothes. A Japanese man who cannot even understand Spanish shares the same abuse and suffering as the pianist and also dies in appalling circumstances. "Clavel," a homosexual prostitute whose johns are his fellow inmates, contracts syphilis and goes insane, gaining in exchange the gift of clairvoyance. The Babelic condition thus extends from the purely linguistic level to the forms of rationality and madness, incorporating an anomalous logic that penetrates to hidden levels of the real. All of these levels coexist and contaminate each other, encompassing behaviors, values, origins, motives, personal histories, race, ethnicity, and sexual orientation. Rife with perversion and degradation, *El Sexto* explores evil in all its variations, demonstrating how the panoptic prison intensifies its effects, making itself, as part of the State apparatus, into the principal factor of human degradation and social shame.

Through the work of language, the textual space of *El Sexto* is saturated and strained, reaching its limits and threatening to explode the discursive rationality and the unstable order of writing. The novel is a melting pot in which marginality, criminality, ignominy, idealism, and belief are mixed together, desires and values are put on display, and political projects, historical developments, and aesthetic sensibilities are all discussed. Perhaps Arguedas's most intensely *political* novel, *El Sexto* explores the world as an anomaly in which, within the interstitial cracks of evil (homophobia, racism, generalized violence), individual humanity fights to break through and survive.

El Sexto was followed by a narrative work that many regard as one of Arguedas's highest poetic achievements, "La agonía de Rasu Ñiti" ["The dying moments of Rasu Ñiti"], which Cornejo Polar considers an "incredible complement" to the prison novel which he considers the antithesis to this short story (*Los universos narrativos* 180–85). Through its use of mythical elements, allusions to social issues such as the condition of the indigenous (particularly indigenous women) working on haciendas in the Andes, the representation of dance and its relation to death and the continuity of culture, the accomplished plasticity of this story impresses an anticlimactic lyricism on Arguedas's narrative trajectory in those years, a trajectory which spanned from the degradation of prison to the totalizing desire of his next novelistic enterprise.

Also of a nature and scope completely foreign to the carceral world of *El Sexto*, the holistic project of *Todas las sangres* is, like Arguedas's previous novel, essentially relational. It seeks to represent the design of a complex, contradictory world and its internal flows: the tensions and forces that motivate it, both on the level of the community and the level of the individual subject. The novel illustrates the process of decomposition of *caciquismo*, or at least the weakening of its power as a matrix of economic and social domination, putting into circulation a series of characters with different affiliations and positions with respect to the deterioration of this power structure and the loss of privilege that this process entails. In this sense, the novel represents the interrelations not just between local economies and transnational companies but also between belief and work, between ethics, aesthetics, and politics. The connections between national and global capitalism are added to the representation of the premodern remnants of the Andean world and its distinct modes of production which generate differentiated forms of socialization, values, and subjectivities. In Antonio Cornejo Polar's review of the novel, one senses the all-encompassing desire of *Todas las sangres* both as a representation of the diverse levels that make up Peruvian reality in that era and in the perception of the course the nation could follow in the future:

> *Todas las sangres* draws an image of Peru as a complex space where at least four social projects are in conflict: that of imperialism, that of the national (and at times nationalist) bourgeoisie, that of feudal or semi-feudal landowners, and that of the indigenous peasantry. Arguedas imagines that it will be the Indians, as bearers of Andean values who are as traditional as they are modern, who will ultimately be the ones to impose their project. (Cornejo Polar, "Un ensayo sobre los *Zorros*" 299)

From the initial curse that opens the novel, in which the landowner Andrés Aragón de Peralta reproaches his sons Fermín and Bruno for their greed, lust, and unscrupulousness, the narrative evolves in different directions to illustrate behaviors and attitudes in relation to power, the world of values, religiosity, passions, and so on. In each character these behaviors and attitudes develop differently according to the characteristics and functions that they are assigned in that world traversed by rivers of blood and structural cracks which stem from the most remote past but which are exacerbated by modernity. The novel constitutes, in this sense, the dissection of a living body, the social body of the Andean nation, marked from the very beginning by inequality and discrimination. In the character of Rendón Willka, to whom we will return later, is concentrated a large part of the tensions and alternatives portrayed in the novel, and he serves as a link between different positions related to the problem of power. He simultaneously represents the force of tradition and the heralding of change, the ancestral and the inevitable transformations of modernization—energies which all converge within him, up to and including his own death, which seems to be an offering to the world that both contains him and prepares him for radical change. Utilizing the techniques of communicating vessels, intersecting narrative and temporal schemes, and multifaceted characters who are transformed throughout the story, Arguedas achieves a dynamic development in which fiction continues to reveal a constant concern for concrete problems in the Andean region.

As a comprehensive novel, *Todas las sangres* includes an important representation of women, who of course also appear in other novels by Arguedas but who acquire here a special relevance, exhibiting, as Melisa Moore has noted, a multiple marginality—of ethnicity, gender, and class. As a link between everydayness and community, between family, fertility, and sexuality, the figure of the woman is a complex character, both at the individual level as well as the collective level, which Arguedas contextualizes by creating fictitious individualities composed of very diverse features and functions. Asunta, Matilde, la Kurku, the women in the market, who are all linked to unrequited love, sexual violence, maternity, and madness, stand out against the backdrop of a patriarchal society in which they intervene in a generally inorganic but persistent way, driving the themes of affective knowledge, the liberation of instincts, and the connection to nature. Moore argues, referring to the woman as a collective character in which forms of incipient consciousness and action are engendered:

> The feminine characters in *Todas las sangres* reveal a contestatory capacity with regard to the individual, but as collective characters, as *cholas*, mestizas, and *comuneras*, they discover the potential they have to form an active resistance that even further displaces the borders between the public and the private and which consolidates their position as defenders of the subaltern group of which they are a part. (*En la encrucijada* 273)[20]

Rama considers *Todas las sangres* to be "in equal parts a novel and a program for governance" (*Writing Across Cultures* 115), carried out through the social consciousness of a writer who understood his intellectual task as a historical mission of promoting a new perspective on the national question, following the paths opened by Mariátegui as well as the elaboration of a cultural plan of action capable of confronting the devastating modernizing drives within the Andean region.[21]

The totalizing representation of social realism that Arguedas offers in *Todas las sangres* has triggered a series of polemics from its initial publication up to the present day. The debates that have developed around this text derive from the desire, made explicit by Arguedas himself, that this work be recognized not only for its literary value but also for its testimonial significance.[22] At the margins of the discussion regarding the interpretation of the texts and focused on the angles that Arguedas's work could have proposed for the knowledge and understanding of Peruvian reality, two conceptual levels which are worth recovering came to light in this polemic. The first is related to the value of affectivity as a cognitive resource for grasping those aspects of reality that do not reveal themselves to the senses or to instrumental reason. In the second place, the polemic precipitated a reflection on the importance of the categories utilized for the configuration of the fictitious world but also of the models that inform language and the methodology of the social sciences that are applied to the study of what Rama called "the Andean cultural area" and which with hardly any elaboration utilize terms from ordinary language (*indio*, *cholo*, *mestizo*, etc.) that require conceptual and ideological refinement.

With respect to the first, the function of emotion in Arguedas's work has been a common locus of critique. Nevertheless, this theme has been insufficiently analyzed in spite of the "affective turn" which has developed in recent decades as a theoretico-critical approach to the study of subjectivity and as an alternative path for the pursuit of knowledge and the understanding of social dynamics.[23] Some headway was already made in this regard in the literary criticism of the 1970s. In *Writing Across Cultures*, for example, Rama discusses the "illuminations" that traverse Arguedas's narrative work, understanding them as "synchronic and structured perceptions of the real" (154) that constitute models of understanding which serve as alternatives to the rational. In these models, passion, intuition, mythical thinking, and lyricism find their place, as if they were related to the "matrices of signification" that, as Lévi-Strauss explains in *The Savage Mind*, transmit the knowledge that the spirit achieves of itself and of the world to which it belongs (Rama, *Writing Across Cultures* 135–36). Infantile subjectivity (which in Arguedas continues to mark, throughout his entire life, a primary and fresh form of approaching the real) and, along with it, lyricism, the ludic and the oneiric, all are part of that "mythic intelligence" Rama detects. This subjectivity requires a new, de-familiarizing, and de-habitualizing language to express itself. In fact, it requires a language that is liberated from the formalizations and norms of ordinary language, in which the basic communicative function obscures expressivity and the emergence of intuitive knowledge (*Writing Across Cultures* 133–55). Hence, Arguedas's search for a utopian and plausible, although artificial and actually non-existent, language that would be capable of transmitting the intermediary place which would make possible the exchange of meanings between cultures, subjectivities, classes, and forms of organizing the social universe and the understanding of individual and collective experience. From this direct experience (in which received culture and sensibility itself are articulated) specific forms of knowledge of the world emerge since, as Aníbal Quijano recalls in the roundtable on *Todas las sangres*, "it is not the consciousness of man that determines his existence but his social existence which determines his consciousness. And a novel of critical realism like *Todas las sangres* is also a form of social consciousness" (Arguedas et al., *¿He vivido en vano?* 75).

However, as Arguedas expressed on multiple occasions, the relation to language supposes not only an affective link of identification with society and nature but also a problem of power in which the hegemony of the linguistic sign establishes itself in the heart of the historical drama of domination and resistance and refers to the processes of appropriation and restructuring of the dominant models. Nothing illustrates this intrinsic and indestructible relation between affect, power, and language better than Arguedas's own words regarding the historical struggle between Quechua and Spanish and the way in which future instances of social struggle can be imagined from within the inescapable frame of modernity. As he explains in the article titled "Entre el *kechua* y el castellano: la angustia del mestizo":

> When I started to write about the life of my people, I was painfully aware of the inadequacy of doing it in Spanish, a language incapable of expressing the skies and rains of my land, let alone our attachment to the soil, to the trees of our valleys, not to mention the urgencies of our human hates and loves.
> [...]
> But now that the man rooted in this land feels the need to express himself and to do it in a language that he does not command, he finds himself in a painful dilemma: the Spanish learned with great effort in school, college,

or university is not fully equipped to express his soul or the landscape of the world where he grew up; and the Quechua he still feels to be his genuine language, in which he can give full voice to his concerns and fulfill his deepest need to express his people and his lands, is an untimely language without universal value.

[...]

This urge to master Spanish will put the mestizo into full possession of the language. And its effect on the Spanish language will be due to the fact that he will never cease adapting Spanish to his deeper need for self-expression, in other words, translating it into every particle of his being, under the command of his Indian self. (Arguedas, "Entre el kechwa y el castellano"141–42/"Between Quechua and Spanish" 15–16)

Inextricably linked to the process of linguistic production, the world of affectivity functions as a space which is in itself *political* and which helps to displace the "magical technologies of public intimacy" that Nigel Thrift speaks of. It constitutes, in this sense, a non-discursive intensity that works to catalyze changes in subjectivity both on a collective and molecular (Guattari) scale, driving the production of a non-rational knowledge and connecting distinct vital instances and diverse subjects, relating subject and object, subject and event, body and non-body, or, as Rama indicates with respect to Arguedas, illuminating the intrinsic relations between the word and the thing. These relations demonstrate substantial, *necessary, and existential* ties that go unnoticed by ordinary communication. Through his linguistic investigation, Arguedas sheds light on this cognitive worldview: he proposes a new way to access the real, the symbolic, and the imaginary, a way which in itself constitutes an alternative to dominant rationality. In effect, the path opened up by Arguedian poetics challenges power with its immeasurably expansive and unstable quality, which is both ludic and lyrical, and in which the instrumental character and conventionalism of the Western conception of language are outstripped by a denotative quality that brings together other realms of knowledge, sentiment, and imagination. In this way, Arguedas surpasses rationality, because affect (which is one of the principal elements of his poetics) always aims at excess; for this reason, intercultural communication appears in Arguedas as the exercise of an excessive, overflowing, performative, and insubordinate language.[24] At the same time, language is fashioned as *one* of the elements that make up cultural semiosis, integrating itself into the complex system of the production of meanings which encompass as well as exceed the semiotic value of the spoken or written word. The meaning is, in large measure, *performed*, staged, and dramatized to achieve the transmission of complex messages that activate another epistemology in which belief, a connection to nature, the mythic dimension, music, sentiment, and the practices of everyday life are articulated and mutually reinforce one another. The oral or written linguistic sign is, in this sense, a *supplement*, a mediation, when it is not a paradoxical obstacle to the process of the transmission of meaning.

Along with the theme of affectivity as a generative matrix of knowledge, Arguedas's work also suggests (as was previously indicated) the need to revise the categories that are commonly utilized to refer to the multifaceted ethnic and racial combinatory of the region through concepts which stereotype the reality to which they refer. Aníbal Quijano calls attention to this point, laying the foundation for his opinion that Arguedas's narrative work, particularly *Todas las sangres*, finds no language to express such nuances and at times falls prey to overly rigid and traditional critical categories in the attempt to conceptualize the processes of social transformation. He refers, for example, to the dynamics of cholification and to the increasing modernization that, by the middle of the twentieth century, had already begun to reach different areas of the Andean region, albeit in an uneven way. Quijano notes, for example, that when speaking of the Indian as such, Arguedas projects an overly static image of this social category, which allows him to call attention to the inequality and marginality of these cultures:

> But, what is the Indian? Somehow, the Indian is something that can *grosso modo* contain various features, elements that come from pre-Hispanic culture but which are completely altered by the influence of colonial and postcolonial Hispanic culture and contemporary republican elements which have, in turn, incorporated elements of Hispanic culture, also reinterpreted and modified. This Hispanic culture has [also] incorporated elements of recent western culture, which have likewise been reinterpreted and modified, but which is still legitimate to discuss, [in reference to] a part of the rural population of the country, within indigenous culture, since all these elements form a relatively (but not completely) different structure from what we can more explicitly call western culture, or the criollo version of western culture in Peru. (Arguedas et al., *¿He vivido en vano?* 58)[25]

To deconstruct the category of "Indian" as an ideological key and principal core of Arguedas's poetics, Quijano leaves the status of fiction intact but cuts ties with a changing, historically conditioned, and conceptually elusive social reality which social science-based analysis must keep on redefining according to its own conceptual and methodological protocols. At the same time, Qujano implicitly calls attention to the dangers of the thingification (mythification, mystification) of an object of knowledge that is above all an object of desire and which, more than simply being part of reality, is a central element in the individual imaginary of the narrator. Based on a strictly referentialist and scientistic interest, sociology describes social reality according to a rationality of progression and change which identifies processes and social actors, factors of continuity and transformation, perceiving the diverse moments of social history as events that occur within a linear temporal order that goes from the past to the future. Other epistemologies admit of diverse conceptions of temporality and distinct spatial coordinates as parameters for knowledge of the world.

Literary criticism tells another story. In her study of social sciences and Arguedas's literature, referring to the inquiries the author of *Todas las sangres* received regarding the way he represented Peruvian society in the novel, Melisa Moore argues that the disagreement between the two disciplinary perspectives is a result of the fact that Arguedas worked with different temporalities at the same time, producing a kaleidoscopic representation of Andean reality that social sciences cannot accept because such simultaneity does not emerge from or result in an organized temporal synthesis. In this respect, referring to compositional aspects of the novel that allow for the consolidation of different disciplinary focuses, Moore indicates:

> Opting for a literary format (the novel *Todas las sangres*) and producing a fabric in which anthropological concerns and ethnographic materials are interwoven, Arguedas is able to reveal not only the simultaneity of these disciplines and genres but also the simultaneity of the chronotopes that are found within them. I have proposed that these chronotopes allow for the intersection of the discourse of historicism and the discourse of archetypes and that these correlate with the different ways in which historical development is perceived. Situating both social actors and specific events within an optic of the "*longue durée*" (Braudel), Arguedas is able not only to show a temporal diachrony but also on this basis attribute archetypical dimensions both to certain characters and to determinate practices and customs. From this emerges, therefore, a hybrid genre in which not only scientific and non-scientific elements are combined but also different spatio-temporal frames that allow for the creation of a more totalizing image like the one Arguedas himself emphasizes in relation to *Todas las sangres*... (*En la encrucijada* 303)

Arguedas's work emerges as a demonstration of subjectivity that, from the perspective of sociology, for example, could not deliver reliable knowledge because the personal point of view is obscured by desire, affectivity, selective memory, individual convictions, and so on. Arguedas's work would thus exist as torn between different regimes of *truth* based on which the object of knowledge is revealed to be contradictory and unsynthesizable, as an antithesis which resists the domestication of a rationality that excludes intuition and affectivity as ways of approaching the real.

It is easy to see the merits of both positions. The social sciences-based reading of Arguedas's work, a theme to which we will return later, has in my view incorporated an extremely useful component for reading literary texts by this Peruvian author, which, beyond their documentary aspirations and their obvious aesthetic value, are read, as Quijano correctly points out, as a particular form of "social consciousness."[26] Stemming as much from the direct experience of indigenous marginality as from his intellectual and literary production, this consciousness informs the ways of conceptualizing reality from an unusually bi-epistemological, dual perspective, which, despite its alternative nature, is expressed in the language of Western science and with the categories that result from the interpretive machinery of disciplines redefined in the context of colonialism and utilized by postcolonial intellectuals in an emancipatory, anticolonial project. In turn, positions which emphasize the specificity of the literary text and its capacity to represent those levels of reality which escape instrumental reason recover *other* forms of knowledge, truths which, along with the observation of social and cultural frameworks, recuperate the perception of the imagined, the desired, and the remembered as simultaneous forms of the processes and modes of being of the real.

Subject to the *double bind* which is consubstantial to the postcolonial condition, the Arguedian consciousness thus transfers to the field of language the irresolvability of a conflict that translates its materiality in terms of the symbolic struggle between resistant forms of subjectivity, sentiments, knowledges, and communicational registers. Arguedas, who explored throughout his entire life the possibility of articulating a dominated society to its oppressor without the former losing its integrity, ever more keenly began to perceive the exclusive hegemony of the latter. The transfer of meanings from one culture to another then appeared to him as a unidirectional process that failed to alter either the status of reality or the fundamental values which sustain it. In this constant battle, Spanish appears to end up winning the game.

But if this complex trajectory of the search for communicative truth would seem to have reached a limit at which the different alternatives have already been completely explored (with mixed results), what is still missing is the intellectual experience of inhabiting the Babelic space which emerges correlatively to the advance of transnationalized capitalism and the impact it has on local cultures—a point which encapsulates Arguedas's ethical and ideological concerns. The setting of *El zorro de arriba* is the port city of Chimbote, a space which includes the migrant worker *slums*, an extreme setting in which the protocols of interlinguistic hybridization and translation, regionalisms and foreign interests which impact the landscape, modes of production and collective subjectivity are all dizzyingly interwoven. The port is home to the disorderly coexistence of carnivalized elements which require new strategies of reading and hermeneutic practice and which are presented in the narrative as a grotesque exposé of human types, interpersonal dynamics, practices, and languages that saturate the world represented there and which assault the reader with their demonstrative and interpellative force.

Taking as its background the prison novel *El Sexto* (with regard to the representation of the coastal regions of Peru) as well as the stories of *Amor Mundo*, the *Zorros* refers to the uncontrollable reemergence of repressed worldviews through the modernizing processes that are excessively debated in the turbulent and cracked surface of a story which definitively intervenes in the bourgeois genre of the novel, twisting its discursivity, its spatiotemporal coordinates, its unities of narrative action, and the concept of heroism. It continues, nevertheless, to exacerbate (if we want to follow the Lukácsian line) the degradation of the world as the general background of the actions that inevitably unfold as vicissitudes between myth and history. The dialogic structure, as well as the inclusion of autobiographical text, links together diverse temporalities—not just past and present, intimate time and collective time, but also the atemporality of myth with the burgeoning historicity of the global changes that shake, as the aftershocks of an earthquake whose epicenter is in the heart of the Western world, the very foundations of the community of Chimbote. The coastal city is presented as a new "Cusco," a center of the world, or a vulva penetrated by capitalism. The paradigmatic space of the city-port is depicted as an underworld profaned by capitalism and tormented by the exploitative dynamics of products and people. The presence of the author intervenes in the writing of the text, which is organized both vertically and horizontally (Escobar, *Arguedas o la utopía* 225) on axes which permit both the unfolding of anecdotal sequences and the inscription of enunciative perspectives, including the narrative function of the foxes. The mythic story of these characters (who originally come from the manuscripts of Huarochirí) produce a discourse that Julio Ortega designates as supra-rational, as a kind of bridge which extends "between the two divided zones of Peru," the sierra and the coast (Ortega, "Discurso del suicida" 272). The crowded and turbulent space of the port represents the crossroads between premodern regionalism and capitalist transnationalization. Chimbote is chosen as the paradigmatic place for the processes of accelerated and chaotic growth that, starting in 1955, impelled the transformation of the fishing population from a community of less than 5000 people to the largest port in the world, dedicated to the harvest of anchovies and the production of fishmeal and fish oil.[27]

Cryptic and unfathomable, at times esoteric, judgmental, rhythmic and ritualistic (when not openly obscene and almost hallucinatory), as well as punctuated by sublime moments of exasperation, the language of the *Zorros* deals a radical blow to *sense*: it constitutes a siege of language as a prison of meanings. The novel is based on a meticulous deconstruction of the word, the phrase, and thought as sites of rationality and possible consensus, effectuating an uncompromising break with Western reason and its epistemological and discursive conventions. Hence, this work has received critical evaluations which, nevertheless, do not fail to recognize its importance and exceptionality. Vargas Llosa has alluded to the language of the *Zorros* as a form of slang or incomprehensible gibberish, an "aphasic language" whose "expressive barbarism" would constitute one of the novel's principal failures. For Vargas Llosa, the *El zorro de arriba* had an initially realist intention that it was never able to crystallize. Based on this aborted reader's contract, Arguedas's text can only reveal itself to be deficient and flawed. In turn, Ortega refers to the language of the novel as "delirious speech" and expresses his concern about the "perilous reading" of the work, in which flaws stand out "because the novel is visibly incomplete and, even more, it is unfortunately damaged" ("Discurso del suicida" 269). For her part, Castro-Klarén avers that, in the *Zorros* and *El Sexto* "what dominates is the desire to denounce reality, which produces weak constructions in the structure and development of the narrative" (*El mundo mágico* 199). Caught between the forces of life and death unleashed by the demonic representation of Chimbote, the narrative of the *Zorros* seems to provoke interpretations that, extending to the work effects drawn from the life/death of its author, consider the text to be in large part a failed project in the same way that Arguedas's suicide confirmed, according to many, that the life he ended in self-destruction was also a failure.

Like the cadaver after death, the novel is a textual body that lies vulnerable and exposed to the gaze of the Other, abandoned, testifying, shocking. As a textual body (as remains) *El zorro de arriba y el zorro de abajo* evokes the residual, ruins, remainders, or in Freudian terms, "the shadow of the object" that falls on the ego, plunging it into the abyss. This resting literary body reveals, as the extreme, melancholic experience that brings it to a close, the "conflict of ambivalence" Freud mentions in his "Mourning and Melancholia." In this essay, Freud analyzes the relation between loss, suicide, and narcissism, and the *double bind* that creates an irresolvable disjunction between object and subject, between the experience of one who narrates his life experience in the final moment before his self-destruction and his simultaneous status as the object of the story, which he submits to the subjectivity that frames and enables writing.

A narrative constructed from these premises can only disappoint traditional expectations of literary reception by confronting the reader, not with a fictional universe configured according to well-known stylistic conventions, but with his own ghostly, subverted image, from the same mechanisms used to construct the story. Converted into a demonic apparatus of dis-identification and dis-narration, and utilizing the deconstructive power of the word as the correlate of the irrational and devastating force of capital, the novel presents an irremediable collapse, a *pachacuti* in which social experience of the known world succumbs and meaning is destroyed, persisting only as the residue of a rationality confronted by the unrepresentable.

El zorro de arriba y el zorro de abajo emphasizes the existence of multiple social, cultural, and linguistic registers as well as the convergence of texts composed in different literary keys (mythical, fictional, autobiographical) that make implicit reference to the sources from which they emerged: local knowledges, the author's own life experience, interviews Arguedas conducted in preparation for the book, Western literary vocation, and the primary source, the manuscripts of Huarochirí, from which the characters of the foxes and the forms of communication that they adopt in their dialog are taken.[28] Orality and writing, high literature and popular literature in turn form the background of this work which draws from and problematizes all of these sources to create among them a conflictive and fascinating proximity. The constant element of death that articulates the story incorporates an intense existential and poetic aspect into the multi-faceted plot of the novel.[29]

Martin Lienhard pays special attention to the theme of the reader profiled in the *Zorros* and to the linguistic strategies that significantly drive "the eruption of Quechua prose in a novel from the Hispanic world" ("La última novela de Arguedas" 179). Drawing support from the foxes' dialogic exchange in Quechua in the first chapter of the novel, Lienhard interprets this insertion of the Quechua responses with Spanish translations as a programmatic option that makes Arguedas's work, and particularly this "subverted and subversive" novel, a pioneering project of the search for a new type of reader for a similarly new mode of literary production. Far from the traditional techniques of indigenism, this accepts "the indigenous narrative moment" directed as a cultural sign to the "internal reader" of the novel. This concept of the "internal reader" designates an abstraction: the figure of a hypothetical receiver who, according to Lienhard, is able to decode everything in the text, not only the linguistic elements but also those pertaining to ritual, mythology, and indigenous symbolism. In this sense, the *Zorros* constitutes a narrative precursor of interculturality, an advance of horizons that are more culturally fluid yet still subject to the hegemony and vampirism of capital.

In the *Zorros*, language floats as if it were a sonic wave transmitted by the *Arguedas-machine*, not so much in Beasley-Murray's sense, in which the machine as an industrial object attaches itself as such to the processes of the production of subjectivity and to different forms of narrative action, but rather as the recuperation of the concept of the "war machine": that which is irreducible to the state apparatus and creates its own territorialities and existential rhythms.[30] In a Deleuzean sense, Chimbote is an *assemblage* in which extreme heterogeneity is articulated around certain dynamics (productivity, industrialization) and takes possession of a space that is as much physical (geocultural) as it is symbolic and existential.

The theme of race is prominent in the decomposed totality of the fictionalized port of Chimbote, although generational, national, and regional differences are added to it, including aspects that come to saturate the story's proliferating *collage*: "Black men, *zambos*, Chinese Indians, drunks, insolent or frightened *cholos*, skinny Chinese, old men as well as little gangs of young fellows, curious Spaniards and Italians were strolling about in the Corral" (Arguedas, *El zorro de arriba* 40/*The Fox from Up Above and the Fox from Down Below*, 43–44).

As Deleuze and Guattari note about the concept of assemblage, what is important is not so much *what it is* as *what it does* with the space that contains it and with the relations (segmentation, nomadism) that traverse it (*A Thousand Plateaus* 257). The logic that reigns in the assemblage of Chimbote is that of dislocation. The presence of myth contributes to the rarefication and complication of discourse and to the ideology that it transmits, but at the same time it incorporates a poetic and achronic dimension in the chaotic explosion of meanings, languages, and desires. The element of magic also rules this same space, which suggests the insatiable alchemy of capitalism: in Chimbote, "these machines and our wharves and trawlers swallow anchovies and defecate gold" (*El zorro de arriba* 100/*The Fox from Up Above and the Fox from Down Below* 125). The organicism that is applied to the descriptions of Chimbote and its dynamics of life and death incorporate a biopolitical dimension that is essential to the study of Arguedas's narrative universe and that acquires an exasperating relevance in the *Zorros*.

In fact, Chimbote is presented as a repository of exploited, suffering, alienated bodies marked by instinct and violence and by the persistent sign of death that connects the narrative to capitalist expansion. *El zorro de arriba* represents in cultural and symbolic code the vampirism of capital and the techniques it deploys above all in peripheral areas marked by colonialist depredation in its various historical avatars. The representation of Chimbote appeals to anomaly and excess as elements of a poetics through which political and social change manifests itself in all its measureless polyphony. The heterogeneity of the *Zorros* is extreme, radical, because it encompasses every level of the narrative: spaces and temporalities, cultural registers, social background, the characteristics and behaviors of characters, economic class, cultural practices, forms of socialization, and communicational strategies, in which there is no lack of technological elements that interfere with the archaic forms of mythical language, novelistic speech, and the lyricism of descriptions. Dances, developments, dialogs, omens, sexual interactions, all give way to forms of transformation and exchange that invigorate the narrative action to the point of paroxysm. A more distinct and contained rhythm corresponds to the mythical evocations and to the omens that are presented in the archaic and judgmental language of the foxes.

The dynamic between the coastal population and the population of the sierra, and the distribution of qualities that almost always favors the latter create the most highly delimited parameters of the conflict between regions which continue to be connected through the nomadic impulses that derive from the modes of production and socialization that the novel represents. But the dominant line is framed by the Andean cosmovision from which the microcosm of Chimbote is observed. Cornejo Polar correctly points out that "[i]n *El zorro de arriba y el zorro de abajo* the Andean elements are of such a magnitude and exercise such decisive functions that it is legitimate to think that in this novel, for the first time, indigenous reason is what accounts for modernity" ("Un ensayo sobre *Los Zorros* de Arguedas" 303).

Nevertheless, the presence of such models of perception and interpretation of reality can only be produced by the "irrationality" of the communicative and compositional exchanges that the text sets in motion. The tangled and anarchic reality of the *Zorros* demonstrates the riotous surfacing of elements that, having been repressed by modernity and exacerbated by the marginalization of centuries, return with a vengeance while also incorporating into the situation new elements that have originated global dynamics. The new world (dis)order of transnationalized capitalism cannot peacefully or harmoniously integrate the already-existing elements nor rationalize their rhythms or curtail their effects. The *Zorros* constitutes the eminently inorganic situation of a global system that is unleashed, intrusively, on specific regions to consolidate the logic of the reproduction of capital, disrupting local logics. Parallel to the forward movement of the author's impending death, which approaches in step with the development of the novel, capitalist exploitation advances and imposes itself as the depredation of nature and as the dehumanization of the social environment. Death seems to be the only possible outcome of a diabolical vicissitude in which what is represented is eminently the final moment of a historical time and of the gaze that perceives it. As Cornejo Polar will point out, the new world that will survive after the final *pachacuti* of the novel still lacks the word. It is for this reason that the Babelic language of *El zorro de arriba y el zorro de abajo* follows silence, the virtual space where the echo of the voices and machines of Chimbote reverberate.

Notes

1. On this subject, the work of Martín Lienhard, a pioneer in the recovery and interpretation of oral and bi/multilingual cultures in Latin America, is of fundamental interest. See William Rowe's study, "La hermenéutica diglósica en los trabajos de Martín Lienhard," in Rowe, *Hacia una poética radical*, 59–64.

2. In this sense, the title *Arguedas o la utopía de la lengua*, which Escobar gave to the book in which he studied "language, discourse, and writing" through the distinct uses and functions of language in Arguedas's work, is entirely appropriate.
3. This use of language refers to the "later" Wittgenstein of the *Philosophical Investigations* (1953), who understands meaning as no longer tied to the descriptive or referential capacity of language he promoted in his *Tractatus* (1921), but rather as a product of the *function* that this language assumes through its concrete uses and effects. If, for Wittgenstein, language is a system of *games*, the rules that govern it should be, according to him, shared, constituted by and within a socialized register that legitimates them and gives them continuity. In this way, the production of meaning no longer depends on the pragmatics of the sign (the ways in which it is used), but rather on the contexts of its actualization and the concrete experiences to which that language refers.
4. [Throughout this chapter, the author makes use of a number of distinctly Peruvian terms Arguedas utilized in his writing which refer to mixing of cultures and races. The terms *mistura* (mixture) and *misti* (mestizo), in particular, are left untranslated here in order to retain the particularity they hold within the Arguedian worldview.—Tr.]
5. [In English in the original.—Tr.]
6. On the concept of the "Third Space" applied to Latin American literature, see Moreiras, *The Exhaustion of Difference*.
7. [Originally published as *Transculturación narrativa en América Latina*, México: Siglo XXI, 1982. The English translation cited here is *Writing Across Cultures: Narrative Transculturation in Latin America*, ed. and trans. David Frye, Durham: Duke University Press, 2012.—Tr.]
8. Escobar already perceived—as Castro-Klarén recalls in her article "Como chancho cuando piensa" ["'Like a pig, when he's thinkin'": Arguedas on Affect and on Becoming an Animal"]—that Arguedas claims for himself a "right to difference" (Escobar 232).
9. Escobar has commented on the dialects that are presented in the different editions of *Agua*: the original 1935 edition, the edition of 1954 that includes *Diamantes y pedernales*, and the 1967 edition published under the title *Amor, mundo y todos los cuentos*. See Escobar, *Arguedas o la utopía de la lengua* (118).
10. The "Vocabulario" ["Lexicon"—Tr.] of Quechua terms included in the original edition of *Agua* was replaced in the 1954 edition by notes or parenthetical translations into Spanish, as Luis Alberto Ratto has noted (Escobar mentions this in *Arguedas o la utopía de la lengua*, 119). See Escobar and Ratto for an analysis of these linguistic aspects of Arguedas's work and for a comparison of the different editions of *Agua*.

11. On the composition of *Yawar fiesta* and the problem of language, see Cornejo Polar, *Los universos narrativos*; Castro-Klarén, *El mundo mágico*; Kokotovic, "Transculturación narrativa y modernidad andina"; and Hare.
12. Here, Escobar's observations on the notion of the "purity" of Spanish to which Arguedas alludes are of great importance, as are his comments on the theme of reception which underlies the concern with language, primarily with respect to the multiple dialects of Quechua and to questions of literacy, the circulation of and access to literature, and so on. (see Escobar 74 and passim).
13. As Silvia Spitta has pointed out in analyzing Arguedas's position "between two waters" [*"entre dos aguas"*], Quechua colonizes Spanish in multiple ways, eroding its codes at all levels: "The use of Quechua words; the elimination of articles; the careless approach to consistency with the Spanish language; sentences that favor the use of gerunds; the lack of personal pronomial forms; the proliferation of the diminutive form and its extension to adverbs and gerunds that normally do not use it; the phonetic confusion between the letter 'y' and the letter 'i' and between the letters 'o' and 'u' and the indiscriminate use of formal and informal forms of address" (166–67).
14. In order to understand some aspects of the conflict of biculturality and the difficult existence of linguistic registers, it is worth keeping in mind Sommer's reflections in her article "A Vindication of Double Consciousness."
15. Bringing together the question of language, and the question of migration and the creation of a *Third Space* of enunciation, Bhabha notes: "To think of migration as metaphor suggests that the very language of the novel, in its form and rhetoric, must be open to meanings that are ambivalent, doubling, and dissembling. Metaphor produces hybrid realities by yoking together unlikely traditions of thought" (in Rutherford 212).
16. On Arguedas as a translator, see also Bernabé.
17. "For Arguedas," Tarica says, "*mistura* was the sign of a historical rupture. If he abandoned it it was because he recognized that the great majority of his readers and critics understood *mistura* as a mimesis of 'indigenous Spanish,' that is, an incorrect Spanish that is difficult for metropolitan readers to understand" (20).
18. In this search, Arguedas discovered the cultural agency of the mestizo and its political potentiality, which is to say, the paradoxical advantages of an interstitial position that sinks its roots into the colonial condition of the criollo, constitutively ambivalent in its Janus-faced quality. Regarding this topic, which we will return to later, see Rama's turbulent and undoubtedly polemical elaborations on the mestizo throughout the essays in the second part of *Writing Across Cultures*.
19. Arguedas was imprisoned at age 26 for having formed part of a university protest against General Camarotta, a representative of Benito Mussolini, who had been invited to the Universidad Nacional Mayor de San Marcos.

20. Moore has produced the most exhaustive study to date on the theme of the representation of women in Arguedas's work, following its development since the author's earliest texts, but concentrating on *Todas las sangres*. What is interesting about her study is that it includes a comparative analysis of the theme of the woman in Arguedas's anthropological work alongside his literary representations, thus allowing one to clearly see the place he assigns to the woman as an agent of an incipient but growing social consciousness in a heavily patriarchal and highly stratified world. As Moore points out, the woman not only has the role of representing a type of subject in which different forms of marginality are combined but also of serving as a bridge between ethnicities and class binaries, between public and private space, between nature and culture, and so on.
21. Gonzalo Portocarrero has summarized the contributions *Todas las sangres* has made to the comprehension of the possible forms of modernization in Peru and the alternatives that the novel presents (which I cite here verbatim, although in a necessarily fragmented way): (1) a modernization headed up by foreign capital and its intermediaries—the agent of this first path is the Wisther-Bozart company; (2) a modernization presided over by a national business community that manages to preserve its autonomy with respect to international capital—this is the path proposed by don Fermín Aragón de Peralta; (3) the neo-feudal project of don Bruno, which implies resisting the corrupting force of modernization; (4) the project embodied by the figure of don Lucas: persevering in path of caciquismo [*gamonalismo*], the path of merciless abuse—this would entail the incorporation of the Christian message this character assimilates with the traditional system of domination. See Portocarrero, "Aproximaciones."
22. Referring to the objections that were made to this documentary aspect of his work, Arguedas said: "If it is not a testimony, then I have merely lived for pleasure, I have lived in vain, or I have not lived at all. No! I have shown what I have lived, and maybe in time what I have lived will not be true. Well, I will accept that, with great pleasure [sic]. There are some elements, yes, which are not exactly sociological, which are not exactly an ethnographic testimony" (Arguedas et al., ¿*He vivido en vano*? 36).
23. For a broad theoretical and critical survey of this development, see, for example, the studies included in the book I co-edited with Ignacio Sánchez Prado, *El lenguaje de las emociones*. Juan Manuel Marcos has also written on the theme of sentiment in Arguedas. Castro-Klarén deals with the theme of affect in Arguedas in "Como chancho cuando piensa" ["Like a pig, when he's thinkin'"].
24. In this respect, see Moraña, "El afecto en la caja de herramientas," which appeared as a postscript to *El lenguaje de las emociones*.

25. According to Quijano, what would be lacking in Arguedas's narrative work (if it requires maintaining fidelity to that testimonialist desideratum that the writer frequently expresses) is a more careful observation of the processes that influence the most important forms of social change. According to Quijano, Arguedas oscillates between various modes of conceptualizing these processes as a substitution for the traditional forms of integration that allow ancient modalities to survive without losing their content. This, which for Quijano is an inconsistency, is rather for Arguedas one of the qualities of postcolonial society that he attempts to represent in all of its nuances. On this dilemma between social science and literature, see Moore, *En la encrucijada*.
26. On the topic of the social sciences in relation to Arguedas's work, see Moore, as well as Archibald, "Overcoming Science in the Andes."
27. See Sulmont and Flores Galindo, *El movimiento obrero en la industria pesquera*, which analyzes the case of Chimbote and the social transformations that resulted from the economic process of industrial fishing and the export of fish products at the international level (the establishment of dozens of fisheries, development in the port for the accommodation of both small vessels and deep-water vessels for harvesting and exporting fish, and the growth of the population from a few thousand inhabitants in the 1940s to more than a quarter million two decades later).
28. Lienhard has emphasized the divided character of the novel, not only in terms of its narrative modalities but also in terms of the way it utilizes oppositions (above/below, which is part of Quechua cosmology; Western/Andean, orality/writing, man/woman), as well as the plurality of narrative perspectives, the fusion of idiolects and sociolects, and so on. Additionally, the positions of the characters, settings, and conflicts demonstrate a constant instability ("La andinización del vanguardismo urbano" 326–32).
29. On *El zorro de arriba*, particularly its links with Andean popular culture, see Lienhard, *Cultura popular andina y forma novelesca*.
30. Beasley-Murray's ingenious reading of the *Zorros* supposes a broader conceptual and philosophical field than he brings to the table. Although he does not develop the concept of the *war machine* in relation to Arguedas's writing, he does correctly suggest the possibility of applying it to this author.

CHAPTER 6

Language as a Battlefield (II): The Narcissism of the Voice

One should perhaps begin by recognizing that Vargas Llosa's achievements at the level of narrative technique, literary structure, and composition of fictitious worlds represent one of the pinnacles of Spanish-language literature, as well as some of the most brilliant examples of literary production in Latin America. As Cornejo Polar indicates, already from his early novel *La ciudad y los perros* (1962) [*The Time of the Hero* (1966)] "Vargas Llosa inscribed himself completely within—better yet: he contributed decisively to [the] foundation—[of] the 'new Latin American narrative'" ("Hipótesis" 253). Although much more ground remains to be covered, his literary texts have been widely studied, from his initial breakthrough writings to his more recent, less-than-solid novelistic offerings. As an author of the era of modernization, Vargas Llosa has made undeniable contributions to the diversification of perspectives on national culture in Latin America (particularly from the point of view of neoliberal thought) on the construction of collective subjectivities, and on the rise of a new phase in the articulation of dependent societies with central capitalism through technologization, the expansion of markets, and the multiplication of resources for the creation and dissemination of symbolic products.

From the very beginning of his career, Vargas Llosa's work has continued to expand, prolifically and diversely, covering an enormous number of themes and culminating in the Nobel Prize in Literature, which he received in 2010 "for his cartography of the structures of power and his trenchant images of the individual's resistance, revolt and defeat." The

© The Editor(s) (if applicable) and The Author(s) 2016
M. Moraña, *Arguedas / Vargas Llosa*,
DOI 10.1057/978-1-137-57187-8_6

conditions that have surrounded most of Vargas Llosa's literary production (including the central position he enjoys at an international level) have been characterized by many as exceptional, particularly for a Latin American author. This centrality has been crucial for the dissemination of his texts in different forms of media, diverse languages, and multiple public, political, and cultural circles.[1] Early on, Cornejo Polar detected a skeptical tendency in Vargas Llosa, not only in relation to the way he examines reality but also with respect to the way he opposes reality and literature, which permits Vargas Llosa, using his undeniable literary virtuosity, to impose a discursive *order* that incorporates a peculiar tension into the referent/meaning relation. Through technically advanced writing which encompasses a broad range of themes, spaces, and narrative styles, Vargas Llosa overcomes the contradictions of reality by submitting a highly controlled final product that Cornejo Polar has interpreted as "a variation of commodity fetishism" ("Hipótesis" 255). According to this criterion:

> [w]hile in narrative (of which Arguedas's work is emblematic) the production of the text, its concrete configuration, and the sense that it bears, all reproduce the conflict of the referent and the perspective it reveals (which in the final instance corresponds to the contradictions of its social environment), [in Vargas Llosa's work] in contrast, a relation of a different kind is created in which, to put it schematically, chaos is represented by order. (Cornejo Polar, "Hipótesis" 255)

Cornejo Polar understands that Vargas Llosa and Arguedas constitute the extremes of a representational spectrum that oscillates between a narrative of capitalist modernization that implies a new order for the Andean region and a literature that represents the phenomena of destructuration of the old social order, a position which Cornejo Polar identifies as a dynamic of "apocalypse and utopia." Based on this, it is possible to implement a form of critical thought that appears to be expressed in literary texts and makes possible the establishment of an alternative historical/political/cultural trajectory. Thus, while Vargas Llosa is able to exorcise the demons of social contradiction and irrationalism within the ordered world of fiction, Arguedas submits a complex vision of a contradictory reality, fragmented and imperfectly integrated into capitalist modernity, in which antagonisms are maintained as the agonizing backdrop of the surviving colonialism Mariátegui spoke of.[2]

In addition to the merits and singularities of Vargas Llosa's literary world, other facets of his intellectual work are worth highlighting here because they complement his poetics and complete his profile in the context of the transnationalized public sphere. Undoubtedly, apart from his narrative universe, where the problematic nature of the referent is filtered and domesticated through the literary devices of fiction, the most prominent aspect of Vargas Llosa's use of language is more closely related to the theme of *discourse* as a cultural practice (to the exercise of mediated enunciation, to communicative rhetoric) than to the problems linked to multicultural or multiethnic representation in the Andean region, a conflictive situation which has haunted Arguedas throughout his entire life. Confronted by these questions, Vargas Llosa developed strategies not unlike those of other writers in the Andean region regarding the representation of indigenous cultures and the conflicts that, according to dominant cognitive models, exist between these cultures and criollo society.[3]

Vargas Llosa's properly *literary* language, to which I referred above, has already been characterized by critics as mundane, sometimes crude, and rife with colloquialisms, obscenities, stifled speech, idiomatic expressions, and proverbs that come together to impress on his writing a sense of orality and a spontaneous, conversational tone. This style frequently includes elements of humor, parody, and irony, thus affirming the value of literature as a form of entertainment that at the same time *intervenes* in social reality at different levels. The constant appeal to the use of cultivated standard Spanish alternates with erudite references and elements of realistic writing that, without wanting to be documentary, aspire to transmit an accurate representation of different types of social sectors and national realities. Vargas Llosa's literary language frequently includes local slang and lexico-syntactical deformations which call the reader's attention to the foreignness of certain characters and to the fractures and dissociations that characterize the fictional world. Above all, Vargas Llosa's work thematizes the dominant culture and the periphery which helps to define it as if this alterity constituted the negative of an image that must be developed, sharpening its contours and leaving behind the spectral, threatening forms that surround it.

Understood as a hermetic and ultimately unknowable space framed by atavistic and mysterious tendencies and energies that exist outside of Western rationality, this cultural alterity (as well as the otherness related to the inscription of class) constitutes the main subject of Vargas Llosa's literature. Above all, what that alterity exposes is its irreducible and disruptive quality and its potential to impact dominant projects and imaginaries. In Arguedas, the conflicting coexistence of diverse cultural registers of identity and otherness compels the creation of intersubjective spaces, the assessment of possible encounters, and the observation of inevitable and dramatic clashes between cultures, ethnicities, and social classes. Alternatively, in Vargas Llosa, the recognition of these dichotomies in turn constitutes the key feature of his fiction because of the capacity of poetic language to expose the alienation of certain social groups and the dissociation from *the social*.

In this sense, the role Vargas Llosa assigns to himself is that of spectator, witness, and narrator of Andean heterogeneity. Also, as Ariel Dorfman once pointed out, Vargas Llosa's work constitutes, as the counterpart to the melancholia of Arguedas's texts, a warning against the bourgeois ideology of fatalism (although such a broad characterization should be understood in the context of the literary texts Dorfman had in mind). His literature thus issues a call for the consolidation of the Western project which promotes the participation of Latin America in the utopia of progress and in the struggle against barbarism and irrationalism.

According to Dorfman, while Arguedas constructs myths and then fights to preserve them, Vargas Llosa helps to destroy them. Nevertheless, the problem is more complex since Vargas Llosa's work is not free from myths, even if they are more personal and less transcendent than those one can see at work in Arguedas's fiction. Updating the role of the messianic intellectual (and of the organic intellectual), which has a long tradition in Latin America, Vargas Llosa's hope appears to boil down to the desire to provide a modernized and indisputable version of the conflicts and potentialities of national culture viewed from a position of privilege and transmitted through the communication technologies that this modernity makes available. His literature, and the entirety of his discourse in general (whether ideological, media-related, or otherwise), orients itself toward a search for universality in the broadest sense of the term. Vargas Llosa's prolific output includes speeches, declarations, interviews, radio and television commentaries, newspaper columns, theatrical productions, official reports, and so on, all of which reveal his need for an omnipresence that would eventually saturate public space. The myth of individual freedom as the basis of democracy and as an abstract site of liberalism persists throughout his entire body of work. His production can be summarized as the attempt to consolidate a singularly prominent and indisputably legitimate enunciative site both as the implementation of that freedom and as a platform for its ideological dissemination.

This process, which will pass through various stages, is directed through what Rowe calls Vargas Llosa's "communicational methods," which, especially since 1975, have been characterized by a notorious and inherent pragmatism. According to Rowe, Vargas Llosa's discursive style supports itself in a verbosity in which the literary comes to the aid of the ideological and the ideological reduces the poetic in lieu of nurturing and deepening it (Rowe, "Vargas Llosa y el lugar de enunciación autoritario" 65–78). Both in his fiction and in his essays, speeches, and interviews, the elements on which Vargas Llosa bases his representations of social antagonism are frequently presented as disconnected or only superficially revealed as part of a totality whose rules of operation and directionality are neither perceived nor developed. As Rowe indicates: "[i]n the same way in which his essays lack a concept of social cohesion, in his fictional work the social is defined by structures of conflict" (ibid. 74).

The most notorious feature of Vargas Llosa's literary production and public conduct is his use and abuse of language for practical and pragmatic ends, such as self-promotion, journalistic activity, cultural criticism, or political discourse, subjects on which Vargas Llosa has expounded throughout his extensive and prolific career. One could even say, following the clues that the author himself presents throughout his texts, that his use of language covers a spectrum that ranges from the quality of *writer* [*escritor*] to that of *scribe* [*escribiente*] or *transcriber* [*escribidor*], from poetics to rhetoric, traversing multiple real and symbolic territories, no longer as narrator but as public intellectual. The use of language to which Vargas Llosa appeals in order to reveal the imagined face of Peru often relies on parody or communicative stereotyping, dichotomies, and even commonplaces that are surprising coming from an ideologue of liberalism. As Lauer points out in his study of Vargas Llosa as an "imaginary liberal," "[t]he essence of liberalism is not denunciation but the formulation of social and political principles that can sustain that individual liberty for those who postulate the doctrine" ("El liberal imaginario" 108). But, as Lauer reminds us, "the liberal critical consciousness has its own rules, and Vargas Llosa broke almost all of them" (ibid. 100).[4]

Through language, Vargas Llosa has accomplished stylistic interventions which introduce us to a fictitious world that is not exempt from humor, parody, or irony but which also lacks neither in scholarly terminology nor in disrespectful or condescending tones, often (although not exclusively) directed toward the lower classes or ethnic minorities. In any case, the function of language and its potential for social impact, its derivations or degradations, constitute a recurring theme in Vargas Llosa's writing. By the same token, the exploration of the limits of literature and the frontiers of language occupies a good part of his texts and reflections. Based on this investigation of language, his fiction manages to penetrate into the territory of canonical aesthetics as well as into hybridized and corrupted cultural spaces where institutional value is carnivalized (military schools, jails, brothels, communities on the margins of dominant culture, the jungle, exotic territories). Practices linked to language are thus deterritorialized, subjected to substantial deformations, and refunctionalized. "Storyteller" [*"hablador"*] or "transcriber" [*"escribidor"*], for example, are terms derived from those that clearly designate the practices of orality and writing, colloquial extensions or deformations that transmit a spurious modification of the primary functions of writing and reading, a form of vulgarization of basic and universal communicative processes. They constitute "derivative" forms that aim to defamiliarize what they refer to, to emphasize more than the nature of the communicative process or its primary function, the *praxis* that allows for the manipulation of spoken or written language as particular technologies of communication. In Vargas Llosa's literary practice, these abilities are turned into skills where the primary function—to speak, to write—is modified and transformed into reproductive, repetitive, and predictable exercises directed to a massive and diversified global recipient. To speak and to write (i.e., to relate, to retell, and thus, to transmit experience, to record the past, to preserve memory) are abilities which carry out a socializing function, forms of dissemination of content designed for a broad public sphere in which individuality is projected into larger contexts. This process of the disclosure and mass diversification of the recipient primordially interests Vargas Llosa, who is an established author of the literary Boom and a producer of highly valued symbolic commodities.

From this perspective, the reference to the "use of language" in Vargas Llosa alludes to the author's public, mass media use of it, not just the use of the linguistic register as a function of literature. It also refers to more vulgarized forms of verbalization in which Vargas Llosa himself becomes a "storyteller" in the sense of a charlatan, a windbag, a con artist, or a blabbermouth, unfurling a loquacity that rivals the eloquence of his literature.

It is interesting to note that this sense of the term "storyteller" we are using (in a different sense, certainly, than this word has in Vargas

Llosa's homonymous work) directly refers to Jean Paul Sartre, who, as is well-known, was one of Vargas Llosa's strongest influences. In his much-publicized *What Is Literature?* (1950), trying to clarify the question "What is writing?" Sartre points out the following:

> Prose is, in essence, utilitarian: I would readily define the prose writer as a man who *makes use* of words [...] The writer is a speaker [*un hablador*]; he designates, demonstrates orders, refuses, interpolates, begs, insults, persuades, insinuates. If he does so without any effect, he does not therefore become a poet; he is a writer who is talking and saying nothing. (19–20, emphasis in original)[5]

Sartre refers here to that which he calls "the verbal moment" in which the word is exercised as a form of action that leaves its imprint on the materials to which it refers. According to Sartre (the main proponent of the notion of *intellectual commitment* that had so much influence in the second half of the twentieth century in Latin America) if the writer remains attached to the stylistic value of words without considering the impact they have on those whom they touch, the communicative function becomes exhausted in its own *performance*, exposing itself as a mere gesture. For Sartre, "[t]he word is a certain particular moment of action and has no meaning outside of it" (21). For communication really to be "worth the trouble," it should connect itself "to a system of transcendent values." On the contrary, "the speaker [*el hablador*] is a pure *witness* who sums up with a word his harmless contemplation. To speak is to act; anything which one names is already no longer quite the same; it has lost its innocence" (Sartre 22, emphasis in original).

In Vargas Llosa, it is the displacement of literature by mass media, of poetry by politics, of aesthetics by rhetoric, which will be analyzed here as an approach which radically differs from what is presented in Arguedas's work. For example, in Arguedas, themes, language, and cultural values respond to an ethico-ideological commitment defined at the crossroads of the *double bind* of domination and resistance and of postcolonial biculturality in which the "civil" use of language (declarations, articles, ethnography, education) is consistent with his intellectual and literary program. Hence, Arguedas's work constantly oscillates between literature and anthropology without perceiving any epistemological fissure between these disciplines, because ethics and aesthetics mutually develop and reinforce one another. Evidently, the difference between Arguedas and Vargas

Llosa has to do not only with a political axiology but also with the position of each one with regard to the problem of the nation and with regard to capitalist modernity as the dominant economic and cultural matrix of our time.

If in Vargas Llosa the function of the "*hablador*" derives from the function of the "storyteller," and the function of the writer from that of the "*escribidor*" (to name some of the formalized and "popular" instances of the utilization of oral or written language), such forms also refer to the changes in communication and to the logics of symbolic exchange driven by technological modernity. Let us look at some examples in his fiction.

One of the narrators of *El hablador*, identified with the author, is not just a writer but also a host of a television program not coincidentally titled "The Tower of Babel," whereas the "storyteller," Saúl Zuratas, is responsible for the mythico-legendary discourse that tells of the life and traditions of the Machiguengas, their struggle to survive, and their cosmogony. Thus, the reader goes from the centrality of the *lettered city* to the suburbs filled with massified, anonymous recipients, confronted by the game of semantics and destined to receive discourses created and recycled through innumerable and uncontrollable mediations. In *La tía Julia y el escribidor*, the character of Pedro Camacho composes unremittingly ludicrous radio scripts, allowing the supposedly autobiographical story of the love between the author and Aunt Julia to fluctuate in counterpoint to the humorous development of radio plays, a massified form of "subliterature" that lends itself to a light and ironic treatment.[6] In *La ciudad y los perros*, the character known as "the Poet" composes short pornographic novels that he sells to his friends. The irony of his nickname is generated from a position that directs shades of meaning and distributes values in the hierarchized world of bourgeois good taste. In this way, both elevated and "inferior" registers, forms belonging to "high" culture and modalities that correspond to popular culture come together and mutually define one another. Popular and degraded forms, however, occupy a marginal, inferior, or subaltern place in Vargas Llosa's cultural universe. His fiction thus sustains itself on Western *master narratives* which organize the plurality of verbal registers offered by culture, distributing hierarchies, and functions.

Although it must be conceded that Zuratas's stories are able to reveal "something primordial, something that the very existence of a people may depend on" (94), *El hablador* is about people condemned to disappear, people who exist outside of official history and on the margins of Western reason. Thus, the storyteller's transmission of cultural memory achieves a compensatory, decorative, and exotic function in the panorama of Andean culture. There is no doubt that what the novel primordially represents is the instance of mediation—that which, connecting memory with the provisional present of the story, produces an *existential discursive territory* in which Machiguenga nomadism is established and suspended, as if in a cultural bubble situated between the continuous present of the modern nation and a community on the path to extinction. In this sense, the novel is the swan song that (en)frames the process of the disappearance of this anomalous enclave of archaism within modernity. This anomaly is illustrated by the disfiguration of Zuratas's face, which like El Lunarejo in the colonial context (and like the recurrence in the text of Kafka's character Gregor Samsa) embodies *difference, in-betweenness*, the inevitable threatening mutation, like barbarism in the heart civilization. The visible sign of interior otherness thus represents the radical alterity that dwells within postcolonial identity and that, paradoxically, helps to define it.

In the very heart of modern, lettered criollo society, literature grows and becomes stronger as a major discourse, sustaining the edifice—the panopticon—of national culture. Thus, the representation of these levels of cultural pluralization which unfold in modernity does not disturb the edifice of dominant values. Storytellers, transcribers, scriptwriters, and pornographers constitute folkloricized and/or degraded forms of communicative functions that have continued to derive from and yield to dominant cultural power dynamics: they are the constitutive outside of the *lettered city* where "high" culture resides; thus, they constitute the *difference* that confirms and reinforces modern identity. As "storyteller" of the criollo nation, Vargas Llosa does not tell the cosmogony of his people but rather of the rituals, ceremonies, and inner workings of capitalist modernity, which he tries to consolidate through a partial and selective (and frequently classist and Manichean) representation of the otherness that sustains it. Thus, he accomplishes a kind of "distribution of the sensible" in Jacques Rancière's sense, understood as the distribution of aesthetic practices that social orders make possible for different individuals and social groups (depending on the place they occupy), thus regulating both the power and ineptitude that they will be able to deploy in the process of symbolic representation.[7] The *distribution* or *division of the sensible* thus constitutes a form of regulation that derives from the relations between aesthetics and politics and that is destined to effectuate "[a] delimitation of spaces and times, of the visible and the invisible, of speech and noise, that simultaneously determines the place and the stakes of politics as a form of experience" (Rancière, *The Politics of Aesthetics* 13, emphasis in original). The displacement and distribution of social functions is inscribed, obviously, within the phantasmatic world of ideology.

In Vargas Llosa's case, media coverage constitutes the most effective form of universality. There is no doubt that the international impact of this writer implies (especially from his own perspective but also in the context of Peru) an overcoming of the local and a recognition of his merits which allows him to voice his positions from the local Parnassus to the World Republic of Letters. According to Lauer:

> [t]he most important thing about the literary figure of Vargas Llosa has ended up being his international fame, which has slowly overtaken his importance as the narrator of Peruvian reality, inventor of narrative techniques, or agile prose humorist. International fame was new to the Peruvian system, which had problems assimilating it and which still reacts to it with a sort of disingenuous mistrust. ("El liberal imaginario" 117)

Vargas Llosa himself often seemed never to stop believing in the influence of his international celebrity. Hence, perhaps, his constant need to reaffirm this fact through various intellectual, political, and media-based strategies ranging from journalism to political hobnobbing, from efforts as a playwright and even as a stage actor to the broad spectrum of his essayistic work—all strategies which demonstrate an insatiable search for celebrity and social influence. The profuse reading that Vargas Llosa has accomplished as a critic of classic works of universal literature reaffirms his profound understanding of the norms and aesthetic principles which rule the Western canon (to which Vargas Llosa has aspired to belong since the beginning of his literary career). His studies of authors like Gabriel García Márquez, Gustave Flaubert, Victor Hugo, José María Arguedas, Thomas Mann, Albert Camus, Juan Carlos Onetti, and others are presented as either individual critical volumes or make up part of books like *La verdad de las mentiras* (1990, expanded edition 2002). To the study of the great authors of renowned and totalizing works like those Vargas Llosa himself aspires to produce—many of them "damned" artists or writers, "*godkillers*" each one in his own right—one can add the numerous studies of painting in which he addresses the work of such disparate artists as George Grosz, Fernando de Szyszlo, Fernando Botero, Egon Schiele, and Paul Gaugin. This variety of undertakings not only demonstrates Vargas Llosa's interest in the literary *métier* and in the visual arts but also, or above all, his desire to control the intellectual field, to mark a direction of reception and interpretation of works he considers important within international registers and which he places on the same level as his own literary work.[8] As has already been shown in the case of *La utopía arcaica*, Vargas Llosa's reading of Arguedas primarily constitutes an exercise of demystification intended to draw more attention to the critic's own persona (his values, positions, and conception of literature) than to the writer he secretly considered his most elusive and reliable opponent. Vargas Llosa does not hide his intention to offer a definitive and, in more than one sense, lapidary interpretation of Arguedas, thus restructuring the territory of national literature—at least on the levels that affect him most directly.[9]

Along with these multiple pronouncements about national and universal canons, his desire for prominence as a transnationalized public intellectual causes Vargas Llosa to proliferate opinions, themes, and mass media appearances, transcending the space of literature and the arts. From the author's romantic aspiration to seek out an ideal solitary and empathetic reader with the sublimity of the poetic word, he moves on to the prefiguration of a collective and massified reader with varied and disparate tastes and levels of reception, marked by the immediacy of mass media and by the speed and simultaneity of information. The search for *universality* that guides Vargas Llosa's intellectual labor is not a search for the universality of humanism (which Aníbal Ponce calls "bourgeois humanism"), but rather a concept of art as an apparatus that delivers a totalizing message directed toward an individual's essence, his or her rational and affective world, whatever his or her geocultural localization, class, or ethnicity. This humanism increasingly appeals to the pragmatic and degraded universality of the market: the vast world in which symbolic commodities circulate and are valorized from the most banal to the most refined registers. From the ideal reader he moves on to the ideal consumer, a capitalist derivation of classical patronage. Toward this new culture-consumer subject (in the broad fields of literature, journalism, imagery, political discourse, technology, and so on), Vargas Llosa constantly projects the word converted into message, judgment, verdict, commentary, or dictum, as if his attempt to launch himself toward posterity necessarily started with capturing the attention of his contemporaries. This concept of the intellectual *mission* as messianism (preaching, haranguing, and even sermonizing) is, nevertheless, the same feature that characterized the lettered criollo (since colonial times). This mission achieved "classical" form with enlightened despotism: the discourse of Reason such as it is defined from the paradigms of Power, spreading out over the people like a paternalistic, authoritarian, monological, conservative, condescending, and exclusive practice that assigns positions and distributes hierarchies within the social pyramid and the circuits of knowledge.

In his newspaper column "Piedra de toque" ["Touchstone"], which was published simultaneously in different national and foreign papers (*Caretas*, *La República*, and *El Comercio de Lima*, Madrid's *El País*, etc.), Vargas Llosa conveyed opinions and analyses of culture, military practices, philosophy, current events, gastronomy, and international politics, many of which were later collected in volumes like those published under the common title of *Contra viento y marea* (1983, 1986, and 1990) [Against all Odds] and in his later book, *El lenguaje de passion* (2002) [*The Language of Passion* (2003)], in which the author seems to want to assimilate himself, as Sergio R. Franco reminds us, to the figure of the "intellectual mandarin" as Vargas Llosa himself once described Sartre. Commenting on this latter work, Franco transcribes the definition that the writer provides for the eminently French (according to Vargas Llosa) category of the mandarin: "a man to whom a vast audience confers the power to legislate on issues that range from great moral, cultural, and political questions to the most trivial" (Vargas Llosa, qtd. in Franco, *In(ter)venciones* 273). Without a doubt, for Vargas Llosa this function constitutes a goal that does not seem out of reach.

Vargas Llosa's all-encompassing ambition, his desire for public recognition and his accumulative technique are also applied in the insubstantial *Diccionario del amante de América Latina* (2006), first published in French (*Dictionnaire amoreax de l'Amérique Latine* [2005]) and primarily addressed to a European audience. Including around 150 entries collected from among the articles and notes that Vargas Llosa produced from the 1950s onward, the collection presents "definitions" of multiple, primarily Latin American writers (Jorge Luis Borges, Julio Cortázar, Jorge Edwards, José Carlos Mariátegui, César Moro, Pablo Neruda, Jan. Carlos Onetti, Octavio Pas, Juan Rulfo, Jean Paul Sartre, César Vallejo), politicians (Fidel Castro, Che Guevara, Alberto Fujimori), and central concepts for the comprehension of Latin America ("cholo," "commitment," "indigenism," "homeland," "tellurism," and "utopia"). The dictionary also includes self-referential notes that include some of the characters of his narrative, places, and so on, as well as references to artists (Chabuca Granda, Frida Khalo, and others.) and places (Lima, Peru, Europe). These articles combine elements of information with anecdotes and personal impressions.

Which model of intellectual corresponds to this philosophy? Within which paradigms of cultural action and based on which traditions of thought should this philosophy be understood? Franco has correctly pointed out that "Mario Vargas Llosa, with greater or lesser nuance, continues to be dependent on modernist [in the Anglo-Saxon sense] thought, a conception characterized by the belief in the unity of experience, of sense determined by referentiality, the logical and scientific supremacy of rationality, and the predominance of universals." The belief, evident in Vargas Llosa, that "reality can be apprehended as a totality and that human beings shared a common level of transcultural and transhistorical experience" explains the conception of art as a totalization capable of apprehending, as Vargas Llosa indicates, "the common essence of the species" (Franco, *In(ter)venciones* 275). A Faustian ideal seems to underlie these all-inclusive intentions but so does the most pedestrian desire for cultural control and the social power associated with it.

In Vargas Llosa the struggle with language thus implies not only the challenge of poetic language but the challenge of utilizing it pragmatically and comprehensively. Within his project he frequently inscribes the "I" as a primary instance of the collective dimension. Thus, autobiographical writing and self-referential discourse in general constitute a modality to which Vargas Llosa constantly appeals as a way of revealing his favorite topics and of strengthening his public image. *El pez en el agua: Memorias* (1993) [*A Fish in the Water: A Memoir* (1994)] is perhaps the best example of this effort.[10] Marked by triumphalism and by the myth of personality, the title of this memoir clearly speaks to the author's self-complacency as well as to his desire to project an overwhelming image of success and popularity beyond the avatars of public life. Alejandro Balaguer's photograph, featured on the cover of the first Seix Barral edition, shows Vargas Llosa, as Beatriz Sarlo points out, with a broad grin, with his arms raised, in the middle of a thick rain of confetti, celebrating his candidacy for the presidency of Peru, glossing over the (far from minor) fact that the writer had lost the election to Alberto Fujimori three years before the book's publication.[11] The memoir constitutes, for the moment in which it was written and for the language it develops, the attempt to frame the status of an overwhelming celebrity that depends (more than on real achievements and collective recognition) on personal conviction and the possibility of controlling public opinion and guiding the reception of his career in the media, the impact of which reaches and surpasses the specific domains of literature and politics.

Throughout this exhaustive recollection of experiences and events, what stands out among the collection of memories is Vargas Llosa' obsessive reiteration of certain terms which are based on practically nineteenth-century dualisms: reason and barbarism, civilization and primitivism, modernity and premodernity, "moral commitment" and savagery, antagonisms which serve to organize the experience of the world and the production of meanings at the literary level. To the Manichean conceptualization of situations, characters, and social realities, we can add the fluctuation of the qualities attributed to certain social groups depending on the role that they play with respect to the "I" that organizes discourse. For example, Vargas Llosa positively exalts the masses when they turn out in support for his candidacy, as in the memorable demonstration at Plaza San Martín, where "the middle classes" enthusiastically applaud him (*El pez en el agua* 48–49/*A Fish in the Water* 40–41). At the same time, he denounces the masses when they present themselves as an uncontrollable mob, as in the case of his preelection visit to Piura, where an "infuriated horde" seems to want to attack him with clubs and knives. This "horde"

> appeared to have emerged from the depths of time, a prehistory in which human beings and animals were indistinguishable, since for both life was a blind struggle for survival. Half naked, with very long hair and fingernails never touched by a pair of scissors, surrounded by emaciated children with huge swollen bellies, bellowing and shouting to keep their courage up... (*El pez en el agua* 574/*A Fish in the Water* 514)

Vargas Llosa explains his decision to run for political office as a response to a "moral reason" that threw him into leadership; his wife Patricia believes, however, that in this leap into politics "moral obligation wasn't the decisive factor [...] It was an adventure, the illusion of living an experience full of excitement and risk. Of writing the great novel in real life" (*El pez en el agua* 25/*A Fish in the Water* 41). According to her, more than anything else, what attracted Vargas Llosa was the possibility of embodying the heroic, novelesque role in which the author's fiction becomes part of a reality and in which he could assign to himself a leading role like the characters he is accustomed to forging in his literature. This approach to political leadership and simulacrum, characterized by individualism, fiction, and egocentrism, belongs to a way of "doing politics" that the Movimiento Libertad, of which Vargas Llosa was a member, assumes as part of its public *performance* in which both the protagonists of political action and their recipients are subject to predictable roles. As Degregori indicates, "The empire of political marketing converted the citizen into a simple elector, a passive consumer of political products: politics as spectacle" ("El aprendiz de brujo" 82). This style of popular interpellation can only be achieved at the cost of an intense reduction of choices and political messages, as well as a substantial simplification of social reality. Degregori argues that Movimiento Libertad did not notice the class-stratified and multiethnic problematic of Peru, a gross oversimplification of the national reality the writer and politician was supposed to represent.

Improvisation, tossing out quick judgments on processes and characters, and ideological opportunism appear to be some of the more prominent features of *El pez en el agua*, a naturally fragmentary text that selectively follows different instances of the process in which public and private spheres collide while sustaining the idea of the author's personal exceptionality and of the circumstances that surrounded his life. Only in some cases, such as in his reflections on the popular demonstrations in Plaza San Martín, does he point to the identification of a national-popular subject that excludes the rest of the citizenry. Vargas Llosa wants to present himself as the candidate of the middle classes but also to renounce the liberal strategy of a broader and more all-encompassing articulation. Notions such as the people and the citizenry are less frequent than one might expect in a public leadership agenda. The people and the citizenry are dismissed as political actors and maintained as abstract and empty categories, useful instead for the articulation of populist discourse (to which Vargas Llosa dismissively refers on more than one occasion as one of Latin America's political deviations). Vargas Llosa's agenda, organized around the modernizing project and the reinforcement of Westernization as a civilizing and developmentalist strategy, feeds on these oversimplified and aristocratic contrasts applied to Peruvian culture and society. One of the most frequently repeated notions is the idea of barbarism, which generally applies to the evaluation of processes and collective events: "Once more in its history Peru has taken yet another step backwards toward barbarism" (*El pez en el agua* 42/*A Fish in the Water* 31) he says, for example, referring to Alan García's project of nationalization and state ownership of the banks, which is one of the catalysts that led to his candidacy. The "imaginary liberal" thus weaves an ideological web, a discourse in which false consciousness creates illusory frameworks of provisional validity, making the personal image shine as the epicenter of a cultural project. This is supported by the pillars of bourgeois individualism and on the primacy of Enlightenment rationality, although in the degraded version that these forms assume in late capitalism. Vargas Llosa himself recorded this state of things in some of his essays and newspaper articles: Progressively, universalism will continue to be reconfigured by the mercantilization of culture, no longer presenting itself as the search for and transmission of ecumenical values of total and integrated consciousness but as the project of capturing diversified and massified global markets. The demand which guides the sort of intellectual action which has in Vargas Llosa a very recognizable paradigm thus does not orient itself (as in classical humanism) toward the search for spirituality and individual improvement. It tends, rather, to strengthen and disseminate hegemonic paradigms of domination and symbolic representation in the context of globality.

In his creative, critical, and political work Vargas Llosa circulates at the level of "high culture," understood as the institutionalized forms of art and literature. To a lesser extent, one could also consider these to be "massive" artistic expressions that conquer a place in the market, which is to say, that manage to secure a consumerist public that legitimates its existence. In a recent article published in the Mexican journal *Letras Libres* with the title of "Breve discurso sobre la cultura," Vargas Llosa explains his concern for the widespread deterioration of the humanities in Latin America because of the ground gained in different contexts by social scientists who, in excessively expanding the category of culture, have made it so that what is traditionally understood as such comes to lose symbolic and social specificity. According to Vargas Llosa, culture has been traditionally understood as: "the vindication of a legacy of ideas, values, and artwork, of a few historical, religious, philosophical, and scientific consciousness in constant evolution and the fomenting of the exploration of new artistic and literary forms and of research in all fields of knowledge" ("Breve discurso").

According to Vargas Llosa, the inclusion of the so-called popular cultures corrupts a category that is associated with artistic selectivity, bourgeois taste, and spiritual elevation. Furthermore, Vargas Llosa argues that the decline of the regard for art and of an education in the humanities began in May 1968 with the youth uprisings in Paris and with the consolidation of the "obscurantist" intellectual leadership of philosophers such as Michel Foucault, Jacques Derrida, and Paul de Man, whom the Nobel Prize winner holds responsible for undermining the humanistic ideal, since, due to their influence, culture "[b]ecomes an incomprehensible, multitudinous, and figurative fantasy. Because no one is educated anymore if everyone thinks they are, or if the content of what we call culture has been depraved to such an extent that everyone can justifiably believe themselves to be educated" (ibid.).

The ex-presidential candidate resented the democratization of the concept of the "humanities" as well as the loss of the privileges and hierarchies that the bourgeois world and its cultural heritage had sustained, spaces in which, with the help of critics like Lionel Trilling and Edmund Wilson, the aura of literature was sustained. Vargas Llosa notes that in the present, in contrast, all categories are disappearing, leaving the world at the edge of the abyss of degradation and chaos:

> No one can know everything about everything—neither in the past nor today was this possible—but to the educated man culture serves at the very least to establish hierarchies and preferences in the field of knowledge and aesthetic values. In the era of specialization and the downfall of culture, these hierarchies have disappeared in an amorphous hodgepodge in which, according to the state of confusion that equalizes the innumerable forms of life christened as "cultures," all sciences and techniques are justified and equivalent to one another, and there is no way to discern with even a minimum of objectivity what is beautiful in art and what is not. Even to speak of such objectivity is now obsolete because the notion of beauty itself has been discredited as a classical idea of culture. (ibid.)

The essay closes with a distressing assertion: "We have made culture one of those attractive yet fragile castles made of sand that crumble at the first gust of wind" (ibid.). This prediction is generalized and formalized in *La civilización del espectáculo* (2012) [The civilization of the spectacle], a book in which Vargas Llosa attacks the "corruption of cultural life by frivolous work," which could lead to the destruction of "delicate material that gives substance and order to what we call civilization."[12] Unable to comprehend the variable borders of *the cultural* and less still the interstitial spaces that exist between institutionalized and inorganic cultural forms, Vargas Llosa takes refuge in a conservative and apocalyptic notion of culture that recasts the debate in the terms that preceded the emergence of mass society and the recognition of popular culture, all which he nevertheless ably represents in his literary texts. In the same sense, what escapes his conceptual universe is the idea that the function of the intellectual could be transformed and that alternative forms of consciousness linked to non-dominant epistemologies could exist. Vargas Llosa also lacks a concept of the idea of *the political* as a productive space of resistance and collective mobilization outside of democratic-republican partisanship and institutionality.

At the other extreme of the spectrum of Andean modernity, Arguedas exists at the intersection of a series of practices, cultural conceptions, and discourses that precisely indicate the struggle of non-dominant knowledges and cosmovisions to be accepted and recognized in the imaginaries of the modern nation. The practices of translation, transdisciplinarity, biculturalism, linguistic hybridity, the coexistence of instrumental reason and mythic thought, the radical fusion of life and work, the presence and impact of affect in understanding the real, the close relationship between materiality and spirituality—these are some of the levels that emerge in Arguedas's writing and that require the deployment of different forms of reading appropriate to grasping the poetic and symbolic specificity of his literature. Indeed, Arguedas's work should be primarily understood as based on the inorganic, dispersed, and fluctuating forms of intellectual labor that Antonio Gramsci defined as being on the margins of the regulation of dominant culture, as a zone of symbolic exchange and interventions, of subversion and vindication of forms of *the social* that make up part of collective interactions even though they are not yet visible or regulated by official discourse.[13] Arguedas's idea of the nation is undoubtedly an idealized, romanticized concept in which he exalts the importance of community space and projects an image of Peru as the realization of a diversified potential of cultures and ethnicities rooted in the pre-Hispanic period. Establishing his historical and literary genealogy in his speech on receiving the Premio Inca Garcilaso in 1968, Arguedas praises Peru as an "infinite country" that possesses an almost measureless wealth: "there is no country more diverse, nor with a greater multiplicity of earthly and human resources; it has all degrees of heat and hue, of love and hatred, of warps and subtleties, of symbols both utilized and inspiring" ("No soy un aculturado" 258/"I am Not an Acculturated Man..." 270). His speech registers, in this sense, a modernist anti-imperialism in which the ancestral spirituality of America is opposed to the technological advances of industrialized countries.[14]

Nevertheless, as Rodrigo Montoya Rojas has clearly explained, the "magical socialism" to which Arguedas alludes in this same speech as a vindication of the affective and non-Western aspect of his thought is far from reducible to the idyllic, anachronistic, or romanticized vision he is sometimes reproached for having. Rather, it has to do with an incorporating gesture that promotes the idea of a vernacular, mixed, and all-encompassing modernity capable of articulating different perspectives and liberating itself from the authoritarian and exclusive productivism of capitalist modernity. The famous declaration, "I am not an acculturated man. I am a Peruvian who, like a happy devil, proudly speaks in Christian and Indian, in Spanish and in Quechua" (Arguedas, "No soy un aculturado" 257/"I am Not an Acculturated Man..." 269) clearly indicates the desire to be defined neither by the terms of European modernity nor as the simple result of the processes of transculturation that constitute a flux of influences and models that expand out from the centers of capitalism toward its peripheries. His claim rejects mechanistic conceptions of the cultural process as much as it rejects categorical and rigid social classifications. It implies a posture that is at once cultural and political, social and ideological, a declaration of principles and a challenge to the paradigms of modernity from a reclaimed position that emerged as a reply to European and North American models, proposing more than the absorption and adaptation of exterior paradigms, a thought of resistance and of cultural and ideological negotiation.[15] However, this declaration also implies that the reclamation of affect is a form of consciousness and a path to social action. Indeed, Arguedas reaffirms pride in constructed identities, the delight of intercultural *jouissance*, the loyalty toward the communitarian spirit, and antiproductive happiness, in which *the national* can be understood not as an oppressive paradigm managed by State apparatuses but as a collective construction that can be redefined from below with an inclusive and integrative direction. The hybrid language of the colonized does not exclude the appropriation of the dominant language but rather its creative and joyful reformulation, its productive and enriching contamination, its counter-conquest.

In Vargas Llosa's case we have seen how *language* no longer works in just its literary function but also as a multimedia propagation of multiple, diversified, and all-encompassing enunciations that spread out and seek to control public space (which we can refer to as *speech for speech's sake* in which language, relieved of creative intention and aesthetic desire, consolidates itself as information, opinion, or critical commentary). In Arguedas we will take note of an additional form of discursive production that has sometimes been interpreted by critics as a *supplement* to literary writing, which is to say, as a parallel activity that can become independent of poetic creation for the purposes of analysis. It is an anthropological discourse that, considered apart from properly literary writing, would constitute not only a cultural but also an ideological complement to

Arguedas's writing of narrative and poetry. With regard to the recuperation of myths, songs, and traditions, as well as to his practice of collecting pre-Hispanic or modern artifacts produced in the heart of the indigenous communities, Arguedas's work reveals the unfolding of a series of strategies for *reading* popular culture that, in their specificity, are productively integrated into the "high culture" to which Arguedas's writing expertly contributed. These levels of popular symbolic production constitute not only the legacies and traditions of the past but document the processes of transformation and cultural mixing in the present. In this way, Arguedas's exploration of cultural artifacts implies a vision, simultaneously synchronic and diachronic, in which the material or symbolic object exposes at one and the same time its temporal trajectory and the processes of *mestizaje* and transculturation that shape it. These processes derive not only from the penetration of modernity into peripheral societies in Latin America (the Andean region in particular) but also from the internal dynamics of migration within national territories and from the hybridities that result from these dynamics. The attention Arguedas pays to the modification of musical instruments and to regionalization allows us to observe variations and continuities in them, as well as the formal changes in musical composition that encompasses chanting and dance, connecting rhythmic elements and magical effects, songs and stories, music and subjectivities that form the fictitious framework of his novels and inform his characters' experiences. Arguedas thus treats the popular cultural artifact in a double register. On a *material and concrete* level, the songs, the artisanal objects, the musical instruments, and so on are recuperated as part of the Quechua-Andean culture the author wants to preserve. On a *symbolic* level, those elements are integrated into fiction, having been assigned specific roles within the narrative, as part of the represented world. Like the terms from Quechua language, the music and the objects that belong to that culture constitute elements of identification and social recognition. In their capacity as cultural signs they function as apparatuses that separate the world of the *mistis* and that of indigenous culture, delimiting identity and alterity, the premodern and the modern, the proper and the foreign. For example, Arguedas describes the *cholos* who arrive in Lima as a growing multitude that assumes the appearance of the mestizos of the city although "the most direct manifestations of their emotions and spirit were not much different from those of the Indian: they played flute and small guitar [*quena y charango*], *pinkullo* and mandolin, harp and lute, they sang *wayno* and danced *kaswa*" (*Indios, mestizos y señores* 92).

In the same way in which, for Arguedas, Andean nature is endowed with music and languages, the objects through which he expresses Quechua culture also speak the language of affect, memory, and dreams. Carnivals and festivals are occasions not just for the expression of feelings and collective ceremonies but instances of consecration and generational transmission of culture, insertions of the particular and contingent into historical temporality. In *Señores e indios* (1976), studying "The Popular Mestizo Song in Peru," Arguedas refers, for example, to the importance of the *wayno* as a document of the collective sensibility of the Indian and as a testimonial element of the stages through which Quechua culture continues to pass:

> In the ancient *waynos* one can study the process of *mestizaje*, just as the age of the earth can be studied and recognized in fossils that have remained embedded in geological layers, with the difference being that the ancient *waynos* speak and tell on their own the spiritual history of the mestizo people. (*Señores e indios* 203)

In Arguedas, ethnographic labor thus acquires the function of a true cultural archeology which, again, can only for the purposes of analysis be separated from the literary project and the ideological program that inform it since, in essence, it constitutes a fundamental aspect of the writer's cosmovision and of the universe he aspires to represent in all of its complex diversity.

Music has a unifying function with regard to the community because it gathers its members together and channels their emotions and desires. Doña Josefa accompanies with her guitar the expression of solitude and abandonment in "Agua," going through diverse localities from Puqui to Abancay, just as in *Yawar fiesta* diverse musical genres evoke the condition of the solitary and dispossessed Indian. Through *waynos* and *harawis* (songs of pain and mourning) the harpist in *Diamantes y pedernales* communicates both the suffering and the hope of purification and relief through music. In *El Sexto* the rhythms of different regions come together as an evocation of the cultural diversity of the prisoners and of their alienated condition, in which harmony is a delirious evocation of a world from which they find themselves definitively removed. In *Los ríos profundos* Ernesto is attentive to the harmonies and rhythms of nature, the bumblebee and the spinning top, the rivers and the trees, fill the air with music and transmit meanings just like languages and images, and music serves as a background to the community's struggle against injustice and the resistance that inequality and abuse inspires in the Indians. In *Todas las sangres* music accompanies work, the fertility of nature, and the display of feelings and collective expectations. In *El zorro de arriba*, carnivalesque scenes exhibit symbols of the chaotic rhythms of industrial exploitation and the social decomposition that comes along with it, advancing the idea of an inverted world covered with disguises that hide its real nature and create an atmosphere of turmoil and a sense of rushing toward death. The rock-and-roll music Maxwell dances to inserts an exogenous element into the transculturated space of Chimbote, creating an atmosphere of exasperated energy and "out-of-placeness." The foxes' dance, in turn, like that of the scissor dancers in "Rasu-Ñiti," introduces an extra-rational, magical, and highly emotionalized dimension into these narratives, revealing the existence of superhuman forces whose influence and significance exceeds the logics and conceptual parameters of criollo culture. This quick overview suffices to out the multiple values and functions that are assigned to indigenous or mestizo music as an element of (self) recognition, expression, and comprehension of the world, in short, as a form of *knowledge* and intuition whose dimensions escape dominant rationality and open up a parenthesis of symbolism and poetry in a world marked by pain and marginalization.

In his studies of the function of music as a "sonorous space" and also as a form of consciousness and of social transformation, Rowe has analyzed the semantic connotations that are associated with references to musical sound and its relations to myth and the social condition and sensibility of the Indian. Rowe emphasizes the importance Arguedas gives to the cognitive value of music and to the "magical world of sound" in general, from which "the spatial categories of western science are subverted" ("Música, conocimiento y transformación social" 73).[16] With a similar impulse, Lienhard studies "the reclamation of Andean culture" Arguedas accomplished through anthropological work as a form of recuperating a cultural patrimony devalued by the dominant culture. Arguedas's ethnographic texts, which Lienhard sees as close to the genre of "travel writing" ("La antropología" 46), demonstrate not only the writer's empathy toward the aesthetic and social values of Quechua culture but his solidarity with the indigenous as a marginalized and dispossessed subject. His study and collection of artifacts allows him to get closer to the dynamics of the cultural market and to the process by which art is transformed into a folklorized product, consequently changing both its function and its meaning. However, Arguedas does not limit himself to studying the evolution of symbolic elements, artifacts, and popular festivals like carnivals, bullfights, or ritual dances but also attends to the modifications of practices like community work, the concept of property, and the forms of socialization that are changed by the effects of migration, the growth of industry, and advances in technology.[17] To refer to only a few of the most well-known examples, Arguedas's ethnographic works on Puquio and Huamanga, as well as the analysis of the evolution that communities in contemporary Peru continue to suffer, accomplish together an "adjustment with regard to indigenous culture," as Rama perspicuously notes (*Writing Across Cultures* 128), that allows us to overcome the nostalgic interpretation of the Inca period and the pretentions to a restoration of pre-Hispanic values and features. These studies emphasize rather the processes of miscegenation driven by the modernizing dynamics from which the multicultural face of contemporary Peru derives. It will be exactly this labor of recognizing Peruvian society from its artifacts and symbolic practices which, following and expanding on Mariátegui's thought, will allow Arguedas to think *national culture* from a new basis insofar as it is a primary platform from which the modern nation can be understood and transformed in order to become an inclusive and egalitarian space.

Arguedas and Vargas Llosa thus represent two very different modalities of the elaboration of a discursive—intellectual, speculative, or analytic— *supplement* of undeniable ideological connotations which, in any case, can be read both in and of itself and in a complementary relation with literary production as such. Thus, we are dealing with two uses of language and two forms of the organization of thought: one, oriented toward mass media, the market, and public image; the other, articulated around a recuperative cultural program and directed to the heart of national culture, as a call for social restructuring and the activation of community values, in the face of the challenges of modernity. These authors ultimately represent two forms of understanding social change, of relating to Western culture and its colonial legacy, and of inserting the local into the larger dynamics of a world in an accelerated process of globalization.

Notes

1. As Cornejo Polar asserts, "It is clear that the productive system that sustains Vargas Llosa's narrative work is significantly more developed and effective than the Peruvian system; thus, his representative status in this specific

situation is partial and indirect. Although he hews to a modernizing dynamic that is common to a more or less broad group of Peruvian authors, Vargas Llosa, escaping national constraints, reaches unthinkable heights within his own country" ("Hipótesis" 253).
2. Arguedas's narrative thus constitutes "the most intense and illuminating aesthetic reproduction of the fundamental contradictions of Peruvian historical development: in essence, from its dismembered socio-cultural constitution, in which various cultural systems converge with their respective languages and distinct modes of production, weakly integrated into a slow and traumatic process of capitalist homogenization that finally arrives with a noticeable delay" (Cornejo Polar, "Hipótesis" 251–52).
3. Certain approaches Vargas Llosa took regarding the problem of how to deal with indigenous language include, for example, the strategy of hybridization (in *El hablador*) or that of "*mistura*"—strategies similar to those Arguedas himself utilized more effectively in many of his own texts.
4. On the topic of Vargas Llosa's "liberalism," see Escárzaga-Nicté, in addition to Lauer's and Degregori's fundamental works.
5. I am grateful to Sergio R. Franco for this opportune reference which confirms the interpretation I offer in this study of the utilitarian and often gratuitous form in which Vargas Llosa makes use of language, in its prosaic rather than in its poetic function.
6. Cornejo Polar asserts that, already with *Panteleón y las visitadoras* (1973) [*Captain Pantoja and the Special Service* (1978)] and later with *La tía Julia y el escribidor*, Vargas Llosa inaugurated the novel of entertainment in Peru. This, in addition to his tendency toward irony and parody, is another aspect through which melodrama repeatedly appears and is channeled in Vargas Llosa's texts.
7. Rancière explains: "I call the distribution of the sensible the system of self-evident facts of sense perception that simultaneously discloses the existence of something in common and the delimitations that define the respective parts and positions within it. A distribution of the sensible therefore establishes at one and the same time something common that is shared and exclusive parts. This apportionment of parts and positions is based on a distribution of spaces, times, and forms of activity that determines the very manner in which something in common lends itself to participation and in what way various individuals have a part in this distribution. Aristotle states that a citizen is someone who *has a part* in the act of governing and being governed. However, another form of distribution precedes this act of partaking in government: the distribution that determines those who have a part in the community of citizens. A speaking being, according to Aristotle, is a political being. If a slave understands the language of its rulers, however, he does not 'possess' it. Plato states that artisans cannot be put in charge of

the shared or common elements of the community because they do *not have the time* to devote themselves to anything other than their work. They cannot be *somewhere else* because *work will not wait*. The distribution of the sensible reveals who can have a share in what is common to the community based on what they do and on the time and space in which this activity is performed" (*The Politics of Aesthetics* 12, emphasis in original).
8. For a study of Vargas Llosa's critical essays, see, among others, King.
9. Vargas Llosa's essayistic and critical work is compiled in various volumes. For a representative example see *La verdad de las mentiras*. For more on this aspect of Vargas Llosa's work, see King.
10. On this text, see Franco, "The Recovered Childhood."
11. Sarlo analyzes the role of the simulacrum as a symbolic modality and the function of electronic aesthetics in Vargas Llosa's and Fujimori's presidential campaigns.
12. Jorge Volpi offers an interesting commentary on this text by Vargas Llosa in his review: "In *La civilización del espectáculo* Vargas Llosa is correct to diagnose the end of an era: the era of intellectuals like himself. Little by little, our ideas about authority and intellectual property become hazy; borders between high culture and popular culture no longer exist; and yes, the world of printed books is fading away. However, instead of seeing in this change a triumph of barbarism, one could understand it as the opportunity to define new relations of cultural power. The solution facing the empire of banality that he so meticulously describes will not emerge through a return to a previous model of *authority* but through the recognition of a freedom that, as vertiginous, ungraspable, and shifting though it may be, is derived from the same freedom for which Vargas Llosa has always fought."
13. Bhabha has referred to the necessity of articulating new forms of humanistic labor that correctly indicate that disciplinary liminality is a space in which the humanities can survive. Arguedas illustrates this idea, namely, that the Western world lives in the present within the limits of its own disciplines, while Vargas Llosa's world continues to be a compartmentalized universe where fusions and exchanges can only belong to the space of fiction, and otherness constitutes at most a disturbance of the dominant identities from which considerable aesthetic dividends can be extracted, insofar as they illustrate a social drama that productively intersects with the thematic necessities of literature. For more on this topic, see Mitchell, "Translator Translated."
14. On Arguedas's relation to the object of technology, see Beasley-Murray.
15. Rama has detected in Arguedas's 1968 speech a manifestation of the writer's complete social consciousness which recognizes and fully accepts his historico-cultural mission. He understands Arguedas's words as a confirmation of the category that Rama himself appropriated from Fernando Ortiz and from the Venezuelan critic and writer Mariano Picón Salas. Promoting a

slightly *self-serving* [in English in the original—Tr.] interpretation of Arguedas's words, Rama says: "He was quite familiar with the mestizo character of Peruvian culture, and he also knew his own role as an agent of transculturation, so the whole problem consisted in finding forms that the ongoing transculturating process of becoming mestizo could adopt that would not destroy the roots of rural communities or provoke anomie in them but that would also not dry up their creative sources and prevent their full incorporation into history" (*Writing Across Cultures* 185).

16. With regard to Arguedas's work on music, artisanal artifacts, and collecting chants and songs, see Huamán 145–91, as well as Rowe's articles in *Ensayos Arguedianos*.

17. See, for example, as Lienhard suggests, Arguedas's "La sierra en el proceso de la cultura peruana," included in *Formación de una cultura nacional indoamericana* 9–27. In general, this entire volume, the texts for which were selected by Ángel Rama, constitutes a very representative demonstration of the themes discussed in this section of the present book.

CHAPTER 7

Toward a Poetics of Social Change: Truth, Modernity, and the National Subject in José María Arguedas

Although the poetico-ideological designs of the authors on whom this study focuses are connected to very different projects, it is interesting to note that both frequently engage in similar modes of reflection, confronting comparable dilemmas related to the representation of Peruvian society and culture. Arguedas's multiple focuses on the observation, recording, and representation of Peruvian popular culture is expressed through a prolific writing agenda that ranges from narrative fiction, poetry, and essays, to education, ethnographic research, oral communication, translation, collecting and archiving (songs, myths, arts and crafts, etc.), to *performance*, such as the one Juan Millones recalls Arguedas staging of his fascinating allegory "El sueño del pongo" ["The servant's dream"] ("Palabras iniciales" 13). His numerous studies of Peruvian popular culture (particularly the forms of indigenous cultural expression) converge with the practice of what is commonly recognized as "high" literature, which, despite its many structural adaptations and innovations, is inspired by European models. All of these cultural access points converge in Arguedas's work at a clearly defined angle: the desire to record, preserve, disseminate, and interpret the legacy of indigenous tradition as a perspective that, still besieged by the countless challenges and aggressions of modernization, contains sufficient force to insert itself into and survive in new symbolic spaces. This tradition feeds contemporary scenarios with a telluric energy rooted in the pre-Hispanic past which is also the hybridized product of new and innumerable transculturating mediations that Peruvian cultural history

© The Editor(s) (if applicable) and The Author(s) 2016
M. Moraña, *Arguedas / Vargas Llosa*,
DOI 10.1057/978-1-137-57187-8_7

has been incorporating for centuries. More than literary textuality, it is *cultural texture* that seduces Arguedas: the rich and intricate weaving of perspectives, languages, materials, and symbols that form the Andean cultural palimpsest, that buries itself deep in the sierra, gets tangled up in the jungle, and returns to the accelerated flows of urban culture, crossed by a multiplicity of traditions, interests, and discourses through which the irredeemable heterogeneity of Andean society is expressed. In this sense, literature is *one* of the privileged forms through which that copious cultural heritage of messages, suggestions, and cultural settings is expressed. It thus represents one of the technologies through which the collective subject is constructed, as multiple and heterogeneous identity—in other words, as *identity in difference.*

Arguedas's work thus focuses on a series of primary objectives that define his intellectual world. I will mention here what I consider to be the three most important levels in this creative inquiry which mark not only an aesthetic horizon but also an ideological and programmatic position that guides Arguedas's multifaceted cultural practice, as well as the construction of his fictitious world. The first of these levels involves reflecting on the function of the intellectual and on the relation between dominant and alternative disciplines and epistemologies in the Andean context. The second pertains to understanding *social change* as the basis for the social transformation of structures, institutions, and collective interactions, making it possible to understand the historical and cultural *long durée* of the Andean region. The third has to do with the elaboration of an operative notion of the *national-popular subject* understood as a potential agent of change and as a political and social alternative to the flat, exclusive, liberal notion of citizenship promoted and managed by the institutions of the criollo state. These three levels are interconnected in Arguedas's work, constituting the ideological axis of his thought and his critico-cultural praxis. These instances of reflection are worth analyzing more closely.

First, as one of his main areas of focus, Arguedas explores the variable *function of the intellectual* in modernity, which is to say, the function of the intellectual *voice* (of the teacher, artist, literato, anthropologist, sociologist, and so on) that interprets and transmits collective cultural heritage and in many cases combines cultural memory, creative imagination, and scientific rigor in a labor dedicated to the community. In this sense, Arguedas's work can be considered a pioneering approach to the peculiar mediating quality and critical function of the modern intellectual as an articulator of cultural levels, ethnicities, and segments of society. These levels are linked together according to persistently fluctuating hierarchies whose transformations accompany the readjustments and nuances of capitalist domination. The intellectual records and organizes the materiality of culture. At the same time, he or she abstracts from that materiality the spirit of *the social*: the values of the community, the density of historical development, and the dimension of collective desire.

The documentary zeal which characterizes a good part of Arguedas's intellectual work is not only a way to access the remote and largely ungraspable sources from which the proliferating identity of the region is drawn. It is also a sign of the region's erasure: every object (songs, myths, dances, artifacts, rituals) is at once presence and ruin, testimony of continued existence and residue of a mostly lost battle against the colonialist cultures that historically established their dominion over the Americas. In this sense, Arguedas's work testifies to his concern for the relations between criollo culture, fashioned in a European mold, and the diverse forms of popular expression which include both thriving mass culture and the more traditional forms of culture developed by indigenous groups within their marginal and subalternized enclaves. This intercultural relation includes the study of the complex links between orality and writing, cultural institutionality and spontaneous forms of production and symbolic representation, dissemination and reception of discourses, objects, and practices, mechanisms of reproduction, preservation and transmission of legacies, artifacts, and systems of communication. Arguedas's meticulous examination of his collections of artistic objects, songs, myths, cultural practices, languages, and beliefs constitutes an investigation of elements which reveal, in their various codifications, traces of the multiple forms of Andean identity.

In its very conservationist and redemptionist orientation, Arguedas's project, focused on the theme of identity, is well aware of the dangers of essentialism and fundamentalism, which have been eroding Peruvian (and more generally, Latin American) thought, crystallizing in nationalist or regionalist discourses of varying ideological valences. Such discourses tend to reduce cultural complexity to a series of ahistorical and homogenizing features, defining identity as a construct in the service of dominant projects and values. Instead, Arguedas resists all reductionism and tends toward an expansive and inclusive thought that goes from the primitive to the modern, from the mythic to the historical, from foundational elements to their multiple historical transformations. He understands that Andean culture is formed through the constant recomposition of all these levels and temporalities. His intuitive fascination with *material culture* relates to comparable developments in the field of study (*Material Culture Studies*, in their Anglo-Saxon modulation), particularly after the Second World War. Arguedas recognizes in the cultural artifact an indisputable cultural inscription of the diverse technologies according to which the human being, from its different ethnic and economic enclaves, impresses its transformative labor on the medium through the production of material and symbolic goods.[1] The approach to the cultural object is thus one of the forms utilized in the study of social behavior and collective subjectivity. It also proposes a nexus between temporalities, forms of consciousness, and levels of intuition and nationality that are traditionally presented as disconnected in ethnographic study. This is the case of the well-known reference to the *zumballyu* in Chap. 6 of *Los ríos profundos*, the spinning top in which music, language, sounds of nature, memory and fantasy, past and present, myth and reality all come together.[2] The top spins before the gaze of the child, organizing levels of perception that would by any other means remain beyond the threshold of consciousness. Cornejo Polar has pointed out the appropriateness of language to the magical circumstance created by the presence of the object. Ernesto repeats the word "*zumballyu*," as if it were an incantation, or as Cornejo Polar notes, "a sacramental, propitiatory allocution" (*Los universos narrativos* 124). As a symbolic link between cultures, the magical object makes time stand still, spinning furiously on its own axis: a buzzing fly, a word detached from its meaning, fascinating rather because of its sound and mystery.[3]

According to this understanding of Arguedas's project, and regarding the disciplinary compartmentalization that some have emphasized in his work, it should be noted that, strictly speaking, this exceptional writer should be considered neither a literary author who did some anthropology nor an anthropologist who produced some literary texts. He is better defined as a transdisciplinary intellectual who appeals to diverse methodologies to approach a complex object, an episteme that should be apprehended through its visible elements and its specters, interpreting the remains left by cultural practices pushed aside by the forces of criollo domination and modernity. In broad terms, Arguedas should rather be considered a *communicator* (as he continued to define himself through his praxis) whose principal function was to establish connections between the elements that configure the total repository of culture. His intellectual mission, such as he conceived it, was to find the communicating vessels between heterogeneous systems of existence and communitarian socialization and to give a voice and a language to those elements silenced or made invisible by modernity.[4] It is useful to note in this regard that in his work Arguedas hoped to reveal not only the primitive materiality of a surviving Incan culture but also the underground sources of modernity: the flow that runs through it, the irrepressible heterogeneity that characterizes it, the technological drives that give it new form, the discourses that define new emancipatory projects, the emergent subjects that continue to be socially and politically active, occupying their place as protagonists of history.

As a cultural worker, Arguedas differed markedly from the notion of the lettered subject [*el letrado*] inherited from colonial times and rearticulated in the republic, referring to the subject that represents a form of power/knowledge legitimated by its establishment in the privileged systems of highly stratified and exclusive societies, where the epistemological dominance of one class coincided with the prerogative of hermeneutic practice. Since independence, and with the separation of church and state, the function of the lettered subject acquired a messianic character and reorganized itself into a combination of spiritual and political leadership. Arguedas also distanced (but did not divorce) himself from the enlightenment conception of knowledge that through instrumental reason allows not just control of the process of acquisition and dissemination of knowledge but also the rule of the *res publica* through pedagogical technologies that reproduce dominant values and interests. Intuition, affect, and belief are thus displaced to the margins of *legitimate knowledge*.

As an intellectual model, Arguedas destabilizes the liberal notion of intellectuality understood as a form of participation in the values bequeathed by Occidentalism, imposed from colonial times as the paradigm of class, race, and gender superiority, and reformulated after the French Revolution as the main instrument for the consolidation of the bourgeoisie. His work de-authorizes every universalist conception, tending rather toward a pluriversal definition in which principles and values are brought together from multiple cultural perspectives and diverse origins (whether rational, affective, magico-religious, or otherwise) that converge in the perception and the interpretation of *the real*.

Finally, Arguedas's critico-cultural practice moves away from the bourgeois model of the Author/Creator of autonomous worlds which are ruled by their own logics and maintain themselves far from the demands and conflicts of the social. For Arguedas, the writer is neither a God nor a privileged exponent of the lettered elite [*élite letrada*] but rather a *producer* whose labor consists in processing cultural materials, preserving their legacies, and disseminating their messages. Neither is this author an *organic* representative of Enlightenment thought or of Western myths. The status of "hybrid intellectual" that critics have emphatically attributed to Arguedas highlights the fact that his work is situated in the intermediary, *in-between*, zone in which cultural power dissolves and fundamental conflicts are expressed.[5]

As a representative of what Lauer called *indigenismo 2* (which, between 1920 and 1940 elaborated a discourse of resistance against the attacks of modernity, reaffirming multiethnicity as one of the bases of national identity), Arguedas's intellectual mission was informed by the necessity of contributing to the project of the refoundation of identity without renouncing vernacular perspectives or betraying the utopia of an egalitarian progress capable of erasing the class and racial divisions and hierarchies that continue to exist within modernity.[6] The magical element Arguedas reclaims as an indispensable component of his thought thereby functions as a metaphor which encompasses everything that reason, dogma, or doctrine cannot. It thus constitutes an *other* form of reason: one that recovers a cognitive level which includes and exceeds instrumental reason and finds in epistemic plurality a form of access to the social and cultural *truth* of the Andean region:

> It was by reading Mariátegui and later Lenin that I found a permanent order in things; socialist theory channeled not only my whole future but, whatever energy there was in me, giving it a direction and making it flow ever stronger by the very fact of channeling it. How far my understanding of socialism went I really do not know. But it did not kill the magic in me. ("No soy un aculturado" 257–58/"I Am Not an Acculturated Man..." 270)

This final realization would cause Arguedas to speculate at length about the nature of magic within his aesthetic and ideological project. This makes it possible to mark multiple differences between the transformative qualities that the author of *Todas las sangres* attributed to the magical element and the superstitious connotations that the notion acquires in other indigenist Peruvian writers (Rowe, "El novelista y el antropólogo" 10). What appears to be even more important is the critical effort to understand the mode in which those ideological elements are filtered into Arguedas's aesthetics, for example, in his work on language and the forms of opacity it assumes in different contexts, obscuring signification and converting language into a carnivalized and performative apparatus. William Rowe notes, for example, how Rendón Willka's bewildering speech metaphorizes the confrontation of two cultural laws as well as of two forms of discursive power: belief and politics, which are articulated in different ways in the search for responses to capitalist (ir)rationality. Capitalism itself is what is ultimately penetrated and intervened into when its communicative codes are subverted and mythical thought embeds itself within it (ibid. 114). In *El zorro de arriba*, where, as Rowe indicates, mythic discourse as such is diluted, the character of "the madman Moncada," however, puts into play other elements through which a different, subversive, and dislocated perception of the surrounding reality seeps. Through a fractured discourse that deconstructs the seething capitalist rationality of Chimbote, and by means of his irascible actions and disguises, Moncada subverts the logic of exploitation and the disciplining of the reproductive worker within capitalism with the ludic unproductivity of a troubled and undisciplined perception of his surroundings. His disturbing and ex-centric presence resists complete assimilation and symbolizes the world threatened by epistemic difference and heteroglossia, qualities which decompose the world into fragments without relation or meaning.[7] Hence, the verbal axis of the *Zorros* is considered the basis of a new poetics and of a new social order prefigured in the novel (Rowe, "Arguedas y los críticos" 157).

Based especially on his identification with leftist thought, spurred on by the experiences of China, Vietnam, and Cuba, and fertilized by the discourses that had traversed the Latin American cultural horizon since the 1960s, Arguedas subscribed to the notion of the intellectual as *cultural worker*, which is to say, as a producer whose superstructural practice was informed by direct contact with the materials and spaces of symbolic production and was defined in terms of solidarity with the lower classes. Arguedas struggled throughout his entire life to consolidate this *discursive position* from both ethnic and class-based perspectives since his position in both categories combined diverse origins and entailed inescapable conflicts. The same is true with regard to the multiple forms of cultural labor in which he privileged direct contact with cultural materiality through fieldwork and the interpretation of data gathered from it and later integrated into his fiction or ethnographic articles. The proximity between cultural producer and *social subject* was a sine qua non condition of his intellectual commitment, especially starting in the 1960s, a period that combined European influences like Marxism and existentialism with the driving forces of liberation theology. From these perspectives he emphasized the necessity of articulating culture and politics, bringing the cultural worker closer to the working class, peasants, indigenous communities, and students, that is, to the most varied forms of *the popular* that have been defined as part of the social transformations of the era. Hence, Arguedas's trajectory also oscillated between his participation in cultural administration, his work in places like the Peña Pancho Fierro (which brought together intellectuals, artists, and activists since its foundation in 1936), and his attention to a variety of popular art forms. His collections of engraved gourds, altars, masks, and pottery, for example (which he organized with the help of his wife, Celia Bustamante, and his sister-in-law, Alicia), constitute an assemblage of craftsmanship that demonstrates the sensitivity and richness of indigenous culture. From all these perspectives, which construct an intricate web of intertextualities and symbolic textures, Arguedas continued to gather materials which helped him to conceive and define his enunciative position and his mediating function as an intellectual involved in multiple discursive communities. Conditioned as much by the private, biographical, affective dimension of his cultural experience as by his public impact, Arguedas is linked in multiple ways to both official and popular culture, to both canonical forms and the most modest and frequently least visible expressions of marginalized communities.

These forms of withdrawal from dominant models of intellectual action are aimed at redefining culture in modern Peru. However, they do not imply a radical renunciation of those paradigms, the effect of which was always present in Arguedas's trajectory in one way or another. But, regarding these models, it is precisely in the imbalances that Arguedas's work continues to reveal that one can notice his persistent inquiry and the progressive decline of conceptions and methodologies that were no longer able to resist the impulses of social transformation that ran throughout Latin America and that now required new epistemological parameters and new forms of collective praxis.

Arguedas's intellectual activity is also defined in the context of a series of theoretical approaches to the study of Latin American society and culture that acquired all of their validity in the region from the Cuban Revolution, which we will review here, although only in a summary way.

It has often been recognized that the principles and method of *North American anthropology* strongly influenced Arguedas's ethnographic work, especially in his earliest period, but the impact of other discourses during that era, such as dependency theory and liberation theology, should not be overlooked. Attention to these discourses implies a reformulation not only of the concept of the progressive, committed intellectual but also the conceptualization of the recipient and his or her expectations and needs as the addressee of cultural narrative. It also entails a redefinition of the object of study: both Latin America in its international context and national cultures as specific modulations within the region.[8]

Dependency theory, which took shape in the decades between the 1950s and the 1970s, helped to define Latin America as a space situated on the margins of large-scale systems of international capitalism and subject to the repercussions of actions at the center that in large measure conditioned national processes in peripheral regions. If the notions of imperialism and cultural penetration were already well-established in the Latin American ideological horizon at the beginning of the twentieth century, dependency theory would contribute in a much more precise way to the analysis of the relations between more-or-less industrialized countries as well as the study of the tense connection between national elites and the sectors of society they dominated.[9] The idea of the center/periphery dualism as a plan for international domination and the conviction that capitalism is based in the exploitation of raw materials in underdeveloped countries on the part of more industrialized nations was popularized as a totalizing explanation of economic and financial dynamics. Dependency theory reacts against all forms of tariff liberalization that would facilitate imports and defends the strengthening of the State and nation-oriented politics. It constitutes a theoretical instrument that makes it possible to account for the profound structural reasons for inequalities of class and race and for social antagonisms at both the national and transnational level. All of these notions formed a complex but intelligible picture in terms of domination and resistance, of hegemony and marginality that, while not free of mechanistic or reflectionistic political economy, encircled in a pedagogically operative dualism the complex international interactions and the deep, systemic crises inherent to capitalism which flared up after the Second World War. All of this makes it possible to perceive the Andean region as a space rife with tension, both internationally and internally, because of antagonisms that affect not only relations with industrialized centers of capitalism but also the links between the centers within the periphery and their own social and economic margins: the capital and the rest of the country, coast and mountains, criollo spaces and indigenous spaces, oligarchy and the common people, and so on.

Conceptualizing the system of domination in these terms makes it possible to delimit the different environments that constitute *the social* and to define ideological positions around the role of dominant culture, popular resistance, regional developmental inequalities, and so on. It also makes it possible to understand the dynamics of *internal colonialism*, a concept that Mexican sociologists Rodolfo Stavenhagen and Pablo González Casanova elaborated starting in the 1960s. This concept has long been part of the critical horizon of the Latin American Left and has been thoroughly employed as a critical approach to the phenomenon of interethnic relations in postcolonial societies.[10] As Walter Mignolo has noted, even though the concept was criticized for the difficulties of applying it to diverse postcolonial settings, in the context immediately following the Cuban Revolution, it served (at least in the Andean region) "to establish a balance between class and ethnicity," thus exposing the *double bind* of the new republics that continue to oppress (as in colonial times) the indigenous population while at the same time advancing national projects in alliance with other colonialist powers (*Local Histories/Global Designs* 105).[11] The conflicting relation between class and race, which is essential to understanding Arguedas, was perceived by the social sciences mostly from the perspective of dependency theory which, at Arguedas's time, was intertwined at different levels with Marxist thought.

In turn, *liberation theology* constituted an alternative to traditional Marxism, in which Christian utopianism was combined with the ideals of socialism, the defense of the poor (the marginalized, the subaltern) as a social victim that must be recognized in all its revolutionary potential.[12] Some critics have detected parallels with biblical motifs in Arguedas's work, finding in *Todas las sangres*, for example, a representation of Christian doctrine as rearticulated by the perspective of liberation theology.[13] Arguedas's personal relationship with the priest Gustavo Gutiérrez supports such an interpretation. Gutiérrez cites part of *Todas las sangres* in his *A Theology of Liberation* (1973) and wrote an essay on Arguedas that he titled *Entre las calandrias* (1990) [Between the calender larks], borrowing words from the end of *El zorro de arriba* which allude to a historico-ideological cycle that is closing ("the closing of the cycle of the consoling calender lark, of the whip," which is to say, of the resigned alienation of the Indian), to the time that opens to the time of "the fiery calender lark," which is the struggle for liberation.[14] Arguedas's earlier works also suggested a similar inclination. For instance, *Todas las sangres* has often been cited as an unequivocal example of Arguedas's liberationist orientation and of his attempt to allegorize the Andean situation through representing the diverse levels of exploitation and inequality that characterize it. In fact, the novel presents a microcosm that is replete with subjects that are easily recognizable in modern Peru: local political bosses, the middle class, Indians and mestizos, representatives of transnational corporations and clergy, all of whom contribute heterogeneous elements from distinct cultural and ideological perspectives and are utilized for the elaboration of the narrative conflict. Some have interpreted the novel as a biblical allegory in which the heroic tenant farmer Rendón Willka represents the Son of God. In a parallel fashion, Willka embodies new forms of social consciousness, principally through the search for a progressive option capable of overcoming the archaic social structure and at the same time resisting the devastating effects of modernization. Social injustice and redemption, oppression and the desire for liberation thus constitute the forces that sustain a narrative in which the religious element undoubtedly plays a role in articulating individual and collective subjectivity.[15]

In any case, what is clear is that Arguedas's work, in whichever of its forms, is defined at the intersection of discourses that delimit an emancipatory project directly accessible to the indigenous peoples of the Andean region, although it is also applicable to other contexts within agitated societies of Latin America in those years. Arguedas's thought, particularly his cultural criticism (understood as a transdisciplinary intellectual praxis), is inscribed within that current aimed at the complete liberation of all people with respect to both their conditions of existence and the recognition of their traditions, legacies, and conceptions of the world. The decolonization and recognition of cognitive models other than those of Enlightenment rationality (to use the current terminology of postcolonial theory) constitute a fundamental platform in Arguedas's work, both for the creation of his fictional universe and in his investigation of real worlds.

If the discourses prevailing during Arguedas's time had an undeniable influence on his work, both national and continental events undoubtedly impacted it as well. We have already mentioned the repercussions of the Cuban Revolution which were felt at every level of Latin American society. These repercussions defined the ideological space in which national liberation movements developed in different regions of Latin America. In Peru, tenant farmer rebellions in the 1960s, primarily in Cuzco, Ayacucho, Cajamarca, and Cerro de Pasco, appeared as a living backdrop in Arguedas's texts and constituted indispensable pillars for the construction of his poetics of social change. His well-known relationship with Hugo Blanco (a leftist political leader from Cuzco with whom he corresponded in Quechua in 1969) has been interpreted as a link which describes, in each case, a different trajectory. Blanco separated himself from criollo culture in order to integrate himself into indigenous communities and their political struggles, while Arguedas emerged from Quechua culture into the *lettered city* and addressed himself to the public of Lima as a trustworthy representative of the indigenous world. Arguedas himself declared that one of his motivations for writing literature was to react against the "false" form in which earlier authors (such as Enrique López Albújar and Ventura García Calderón) represented the indigenous in their literary texts: "In these stories the Indian was so disfigured and the landscape so sickly-sweet and ingenuous, so awkward that I said to myself: 'No, I have to write about this the way it really is, because I have enjoyed it, and I have suffered it'" (*Primer encuentro de narradores* 41).

Arguedas's search for truth supported in his own personal experience and commitment is the basis of a literature which contains the traces of both testimonialism and the subjectivity of one whose writing is guided by an ethico-aesthetic mission that intends to correct earlier accounts. Arguedas's literature proposes, even if in a fictitious register, to rewrite history (not so much real history as the possible history of modern Peru) from a perspective that makes it possible to incorporate elements that have been hidden or suppressed by official discourses. Thus, for example, *Los ríos profundos* describes the *chichero* rebellion, and *Todas las sangres* closes with the dream of collective uprising in the Andes, represented like a subterranean river whose roar announces indigenous insurrection. Arguedas's literature thus attempts to bring together the real and possible agents of collective change, making documentation, ethnography, material autobiography, myth, and historical imagination converge in texts that set out an alternative to the linear and logocentric story of Occidentalism. And it does this by reappropriating the bourgeois genre *par excellence* (the novel) and in the (sometimes hybridized) language of the colonizer, but principally from the ever-more porous limits of the *lettered city*, whose walls—less solid than those Ernesto wonderingly observes in *Los ríos profundos*—cannot contain the force of new representational forms and new languages without transforming the material of literature and the definitions of the literary itself.

The decolonizing project that characterizes Arguedas's work also contains the relation that his narrative establishes with nature. Through the artistic and symbolic artifact, it establishes transhistorical and transcultural connections that illuminate the complex social fabric of Peru. At the same time, Arguedas's ethnological work nourishes and preserves historical memory, contributing ineluctable elements for the elaboration of new forms of social consciousness.[16] Without forgetting the poetic register, in which language, however it is embodied, energizes the global production process of meaning, writing, and orality, Spanish and indigenous languages, *mistura* and "clean language" [*"lengua limpia"*], everyday objects, community practices, imagination, and memory all flow together in the symbolic magma of culture, making it possible to understand the present and transcend it with the utopianism of potential emancipation.[17]

Nevertheless, Arguedas's transition toward the decolonization of knowledge did not occur without tensions or ideological contradictions. His anthropological work (which was carried out most vigorously between the publication of *Yawar fiesta* in 1941 and the publication of *Los ríos profundos* in 1958) grew out of the orientations current in the discipline during that period in North American academia, serving as an ideological basis of the developmentalism that would have so much theoretical and practical impact in the following decades. It is also certain that these ideas at least partially informed Arguedas's knowledge about the necessity of understanding the process of social change and the cultural practices which accompany it. In this sense, it is useful to remember, as Martín Lienhard notes, that Arguedas believed in culture as a *continuum*, in the *long durée* of history. In other words, he believed in the temporal prolongation of deep structures and in the slow impact of social changes and ruptures that, although they may be immediately imperceptible, broadly affect subjectivity and collective behaviors without the subject of history having to become fully aware of the process that is taking place before their eyes ("La antropología" 51). Hence, Arguedas conceived social change as the result of modifications that were being produced in social reality as a consequence of the transformation of profound politico-economic layers, which is to say, as an incorporation of the fracturing of traditional structures that continue to give way to new forms of conceiving *the social* and of organizing *the political*. Nevertheless, any assessment of this change, whether positive or negative, will depend on, among other factors, the rhythms that social transformation assumes. This is evident, for example, in Arguedas's works on Puquio and the Mantaro Valley, where he observed the effects of modernizing acceleration (increased commerce, growth of infrastructure making it possible to expand links with coastal areas, construction of houses in indigenous communities, etc.). As Arguedas notes in his article on "Cambio de cultura en las comunidades indígenas" ["Cultural change in indigenous communities"] in Puquio, social transformation established a conflict between objective and generational rhythms that ended up significantly affecting the level of language and community interrelations:

> the old Indians bitterly contemplate change because it has been brought about so quickly, and an extreme difference exists between the behavior and the ideals of the young tenant farmers and the older generation. "They speak a language now that we don't understand. We aren't even able to speak at the council meetings," an old and wise Chaupi leader told us in a lamentable tone... (*Formación de una cultura nacional indoamericana* 32–33)

The devastating effect of social change thus creates discrepancies in the social *habitus* which only gradually assimilates new forms of social consciousness.[18] Literature illuminates precisely these continuities and ruptures. In it, inorganic, spontaneous, and often contradictory forms are produced from which the collective epic unfolds in everyday social struggles.

Responding to the objection of historian Nelson Manrique, who sees in Arguedas the anthropologist of the 1950s "a culturally colonized intellectual" (88, qtd. in Lienhard, "La antropología" 54) whose disciplinary tendencies threatened what Flores Galindo defined as the "Andean utopia," Martín Lienhard underscores the writer's conviction that the Indian's miscegenation and adoption of a capitalist mentality was already an inevitable situation that Arguedas tried (not without a considerable degree of ideological conflict) to incorporate into his understanding of regional processes. For this he utilized the instrument of anthropology as a direct form of accessing the conflictive nature and the particularism of the Andes. To him, these levels are not the basis for an Incaist proposal, or for the recuperation of pre-Hispanic forms of sociality, but rather a repository of community values that can be integrated into a peripheral modernity, making it possible to absorb both heterogeneity and the specificity proper to the Andean region. For this reason, Lienhard is right again when he points out that utopia in Arguedas is in no way "archaic," as Vargas Llosa would contend. Rather, it is a "disarchaicizing" intention that guides Arguedas's project, completely focused on the problematic nature—and in the criticism—of Western modernity (Lienhard, "La antropología" 55 n. 13).

Developmentalism and Andeanism thus constitute two perspectives that Arguedas understood as being in a not-necessarily-antagonistic but rather heterodoxly dialectical relation, since the possible synthesis of both positions could come to suggest a modernization capable of saving the elements of indigenous culture without removing the latter from the historical process of incorporation into modernity.[19] This form of ideological commitment was attenuated in the following decade when leftist thought became stronger at the continental level. Arguedas made further progress on his conceptualization of the *Andean political subject*, passing from a principally ethnic configuration to a more popular and inclusive dimension that included mountain and coastal populations, Indians, *cholos*, and mestizos.

Enrique Cortés has analyzed the step that Arguedas's thought took from the abandonment of the discrediting of the mestizo accomplished by Valcárcel to the ignorance of the quantitative and cultural importance of this social segment of modern Peru, culminating in his claim as a political agent based on factors beyond the purely racial:

> For centuries, European and indigenous cultures have cohabitated in the same territory in unceasing mutual reaction, the former influencing the latter with its ever-expanding media that offers its powerful and incomparable dynamic, and indigenous culture reacting and defending itself thanks to the fact that its interior assemblage has not been broken and that it continues in its native environment. In this timespan, one has not simply intervened in the other, but rather, as a result of this incessant mutual reaction, a new character has appeared, a human product that is unleashing an extremely powerful and increasingly important level of activity: the mestizo. We speak in terms of culture; we don't consider at all the concept of race. In Peru, anyone can see white Indians and copper-skinned subjects who are Western in their behavior. (Arguedas, *Formación de una cultura* 2, qtd. in Cortés 175)[20]

In this way, Arguedas makes it clear that his awareness that the conceptualization of the Andean social subject as *national-popular subject* in the political sense requires a social and ideologically cohesive operation. Such an operation should be based not on differences of race or class but rather on the *similarities* of the different sectors that suffer social inequality and are motivated to develop projects of resistance and collective emancipation.[21] This process implies a critical and revolutionary view with respect to the system of domination and to its various forms of economic, social, and cultural manifestation.[22] It also requires special attention to the processes of transformation of the modes of production in the context of regional modernization and of its impact in different geocultural spaces. Arguedas is attentive to the changes taking place at the national level—for example, the migration that turns the port of Chimbote into a space crossed by social groups from different origins and by economic and financial flows that penetrate and alter earlier rhythms. In these contexts, the drives of transnationalized perspectives are superimposed over traditional mentalities. All these social dynamics end up "Andeanizing" areas that had been until that time radically differentiated from rural zones. Arguedas recorded the way in which these demographic changes impacted the structure and the composition of Peruvian society and changed their imaginaries. Thus, many shades of *mestizaje* emerged. The *cholo*, for instance, emerged as a transformation of the Indian and as a result of miscegenation, making it possible for this social group to be considered, in this sense, as one of the historico-social avatars that resulted from the pressures of economic change in the periphery of capitalism. The culture of the sierra thus continues to affirm itself in coastal areas and claim a place in an increasingly hybridized national culture.[23]

The theme of the *cholo*, extensively covered by sociology, directly touches Arguedas's literary world since it points to the emergence of new forms of conceiving the national. In *Dominación y cultura: Lo cholo y el conflicto cultural en el Perú* [Domination and culture: The *cholo* and cultural conflict in Peru], Aníbal Quijano analyzes the characteristics of this social group associated with the theme of social change and the modernizing processes that give rise to migration and transformations of collective subjectivity. The *cholo* is a mobilizing factor that alters traditional stratifications and that leads the way to new forms of political and social agency that respond to both the pluralization of Peruvian society and the pressures of economic development which present distinct characteristics and levels of intensity in diverse regions.[24]

Together with the complex theme of becoming-*cholo* [*cholificación*], the categories of *mestizo*, *mestizaje*, and *miscegenation* have been reformulated numerous times. Marisol de la Cadena has studied the theme of mestizo in Andean society, and in particular the ethnic and cultural aspects associated with it, as well as the different historical and regional forms of hybridization that characterize it. In his 1958 speech, Arguedas had already called attention to the "*indomestizos*" who "were deserting" their communities in their choice for an urban life more connected to the benefits of modernity (Escobar, *Arguedas o la utopía de la lengua* 49). Attention to these racial and class-based interactions has allowed for extensive reconsiderations of the cultural role of this new sector and of its forms of social action and symbolic representation, especially since José Carlos Mariátegui repositioned the "Indian question" within national culture and thereby reconfigured the perspective of Peruvian society.[25] Ángel Rama has been particularly critical with regard to the mestizo and to the indigenism promoted by this new social stratum activated principally by the processes of urbanization and industrialization that developed in the inter-war period. For Rama, indigenism constituted "a mestizo movement—call it a *mesticismo* [...] that dared not reveal its true name" (*Writing Across Cultures* 97). According to the Uruguayan critic, the indigenist movement (and no longer only its literary representation) protected itself in ideological ambiguity and in the very broad principles of social justice and the vindication of the rights of marginal communities to advance an opportunist agenda in which the theme of the indigenous was included "as a referential element" that was never able to transcend its lower middle class boundaries during the process of upward class movement. For Rama, from Bartolomé de Las Casas's accounts of the destruction of the Indies to Jorge Icaza's *Huasipungo*, indigenism consistently produced:

> material for consumers from the same overall culture, the members of which were drawn from different strata (Spanish, criollo, mestizo) during successive eras. All dealt with a somewhat exotic theme, with aims that cannot be found in their discourse of explicit denunciations (moral, political, metaphysical, and social [...]) but rather in their literary and artistic sources, their aesthetic structures, and their cultural worldviews—those worldviews being the implicit facts that led to the creation of, and therefore set the tone for, the corresponding texts. (*Writing Across Cultures* 98)

Rama reproaches this mestizo literature for having "no real way of evaluating" indigenous culture in the present and for having perpetuated the perspective of the dominant culture over those of the dominated:

> The indigenista movement saw and explained the Indians using resources drawn from the emerging mestizo culture, which frankly was none other than the bastard child of its father, the eternal white conqueror, and was at that moment devoted to demanding the recognition and legitimacy that its progenitor had denied it. It took from the dominant culture all of the elements it considered useful, simplifying and clarifying them through its close contact with the actual functioning of the society in which it existed—that is, through its tough determination to survive in a hostile environment. (ibid. 99)

The great leap Arguedas made with regard to the indigenous question is his consideration of the values of that culture in the contemporary era, eschewing the nostalgia for the Incan Empire that had guided the delirium of restoration of many of his predecessors. From this point, moving through critical observation of the processes of social hybridization resulting from economic transformation, he arrived at the recognition of the "positive value of the mestizo social strata" (ibid. 126). As Rama points out, this enterprise

> was no easy task. Arguedas did not draw close to the mestizo without uneasiness and suspicion. He felt repelled by the mestizo's disconcerting ambiguity and his seeming antiheroism. He saw him as closely dependent on the landlords and carrying out the lowliest chores; he also saw the speed with which he could shift from one side to the other without clearly committing to either, but above all, he was bothered by his lack of morals. It called for a great effort of understanding to take a realistic measure of the mestizo's social situation, his way of life in a land that belonged to everyone else but not to him, forcing him to develop conditions adapted to a hostile environment. (ibid.)

Arguedas, who is perfectly conscious of the ambiguities and anxiety provoked by the mestizo's interstitial condition between classes, races, and historical moments, seemed to consider that resistance to the transformations brought about by modernity can only be relative and concentrated the cultural sphere as a laboratory of change and social resistance. If he sees in the mestizo a thriving segment of society advancing as a protagonist at the economic and cultural level, the Andean masses, characterized by their heterogeneity and fluidity, appear as the broad sector from which the foundation of the national-popular subject as agent of history continues to be defined. Nevertheless, it is obvious that the political action of which the mestizo is capable was not yet set in stone during the years when Arguedas was reflecting on the material basis of his "Andean utopia." In his work he correctly emphasizes the productive plurality of these bases, showing them to be a true palimpsest of signification through which diverse and sometimes divergent perceptions, messages, and objectives circulate. It will be later, in the face of the progressive emptying of state politics and the perspective opened up by the social movements that became active toward the end of the twentieth century and occupied the spaces left open by the exhaustion of party politics, when many of the exploratory lines at the symbolic level of culture will go on to become settled politically in some regions of the Andes, although not quite with the force Arguedas foresaw.

In any case, it is useful to retain the idea that, through the discursive network of his era (and while he performed the work of founding alternative forms of knowledge, interpretation, and representation of the social) Arguedas also delineated (along with an epistemological project) a critico-hermeneutical praxis capable of promoting a new reading of cultural texture and its hidden symbolic messages. He recognized that neither European nor Anglo-Saxon models constitute unassailable paradigms of rationality and modernity any more. The pluriversal vision Arguedas reclaims as the basis for understanding Peruvian social and cultural reality is crossed by deep rivers of meaning, intangible designs, and collective dramas that have been invisibilized by liberal ideology and hegemonic knowledges. His work is oriented toward the disclosure of a truth that escapes the disciplinary protocol and rationalist and exclusive myths of Occidentalism. His thought neither ignores nor disregards these perspectives but de-centers and de-universalizes them: it converts them, rather, into marginal and provisional tools in the search for an inclusive and necessarily *impure* knowledge founded in the specificity of the local and in its irremediable heterogeneity. This "provincialization" of Occidentalism is not ignorant of either *colonial reason* or the complicity of the knowledges that have at various times accompanied the political and economic hegemony of Europe and North America both at the transnational level and in the space circumscribed by the nation state. However, it also assumes that, for the recuperation of history proper, which has been traditionally obscured by dominant versions that hide the truth of domination and failure, it is necessary to appropriate existing knowledge in order to subvert dominant paradigms. As Prakash notes, "There is no alternative but to inhabit the discipline, to dig in the archives, and to push the limits of historical knowledge to convert its contradictions, ambivalences, and lacunae into the basis for its re-inscription" (311).

The polemic between literature and social science, promoted in Peru by this reading of *Todas las sangres*, is based in the latter's academicist pretensions, which reveals the disciplinary privilege and attachment to privilege of certain forms of theorizing the social that coincide neither with the nature of the object of study nor with the evolution of knowledge itself, particularly in postcolonial Latin American societies. In these latitudes, the very hybridization of the cultures and societies which continue to show the scars left by colonialism de-authorizes *without any further ado* the application of positivist classifications and critico-theoretical categories developed in and for other cultural realities. The roundtable debate on

Arguedas's novel that took place at the Instituto de Estudios Peruanos (IEP) in 1965 revealed not the insufficiency or the unfitness of literature for capturing the complex and often paradoxical and contradictory reality of Andean society but rather the incapacity of certain areas of knowledge to grasp the specificity of the processes and the exceptionality of imaginaries which lay beyond established models. Categories such as class, race, and social status, the Indian/*misti* dualism, as well as the essentialization of the diversity between the mountain and coastal regions of Peru have shown themselves to be insufficient for understanding social phenomena that consist precisely in the mixing and blurring of the conceptual and ideological borders of these notions, which eventually go on to be replaced or complemented by other new ones that refer with greater precision to the processes of social transformation, the circulation of meaning, and the transgression of geocultural limits. Phenomena like migration bring together subjectivities, commodities, and languages in the same way that the effects of technology already transformed spaces and temporalities in Peru in the middle of the twentieth century, creating flows and simultaneities that would have seemed unthinkable only a few decades earlier. The persistence of premodern elements in modernity led Aníbal Quijano, one of Arguedas's critics, to elaborate his foundational category of the *coloniality of knowledge/power* as an attempt to explain the perseverance of colonial structures in the present as well as the possible and conflicting coexistence of very diverse registers, cultural systems, and forms of domination that are articulated in the impure and fluid space of *the modern*. The processes of becoming-*cholo* (which Quijano himself studied at the same time as Arguedas) show the need for making thought more flexible—not in order to make it less rigorous or to distance it from sociological evidence of experience, but to make it possible for theory to encompass transformations of the real, which are faster and more chaotic than changes in the realm of ideas. Arguedas understood these same demands, and so his literature reveals a complex and contradictory world, one that is not anachronistic but postcolonial by nature, where the coloniality of knowledge/power is firmly entrenched within modernity and affects the very constitution of the fictional world and poetics of social change that sustain it.[26] In fact, in the following decades postcolonial thought theorized what Arguedas's narrative announced and poeticized. In short, I am referring to the processes of social and cultural hybridization, to the emergence of new social subjects that incorporate the racial only as *one* of their constitutive elements, to the importance of *difference* as a fundamental idologeme for understanding the processes of social (self-)recognition, to the difficulties of theorizing *otherness* and critiquing modernity from a supposed theoretical *outside* that allows us to elaborate in only a relative way our distance from the object of study, the function of *mimicry* as a strategy of appropriation and refashioning of dominant models. In effect, Arguedas helped make clear the importance of border knowledges, which are neither Western nor indigenous but transculturated in both directions and connected through a process of reciprocity and tension that frequently results not in a harmonious synthesis but, as Antonio Cornejo Polar warned, in the perpetuation up to the present day of antagonisms derived from inequality. In the early decades of the twentieth century, Mariátegui's heterodoxy paved the way for these later developments. His perspective made possible the comprehension of the hybrid and antagonistic systems that form Peruvian reality as well as the importance of myth and affect in the formation of collective subjectivities and the premodern enclaves proper to postcolonial societies, topics that theory today always incorporates in analyses of social conflict and emancipatory alternatives.[27] The social sciences, in their critique of the traditionally humanistic perspective represented by literature, constantly look for a universalist focus connected to the register of the real and a pedagogical function of fiction in support of national projects. Arguedas's literature and the poetics that his work attempts to deploy as a symbolic form of approaching the problem of social change is too innovative and too opposed to dominant models to be absorbed, due to its fragmentarism and its poeticization of the drama of inequality and the epic of collective resistance. Its cultural and linguistic performativity challenges the interpretive resources of the reader who tries, with varying degrees of success, to comprehend it within canonical parameters.

Social sciences (which in the case of Peru were temporarily able to capture a large part of these processes within their disciplinary purview) were much more limited in their transdisciplinary shift and their comprehension of the voices of fiction not as a register of punctual reality but as forms of perception that inform historical imagination. Social sciences demanded of literature a simplification of the material it represented so that it could fit into existing categories and transmit predetermined aesthetic-ideological positions without accepting the challenge of a reality that overflowed the parameters of theory and dominant epistemic and methodological paradigms. When Arguedas was accused of offering an *indigenist* solution to Peruvian social conflict in *Todas las sangres*, particularly with regard to the problem of the peasantry, his critics implicitly emphasized the heterogeneity between the world represented and the narrative perspective (whether that of the characters or of the author himself). Thus, they assumed that the point of view of sociology, for instance, could diminish or even eliminate the distance between experiential evidence and story and that literature could have the capacity—or even the mission—of describing imagined universes where the rebellious diversity of the real is domesticated. They could not admit that, outside of all testimonial obligation, literature is rather a space for impure and ludic nature, symbolic negotiation, a laboratory of signs and meanings. The process by which experience is transformed into discourse is, in fact, frequently impeded by representational strategies that alter the real in order to become less familiar with its attraction or to expand its search into inconceivable territories, provoking effects that open up to distinct forms of interpretation and aesthetic enjoyment.[28]

Neither were the social sciences able to take responsibility at that moment for the dimension of affect that to an important degree dominated Arguedas's literary world, a world replete with passions, intuitions, and desires that were not always represented in the register of instrumental reason. Castro-Klarén has referred to the function of what she calls "cognitive affect" in Arguedas, elaborating on the importance that the writings of Huarochirí had for his imagination, introducing through the world of belief (myth, the sacred) a dimension of being/existing as typically Andean, a feature that Arguedas expresses in all of his work but in a particularly brazen way in *El zorro de arriba*.[29] Other critics also elaborated on the important function of sentiment (anger, love, hatred, gratitude, tenderness) as a configuration of the "profound self" of Arguedian narrative and highlighted the mobilizing force of the feelings of reciprocity that characterize Andean sociality.[30] Feelings of love and tenderness, which have a constant presence in Arguedas's work, paradoxically complement and complete the idea and function of violence that is always latent in his stories. As Slavoj Žižek and Peter Sloterdijk (reworking Walter Benjamin's ideas) remind us, anger and resentment can be utilized for emancipatory purposes and are linked to the love of one's neighbor and the desire for justice.[31] Arguedas himself pointed out, referring to his earliest stories: "*Agua* is a pure outgrowth of the Andean world; it was inspired by hatred and tenderness." He adds: "*Agua* was indeed written with hatred, with the rage of a pure hatred: that which grows out of universal love, there, in the regions of the world where two sides confront each other with primitive cruelty" (*Diamantes y pedernales* 7).

This point of convergence between love and hate is precisely where the dilemma of language is generated, the *double bind* that Arguedas refers to as a "difficulty," as a "disturbing problem" in which the dimensions of the local and the intimate, hindered by modernity, surface as inescapable traces of individual and collective subjectivity. It is also the source of the "subtle disorderings" (to which we referred earlier in this study when analyzing the problem of language), the disruptions of the communicative pact, the deconventionalization of the system of signs, the clouding of language as the metonymic representation of the invisibilization of the subject and of its necessary appearance as rupture and subversion. Arguedas once again:

> Another disturbing problem stood in the way of actualizing my burning desire. How can I describe those hamlets, villages, and lands: in which language can I narrate their life? In Spanish? After having learned, loved, and lived it through the sweet intensity of Quechua? This seemed an irresolvable difficulty. (ibid. 9)

All this introduces varying degrees of importance and multiple strata of meaning into a narrative in which ideology always appears as a relatively domesticated form of affect but also as a space of potential violence and in which the force of the subjective, the affective, and the private compete with political, social, and economic factors in the configuration of social projects and behaviors.[32]

The polemic around *Todas las sangres*, particularly regarding the figure of the tenant farmer Willka, touched on the theme of the construction of identity in postcolonial societies and the need to understand these instances of social (self-)recognition beyond all essentialism and all stability. Subject to the processes of accelerated modernizing transformation as well as to the phenomenon of the persistence of colonial structures in modernity and the emergence of new subjects and social behaviors that accompany the processes of migration, becoming-*cholo*, industrialization, and technologization, identity can only be understood as a necessarily relational, fluid, variable, and multiple formation. In this sense it constitutes not an essentialized stage but a construct susceptible to changes and combinations in which a form of definition ("I am a tenant farmer," Willka says) does not exclude other possible identifications, other processes of the negotiation of subjectivity, desire, and ideology.

Without denying the importance of the factors of class, race, and gender, or the force of the State as manager and administrator of *difference*, the processes of identification encouraged by modernity combine distinct forms of *affiliation* within the parameters of *the social*, making possible different modes of defining homeland and territorial belonging, of understanding the relation to the land, of establishing familial relations, connections to the mother tongue, the phenomena of belief, and political sentiment. As Moore reminds us, before the critiques delivered at the roundtable at the IEP referring to the character of Rendón Willka, Arguedas points out that, for this character:

> no contradiction exists between his magical and rational conceptions of the world. Before reflecting a syncretic vision comparable to a *mestizaje* that frequently hides the phenomenon of acculturation, the process of becoming-cholo that Rendón represents is typically uneven and gives us evidence of a process of partial or selective transformation in which different levels of cultural penetration are combined, both in urban and rural environments. In other words, it shows that the *cholo* can be more or less Indian or criollo according to his particular geocultural situation. (Moore, "Encuentros y desencuentros" 273–74)

This is the uneasy and inescapable social diversity of the Andean region that Arguedas is interested in exploring, in which the constitution of the collective subject constantly fluctuates and recomposes itself, making it so that its "nature" escapes any type of stable categorization due to the dynamics imposed on it by the processes of migration and miscegenation exacerbated by modernity. In this investigation, Arguedas takes more than one approach to that complex and obscure "object of desire," the culture of the Other (which is his culture), without disciplinary or epistemological restrictions. There is no place in his program for identitarian essentialisms that would place the subject outside of history and make its story unnecessary. The only guidelines for situating forms of social (self-) recognition (not *identities*) are those which understand subjectivity and its collective processes as eminently fluid and relational, constantly changing and developing.

As we have seen, the paradigms of the Quechua cosmovision combine and sometimes mix together in Arguedas's work in an unrestricted and undisciplined way with European "high" culture, extra-rational forms of approaching the real (the reclamation of affect, intuition, and myth), together with the cognitive models passed down from the colonizer and successively reaffirmed in the diverse avatars of capitalist modernity without it being necessary to choose or hierarchize those legacies. It is inspired equally by the airplane and the gods of Huarochirí, the utopia of popular revolution and the notion of *pachacuti*, the magic of the "word-thing" and the power that it can come to deploy at the level of sentiments, actions, and concepts. It understands that all these elements compose in and of themselves and in their interactions the complex world in which they happen to live. To grasp this complexity, to study its socio-cultural frameworks, and to communicate it in a symbolic way, Arguedas thus refined his representational resources, discarding neither realism nor fantasy, neither Spanish nor Quechua, nor any of the aleatory formulas that he was able to propose, both at the linguistic level and within the literary proper, for the search for an elusive and pressing reality marked by both ancestral and contemporary tragedy. However, Arguedas's "inspiration" did not respond to romantic impulses or refer to elevated or transcendent levels of aesthetic and ideological enlightenment. Rather, it derives from profound and contradictory but always concrete and historically—ideologically—situated forms of social consciousness. It constitutes, in this sense, a particularized form of production of the *political unconscious* that Fredric Jameson theorized as the symbolic place in which the hidden contents of history and the diverse stories constructed to comprehend it are to be found. If all narrative is, as Jameson argues, a socially symbolic act organized on the basis of ideology, it is from such a focal point that the process of literary production (which in Arguedas's case fosters a reappropriation of past elements and values from the problematic present of the Andean region) must be understood. Jameson establishes the dilemma—the *double bind*—of historicism, which is presented as the desire to grasp the grandeur of the ancient or the archaic (which, in Arguedas's case, as in Mariátegui's, is the remote world of the Incan Empire and its cultural legacies) from the conflictive nature of the present time. Inappropriate forms of relating to and reappropriating the past continue to exist, namely, those which superimpose onto the text—or onto cultural textuality—a "rewriting" that denaturalizes cultural representation. As Jameson notes:

> This unacceptable option, or ideological *double bind* between antiquarianism and modernizing "relevance" or projection demonstrates that the old dilemmas of historicism—and in particular the question of the claims of monuments from distant and even archaic moments of the cultural past on a culturally different present—do not go away just because we choose to ignore them.

[...]
[O]nly a genuine philosophy of history is capable of respecting the specificity and radical difference of the social and cultural past while disclosing the solidarity of its polemics and passions, its forms, structures, experiences, and struggles, with those of the present. (*The Political Unconscious* 18)

There are in Arguedas's literary project important traces of this historicist concern that respects above all "the specificity and radical difference of the social and cultural past" while deploying a solidary passion for a present in which marginalization and inequality for indigenous cultures continue to exist. Arguedas's work implicitly reads and re-reads the narratives of colonialism that have preceded the existence of the nation as well as the narratives of modernity which have shaped it since independence. Based on these narratives, it proposes to drive a new reading of the Andean question, not of its empirical history but of the canonical stories that sustain it. His work thus inaugurates a new hermeneutics of capitalist modernity and the peripheral heterogeneities that subvert the transculturating process that intervenes in local cultures. His narrative establishes a new symbolic contract with the reader, one that Boom literature had neither undertaken nor foreseen, attentive as it may have been to machinations of the global markets in which circulated a literature that had transmutated from text into book, which is to say, from symbolic discourse into commodity and which, as such, is sold for its exchange value on international markets.[33] Arguedas's work strengthens and in some measure exacerbates or hyperbolizes the local (the singular and contingent). This is the hard core of his narrative. Arguedas unravels the tremendous contradictions and ruptures that involve the broad transculturating program that in high modernity implements epistemological domination of the periphery by a capitalism that thenceforward expands as a contemporary stage—as a "superior phase"—of originary colonialism.

Arguedas's narrative covers a broad spectrum that runs from recording atavistic elements to fascination with technology.[34] As writer, ethnographer, educator, and so on, he was seduced by the processes of urbanization and transformation of subjectivity as much as by the persistent continuity of communal forms of socialization. He also always remained alert with respect to the impression that Western models continue to leave on heterogeneous Andean culture, de-naturalizing its traditions and gradually erasing its tracks. Arguedas thus deploys a "mode of artistic production," to use Jameson's terminology, that recognizes an "ultimate horizon" in history for the analysis of culture and its aesthetico-literary register. I am not referring here to a reading of the actual development that crosses through a determinate community but to the comprehension of that course in its profound, intrahistorical significance and in its *imaginary* dimension in which expectations, experiences, and desires are combined in order to produce the collective dimension of the social and the plural memory it preserves. This form of *synthetic truth* that is supported in the materiality of the socio-cultural texture (interactions, objects, beliefs) implies a specific form of understanding the relation between history and discourse, reality and language. It also supposes a commitment to the *truth*, understood not in its objective, ontological dimension, as accordance with reality, nor as correct representation, but as a *quality of the subject*, which is to say, as the capacity to grasp and interpret reality from the profound experience in which ethics and politics, knowledge and the hermeneutics of the social converge. It is the commitment of the subject to the revelation of the object which makes it possible to uncover its truth; it is its search that makes possible its discovery, its interrogation that allows a response to emerge. This is the point at which attention to cultural *difference* gives way to the critical representation of politico-economic *inequality*, and the literary/anthropological project acquires its highest ethical and ideological dimension.

Notes

1. The study of material culture was developed principally in the USA and in Europe during the twentieth century, although it first emerged in the previous century. As an interdisciplinary enterprise, the study of material culture is concerned with history, the uses and meanings of objects and artifacts belonging to distinct cultural and historical contexts, as well as the social relations that are established around them. In this sense, the field of material culture is linked to consumer studies, environmental studies, the circulation of commodities, the establishment of value, the uses of the object, the construction of identities, commercial transactions and exchange, the preservation of cultural legacies, the institutionality of museums, and other related themes. The principal disciplines which converge in the study of material culture are anthropology, history, archeology, sociology, philosophy, cultural criticism, economics, and others. For an example of general studies with this orientation, see, for example, Thomas J. Schlereth, ed., *Material Culture: A Research Guide*; Arjun Appadurai, *The Social Life of Things*; and the *Journal of Material Culture*. In some cases, the study of material culture rests completely on the

analysis of the circulation of commodities, recognizing as one of its theoretical foundations Georg Simmel's early study, *The Philosophy of Money*, from 1907, and Marx's work on capitalist production and political economy. In other cases, the orientation has more to do with Bourdieu's analysis of social behavior or with the more semiotic orientation of Baudrillard.

2. On the significance of the *zumballyu*, see Huamán 286–92. His book is also useful for comprehending the meanings of other Quechua references in Arguedas's work.
3. Moore highlights the unifying importance of the *zumballyu* as a hybrid element and as a "magic mediator," indicating that, "as with the bull and the bullfight in *Yawar fiesta*, the *zumballyu* dramatizes both the socio-cultural diversity of Andean society and the possibilities of its integration" (*En la encrucijada* 305).
4. Julio Ortega emphasizes (although he is referring strictly to the literary world created by the author) Arguedas's condition as the communicator of a plural model appropriated in order to represent a highly stratified and culturally differentiated society. In this sense, *Los ríos profundos* constitutes a fictional representation of the social drama that derives from the tense coexistence of different systems of communication which assume diverse models of perception as well as different ways of transmitting, hierarchizing, and processing information—hence, the plural configuration of the narrator and his tendency to redouble into an authorial "I," a witness "I," and a protagonist "I." Some of Ortega's observations on the theme of communication can be applied to Arguedas's anthropological work as well as his work as a cultural critic more generally.
5. Ann Lambright works the useful notion of "hybrid intellectual," understanding it to mean a member of the *lettered city*, generally white and of urban origin, who identifies with indigenous communities and whose social conscience prepares him to struggle on their behalf (56–57). Lambright studies this *hybridity* not only in terms of ethnic exchange or co-belonging, but also in relation to nationalist ideology linked to the notion of gender, the representation of the feminine in Arguedas's work, and the functions that are assigned to it, at an aesthetic as well as an ideological level, within the author's fictitious world. Used in this way, the notion of hybridity, which ends up encompassing too many levels, is expanded toward other territories, broadening the possibilities of analysis but also diluting—and at times easing—access to the possible theoretical valences of this notion.
6. Castro-Klarén has proposed the notion of "indigenist realism" with regard to thinking about Arguedas (*El mundo mágico* 21), an author whose commitment to historical reality is not diluted by the undoubtedly poetic dimension of his texts, which are always rooted in a worldview strongly influenced by indigenous epistemology.

7. Rowe concludes his article on "El novelista y el antropólogo" ["The novelist and the anthropologist"] with a reflection that, in and of itself, could guide new readings of Arguedas from a postcolonial perspective: "Insofar as the Andean response is displaced from an imaginary praxis to a real praxis and the borders between the two worlds are disappearing, the mythological universe is entering a crisis at the same time that capitalist Peruvian culture is losing its monolithic and impenetrable appearance. In spite of—but also because of—its use of myth, magic, and religious symbolism, Arguedas's work stages the necessity and the difficulty of going beyond mythology" (116). I think, however, that Rowe's last assertion is debatable since myth carries out an articulating function of significant ideological import, as Mariátegui already pointed out, making the world intelligible and incorporating categories of perception and analysis that Western rationality relegates to the margins of accepted knowledge.
8. On the theme of North American anthropology and the discipline of anthropology in general as an instrument of imperialism, as well as on the relations between anthropology and "magical" thought in Arguedas, see Marisol de la Cadena, "La producción de otros conocimientos y sus tensiones: ¿de la antropología andinista a la interculturalidad?," and Degregori and Sandoval, "Dilemas y tendencias," *Saberes periféricos*, and other texts. Ladislao Landa Vásquez formulates the idea of "anthropology at home," referring to the local view Arguedas exercised within his own environs, in which he brought together the observed, the recorded, and the lived. This would give Arguedas the status of "native informant" ("self-ethnographer"), a condition in which first-hand knowledge of one's own culture is combined with subjective elements (affectivity, desires, etc.) which distinctly affect the anthropologist's interpretation and account of his or her object of study. In this regard, see Strathern, as well as Geertz on the problems of ethnographic writing.
9. Although the origins of dependency theory are generally linked to the crash of 1929 and to the effort to understand the world crisis of capitalism and the elaboration of regional alternatives, in Latin America this tendency was disseminated by the Argentine economist Raúl Prebisch, who directed the Economic Commission for Latin America (ECLAC) between 1948 and 1962. Thus, in different contexts within Latin America, a debate developed about the protectionist role of the State, the role of international markets, and the center/periphery configuration as a structure of capitalist domination. The principal representatives of dependency theory are Theotonio Dos Santos, André Gunder Frank, Celso Furtado, Ruy Mauro Marini, Enzo Faletto, and Fernando Henrique Cardoso. Dependency theory analyzes the benefits of state control and rejects the pressures of the international market, promoting instead protectionist barriers and stimulating import substitute industrialization.

10. González Casanova writes: "The definition of internal colonialism is originally linked to phenomena of conquest in which native populations are not exterminated and form, first, part of the colonizing State that later acquires a formal independence or initiates a process of liberation, of a transition to socialism or a recolonization and return to neoliberal capitalism. People, minorities, or nations colonized by [another] nation-State suffer conditions similar to those that characterize colonialism and neocolonialism at the international level: they inhabit a territory they do not govern; they find themselves in an unequal situation, facing elites from dominant ethnicities and the classes they compose; their juridico-political administration and responsibility concern dominant ethnicities, the bourgeoisie, and the oligarchies of the central government or its associates and subordinates; its inhabitants do not occupy the highest political or military positions of the central government except when they have fully "assimilated;" the inhabitants' rights and economic, political, social, and cultural situations are regulated and imposed by the central government; in general, the colonized within a nation-State belong to a distinct 'race' from those who dominate the national government, a 'race' which is considered 'inferior' or at most is converted into a 'liberating' symbol that forms part of the state's demagoguery; the majority of the colonized belong to a distinct culture and speak a language different from the 'national' language" ("Colonialismo interno" 410). See also Stavenhagen and González Casanova, *De la sociología del poder a la sociología de la explotación*.
11. As Mignolo notes, Silvia Rivera Cusicanqui also covers this concept in her studies of the indigenous peasantry in Bolivia.
12. Liberation theology has its origins in the 1960s, and its principal representatives include Peruvian priest Gustavo Gutiérrez Merino, who published *Historia, política y salvación de una teología de liberación* in 1971 [translated as *A Theology of Liberation: History, Politics, and Salvation* in 1973—Tr.], Brazilian Leonardo Boff, Colombian Camilo Torres, who was a member of the Colombian National Liberation Army, and others. This movement articulated Christian transcendentalism with a Marxist emphasis on economic processes and the struggle between classes as fundamental elements for the comprehension of social injustice. It focused on poverty as a mobilization point for transformative social action against inequality, thus elaborating the notions of the social victim, solidarity, and structural sin, making itself into an alternative to capitalism as well as into a different path toward socialism than the traditional avenues of partisanship and orthodoxy. The relationship between Gustavo Gutiérrez and Arguedas would be documented in *El zorro de arriba y el zorro de abajo* and in Gutiérrez's book, *Entre las calandrias*, which he dedicated to his friendship with Arguedas. In this regard, see Gutierrez's *A Theology of Liberation*, as well as Boff and Dussel.

13. In this regard, see, for example, the section of Klára Schirová's "*Todas las sangres*: la utopía peruana" entitled "El dios de los pobres," in *Arguedas en el corazón de Europa* 118–26.
14. Based on these elements, the religious connotations that Arguedas's work may have had have been exaggerated in some cases by voluntarist readings, such as that of Gutiérrez himself, who insists on the importance of the Christian God in Arguedas's work. In any case, the relations between theology and Latin American literature have yet to be exhaustively investigated. In this regard, see Schirová and Rivera-Pagán. On the role of religion in Arguedas's work, see Trigo.
15. "From the point of view of form and content, *Todas las sangres* has all the features of a mythic novel or biblical allegory [...] Willka's trajectory symbolizes the life, death, and resurrection of Christ. His pilgrimage to Lima, the awakening, the return to San Pedro, the organization of communities, and the redemption of death together with the signal of messianism repeat and affirm the Christian cycle of suffering and salvation" (Schirová 120).
16. Arguedas's first anthropological work was his doctoral thesis at the Universidad Nacional Mayor de San Marcos entitled *Las comunidades de España y del Perú*, written on the basis of fieldwork undertaken in Spain in 1958. He described this thesis as an "irregular book, a good chronicle [that] is, for all that, somewhat novelesque and peppered with a certain academic nuance" (Millones, "Una mirada" 22).
17. In terms of cultural recovery, it is worth recalling Arguedas's recuperation of Andean stories based on those collected by Luis Gilberto Pérez, who served as Arguedas's source on several aspects of Quechua culture. Arguedas published these texts in Quechua with his own Spanish translations in the journal *Folklore Americano*. It is interesting to note both the proliferation of mediations and the documentary function assigned to literature as a space of cultural (re)cognition and recuperation of marginalized writings. In this regard, see Bueno Chávez's article.
18. Lienhard correctly notes that "In contrast to Luis Valcárcel's messianic, indigenist dithyramb in *Tempestad en los Andes*, the mestizo messianism that animates José María Arguedas's article [referring to "La canción popular mestiza," collected in *Indios, mestizos y señores*]—the definitive conquest is not too far off—does not point to a violent social tempest but rather a *change in mentality*" ("La antropología" 50, emphasis in original).
19. Examples of these positions can be seen, for instance, in Arguedas's texts on Puquio and the Mantaro Valley, collected in *Formaciones de una cultura indoamericana*.
20. On Arguedas's ethnographic work and his elaboration of the notions of *mestizo* and *mestizaje*, see De la Cadena and Kokotovic, *La modernidad andina*, especially its second chapter, "Del desarrollismo al pachakutiy"

(93–131). On Valcárcel, see Escobar (30–35), and on the difference between this latter and Arguedas, see Cortés.
21. I agree with Cortés in his discussion of Manrique and Flores Galindo's considerations on what would in Arguedas be, according to these scholars' perspective, a contradictory and harmonizing discourse on the theme of *mestizaje*. I think Arguedas's notion of *mestizaje* is conceptualized from a certain strategic essentialism insofar as he is trying to propose a category that would allow him to delineate a political agent, which is to say, an (in principle) cohesive cultural and ideological structuration that can rise above internal antagonisms and differences to consolidate an agenda for political mobilization.
22. After the considerations expressed by Mariátegui, who tried to analyze the position of the mestizo in its historical moment in relation to other segments of society, the theme of the mestizo has been studied very soundly by Flores Galindo in *Buscando un inca*. See also Alberto Escobar, "En torno del mestizo," in *Arguedas o la utopía de la lengua* (48–56), and De la Cadena, *Indígenas mestizos*, where on the basis of this concept he studies the condition of individuals of indigenous but trans-territorialized origin, whose experience in urban centers does not change, however, their identification with indigenous culture. See also his article "¿Son los mestizos híbridos?"
23. As was previously observed, with respect to these representations of social change in Arguedas's work Flores Galindo noted the fact that this narrative seems to follow the itinerary that describes the expansion of the internal market in Peru: "A parallel can be established between the expansion of the road system, the growth of commercial agriculture, and the intensification of exchange as well as monetary and commercial flows with the development of Arguedas's work" (*Dos Ensayos* 15). Flores Galindo even connects this Arguedian thematic to the writer's own biography, the travels of his father (a lawyer) in a fully developed country, young José María's re-enrollment in schools in Ica and Huancayo, and his further studies in Lima. In this respect, see Cornejo Polar's studies of the migrant subject as well.
24. Quijano sees this process as an uneven development that cannot be applied without examining the different contexts in which it occurs. See Moore's discussion of the topic in *En la encrucijada* (163 and passim), as well as Matos Mar's foundational book.
25. It is important to see here the substantial change the concept of *mestizaje* underwent in the context of populism in the inter-war period, not only in Peru but, of course, in Mexico as well, after the impact of the Mexican Revolution. In this period, the notion of national culture and the conceptualization of the Latin American political subject (particularly in the Andean region) substantially changed. In this regard, see Moraña, *Literatura y cultura nacional en Hispanoamérica: 1910–1940*.

26. Moore reconstructs the terms of both the debate itself and the intellectual horizon of the era in which it occurred, and in which the recent works of Henri Favre on the peasants of Huancavelica and Quijano's influential study of the emergence of the *cholo* segment of Peruvian society had circulated. Nugent has written more recently about this latter theme in *El laberinto de la choledad*. Moore also recalls the fact that the character of Rendón Willka, who raised so much controversy at the roundtables of 1965 for the way he related to other characters that represented capitalism (the landowning patriarch Andrés Aragón y Peralta and his sons Fermín and Bruno), is himself a product of internal migration in Peru, an ex-Indian or *cholo* embodying both the skepticism and the adaptability of this social category. In spite of his distrust of party politics (including communist politics) as a politico-ideological structure, Willka shows himself capable of responding to the challenges of modernity, accepting of the changes imposed by technology, and negotiating forms of functioning within the new social parameters of the epoch. In this sense, he does not represent an "anachronistic" form of social inclusion but rather illustrates the very ambiguities and contradictions of a new social subject in a setting undergoing profound transformations.
27. On Mariátegui and postcolonial thought, see Moraña, "Mariátegui en los nuevos debates: Emancipación, (in)dependencia y 'colonialismo supérstite' en América Latina."
28. It is interesting to note that, revealing the disciplinary hierarchization of the era, Arguedas defended himself from his critics' attacks by appealing largely to the same language of social science, indicating the imprecision of particular terms ("Indian," "*cholo*"), citing the example of the four servants ["*pongos*"] from Huancavelica, and maintaining that all social realities and all analytical categories are necessarily relative to the specific place to which they are applied, thus claiming the dimension of the particularity of the local and the need to historicize processes and contemplate their geocultural variations. In this regard, see Moore, "Encuentros y desencuentros." When Arguedas was questioned by literary critics such as Oviedo and Salazar Bondy, he was even more disconcerted by the claim that they advanced regarding the lack of documentation in Arguedas's novel.
29. Castro-Klarén considers the unfolding of affect derived from Huarochirí's manuscript, which presents the shamanic world as a form of knowledge that Arguedas had tried to incorporate into his writing. More than the mere right to "be different," or the text's evident thanatic directionality, *El zorro de arriba* is so excessively marked by affect that it tests the limits of writing and of life itself. On "machinic affect" in the *Zorros*, see Beasley-Murray.
30. See, for example, Castro-Klarén, as well as Portugal ("AGON: la imaginación melodramática"), Moore ("Encuentros y desencuentros," 275–76),

Fernando Rivera-Díaz ("El zorro en el espejo," in Sergio R. Franco, ed., *José María Arguedas: hacia una poética migrante*, 178–82), and Marcos.
31. See Žižek, *Violence: Six Sideways Reflections*, especially the section dedicated to divine violence. Žižek reminds us of one of Che Guevara's most famous quotations: "One must endure—become hard, toughen oneself—without losing tenderness" (204). Žižek's reflections on Benjamin's concept of mythic violence ("that [which] demands sacrifice," 199) can be applied to moments in Arguedas's narrative work.
32. Arguedas's prologue to *Diamantes y pedernales* (the Arca/Calicanto edition which only includes one of the novels to which the author refers in his introduction) is very conceptually rich regarding such topics as the dilemma of language, translation, the affect/ideology/language relation, language as fiction, the links between universality and regionalism, and many others.
33. On literature as exchange value in the Boom era, see David Viñas, and on this literary movement more generally, including its cultural and ideological significance, see Rama, "El 'boom' en perspectiva."
34. On technology in Arguedas see Sergio R. Franco, "Tecnologías de la representación" and Kraniauskas.

CHAPTER 8

Which Truth? Otherness and Melodrama in Vargas Llosa

Without a doubt, Vargas Llosa's prolific literary production has run a very different course than José María Arguedas's. The themes that seem to concern him most persistently, linked in a more or less oblique way to the problem of *truth* (which in Arguedas's work takes on dramatic overtones), refer to the opposite of this latter concept in Vargas Llosa's narrative and essayistic production. Although the problem of morality is a recurring topic in his essays and journalistic work and in fact appears to saturate all of Vargas Llosa's literary production, the elusive and artificial style with which his writing approaches the explicit or implicit discussion of these topics is undoubtedly symptomatic. In fact, Vargas Llosa's constant reference in his work to the notions of lying, falsehood, pretense, simulation, farce, invention, unreality, charlatanry, fiction, pastiche, and simulacrum reveals a perpetual uneasiness about the ways in which the task of literature is defined by its social practice and ideological performance. In particular, he is interested in exploring the field of literature's influence, its relation to distinct forms of symbolic interaction, the ways in which it affects discourses of power, its interpellative capacity, its political dimension, and its range as a rhetorical strategy and ideological resource. One could say that this persistent investigation of the nature and function of literature is evidence of a need for legitimation and in large measure the reclamation of a form of work that, from the neoliberal point of view, is frequently considered marginal within the logic of capitalist productivity. In Vargas Llosa's ceaseless opinions on the function of art and the sources of poetic inspiration, one can see an attempt to articulate a coherent and irrefutable conception of the position of the writer and of literature—its specificity and relevance—within the sheltered but fluctuating space of the *lettered city*.

As we have already seen, in Arguedas the problem of truth is linked instead to the uncovering of hidden levels of the social problematic, and it inevitably passes through the epistemic struggles related to the theme of the decolonization of thought, the challenges posed by coloniality, and the remnants of ancestral cultures in their struggle against the forces of modernity. Thus, it becomes obvious that there is a need to conceive of alternative modes of being modern based on new forms of social consciousness. In Vargas Llosa, however, the theme of truth refers rather to the level of representation of a given, contingent, immediate reality which the narrator approaches through representational strategies that manipulate the perception and interpretation of the fictional world, distorting, delaying, or hastening its manifestation to the reader. Vargas Llosa works on the smokescreen that hides the real, which in all its corrupt materiality awaits the gaze of he or she who discovers it. But for Arguedas, behind this smokescreen lies an ethical, historical, and epistemological abyss. His literature thematizes that limit situation on the basis of poetry, not without that trace of melancholia that is essential to utopian thought. Vargas Llosa records the degrees and forms that degradation assumes in an inescapably real world, and in this final, definitive sense: the world of *the-history-that-is*, the world of capital, the market, the material and symbolic power that, like a war machine, moves the relation of the human being with its environment, its own body, and others' bodies. The commerce of meaning thus cannot itself follow both courses, nor can the conception of the *truth* approached by the word be supported on the same foundation. In Arguedas, penetrating the layers that separate us from the historical and social truth is an affective practice, a phenomenon of belief; in Vargas Llosa, literary writing implies the deployment of subterfuge and tactics, a *mise-en-scène* in which reality and literature confuse their respective territories, where politics can survive as a spectacle, lies as truth, falsehood as the production of meaning, fiction as history—in sum, a scenario in which all that is solid melts into the text.

In addition, both writers are differently positioned with respect to the topic of posterity. The incentives of recognition and fame and the construction of a public image (which Vargas Llosa places at the forefront of his intellectual enterprise and approaches with total dedication and enthusiasm) was never able to penetrate the dense cloud of anxiety that seemed to surround Arguedas at all times, nor could it pierce the joyous vitalism that at the same time characterized the latter author's life experience. Vargas Llosa's determination to elevate literary practice to a position of cultural prestige, professionalization, and international impact should be understood, at least in part, as a reaction to what he believes is the profound lack of recognition of lettered labor [*labor letrada*] within Peruvian national culture, a situation for which Vargas Llosa has expressed particularly bitter contempt on various occasions.

One of the most exemplary articles Vargas Llosa has written on this topic is from 1966 and is dedicated to one of his colleagues from that era, Sebastián Salazar Bondy, as a posthumous homage.[1] Vargas Llosa expounds on the situation of the writer in Peru, including the frustrations, persecutions, and insults to which the writer is subjected, confirming that "every Peruvian writer is defeated in the long run" ("Sebastián Salazar Bondy" 92/61).

> In a society in which literature plays no role because the majority of its members do not know how to read or do not have the necessary conditions in which to read and the minority that have these opportunities do not read, then the writer is an anomalous being, without a precise place, a picturesque and eccentric individual, a sort of harmless madman who is allowed his freedom because, after all, the madness is not contagious—how can he harm others if they do not read? Yet, even so, he should be kept in a straight-jacket, at a distance, treated with caution, tolerated with systematic mistrust. (Vargas Llosa, "Sebastián Salazar Bondy" 93/61–62)
>
> But Peru is an underdeveloped country, that is, a jungle where one has to earn the right to survive by force. (ibid. 95/63)

To support these claims, he cites Salazar Bondy's own words from *Lima la horrible*: "Aesthetic concerns encounter a tenacious obstacle in Peru: they are apparently gratuitous. Since it lacks use value for indoctrination or sensuality, beauty created by artistic talent has no function" (ibid. 93/62). And he adds:

> Yes, Peruvians can be poets and writers when they are young. Then the milieu begins to change them: it reclaims and assimilates some, it defeats and abandons others, leaving them morally defeated, frustrated in their vocation, taking sad consolation in laziness, scepticism, bohemian behavior, neurosis, or alcohol. Some do not deny their vocation as such, but manage

to shape it to the environment: they become teachers, they stop creating to teach and research, both necessary activities, but essentially different from those of a creator [...] When they go to the grave, the majority of Peruvian writers have been corpses for a long time and Peru is not usually moved by those victims that it destroyed, ten, fifteen, twenty years before their death. (ibid. 113/68–69)

It does not seem too risky to hazard that the conditions of the Peruvian milieu Vargas Llosa so exasperatedly describes are precisely those that he himself wanted to overcome through a determined process of professionalization and entry into the prestigious settings of world literature.[2] Perhaps his early awareness of the limitations and pettiness of the national milieu was one of the incentives for him to secure a position in the spaces of international letters, which he perceived as less sullied (or at least more gratifying and controllable) than the parochial settings from which he emerged due to the distance this allowed him to place between himself and his personal and institutional contacts. This is also perhaps where one should look to find the key to understanding the public stature that Vargas Llosa continues to fashion for himself, as well as his political ambitions, his omnipresence in mass media, his participation in commissions, tribunals, and debates which all afford him the opportunity to place himself above the majority of his contemporaries by occupying prominent positions. It is also possible that the restrictions of intellectual work at the merely national level have intensified his individualist tendencies, his desire to professionalize and control the sphere of culture, to break free of the ideological discipline of socialism, and to tirelessly search after power and recognition.[3] Finally, perhaps it is also within these parameters that one can understand his elaboration of a poetics informed by elements of romantic-idealist sublimity that place his literature on a transcendent and spiritualized plane, clearly differentiating it from the more pedestrian and quotidian work of other writers. These sublime aspects that Vargas Llosa claims for his work include the idea of the creative *vocation* qua vital impulse elaborated by José Enrique Rodó at the beginning of the twentieth century within the framework of an Arielist (elitist and humanistic) vision of culture, the enthusiastic and indiscriminate *rebellion* of the artist as proof of the non-conformist and transgressive spirit that elevates him above established powers, the idea of *demons* as superior forces of enlightenment and creative power, the *struggle against evil* in defense of the universalist and abstract principles of community *morality*, staunch *individualism* as estrangement, and intellectual aristocratism. More tortuous is the relation that can be found between the rejection expressed in Vargas Llosa's *limeño* provincialism and his adherence to neoliberalism, between the restrictions he feels are imposed by national culture and the conception of a modernity built on the immolation of indigenous communities, or between the fear of not having surpassed the limits of a modest and unequal peripheral capitalism and the universalism of values and principles that constitute an empty rhetorical pretext that fails to justify his disdain for the working class and its will to power.[4]

Neil Larsen has insisted on the futile, "inane" quality of Vargas Llosa's ideological principles: his faith in Peru as the proper place for the flourishing of modern liberal *individuality*, his *fictionalization* of the ideological, the result of a social reality that has been systematically neglected and displaced in one way or another by consistently self-centered narratives; his perception of the "truth in lies" as the principle by which reality is substituted by the simulacrum, even in the arena of politics proper. The *knowledge* of the real is thus transformed into an act of faith, as when he postulates that poverty has been "chosen" by marginal populations and that nations can "decide" their own progress and prosperity, as if there were no objective conditions beyond desire and free will.[5] However, it is precisely those social processes and historical developments that in large measure determine the forms of social consciousness and strategies that transform reality to which it is necessary to return to contextualize Vargas Llosa's project.

In his 1975 article "Albert Camus y la moral de los límites" ["Albert Camus and the Morality of Limits"] exalting the figure of Meursault, the protagonist of *The Stranger* as a "martyr to truth," Vargas Llosa demonstrates his admiration for this *elemental* (in the strongest sense of the word) representation of the total desacralization of existence and of the repositioning of faith in the place of morality as a superior moment of politics. Meursault has "the vice of telling the truth," a virtue that Vargas Llosa lauds, allocating to the character a tinge of anachronism and an affected superiority that the Peruvian writer undoubtedly would like to integrate into his own individual nature. Enamored of this image that elevates the spirit blessed with these qualities above all others and which recognizes individualism as the key to axiological excellence and civic virtue, Vargas Llosa thus effectuates a notorious and significant shift from enthusiastic admiration for Sartre to fervent support of Camus. According to the Peruvian author, Camus' positions leave much more room for personal liberty and for the establishment of ethical principles that each individual can define for himself or herself.[6] This shift in Vargas Llosa's intellectual preferences is one of the most significant in his career, not only for its ideological implications but also for the terms on which it was established. It will be helpful to briefly review these terms as an illustration of the broader process the Peruvian author continues to follow today.

Although Vargas Llosa continues to hold Sartre in high esteem, his support for the French philosopher, as is well-known, has passed through various stages. In his article "El mandarín" ["The Mandarin"] Vargas Llosa recognizes that his admiration for Sartre changed after the latter downplayed the importance of literature in relation to other demands of social struggle in an interview with *Le Monde* in 1964. This attitude of staunch commitment to social causes—which Vargas Llosa considered confusing and excessive, as well as ignorant of the specific cultural contributions literature has made to the struggle against injustice and inequality—led him to feel personally "betrayed." He describes Sartre as a "thinking machine," for whom everything seemed to be an "epiphenomenon of intelligence," leaving no room for the joy, humor, or playful moments that Vargas Llosa believed were an essential part of life and, ultimately, literature. Although he acknowledges that Sartre was one of his earliest introductions to the theme of the civic function and responsibility of literature, Vargas Llosa resents the French philosopher's austerely reflexive style. He finds in his idea of the committed intellectual a restrictive notion of creative freedom, "rubbish" that caused him "consternation." This allows him "to argue with [Sartre] in my mind and to debunk him with my questions," formulating in "The Mandarin" a series of rhetorical questions:

> What coefficient of proteins per capita did a country have to achieve before it was ethical to write novels? What indexes of national income, education, mortality, health had to be reached for it to be moral and paint a picture, compose a cantata or make a sculpture? What human endeavours can withstand the comparison with dead children more successfully than the novel? Astrology? Architecture? Is the palace of Versailles worth more than a dead child? How many dead children are the equivalent to quantum theory? (*Contra viento y marea* I 400/*Making Waves* 142)

The reductio ad absurdum argument with which Vargas Llosa chooses to address the otherwise hackneyed theme of the social function of literature (lending it the form of an interpellation directed to one of the most influential philosophers of the twentieth century) is overwhelming, to say the least, especially taking into consideration the politico-ideological frame of the post-1960 era. In that period, existentialism and Marxism proposed a radical rearticulation of the cultural sphere in a time of broad social change and collective consciousness-raising. The "imaginary socialist" that Vargas Llosa still was at the time participated in the utopia of social transformation, inspired by the thought of the same authors he would later denigrate when his leftwing convictions were diluted in sea of neoliberalism. In spite of his belated yet forceful disagreements with the French philosopher, Vargas Llosa was grateful to Sartre for having at an earlier moment given him conceptual weapons with which to fight provincialism, aestheticism, folklorism, and Manicheanism, deviations he attributed to many of his contemporaries.[7] Thus, when asking what Sartre's work has to offer a Latin American student beyond a considerable amount of information about the new directions of contemporary narrative, he says it

> could save him from provincialism, immunize him against rustic folkloric vision, make him feel dissatisfied with that local colour, superficial literature with its Manichean structures and simplistic techniques—Rómulo Gallegos, Eustasio Rivera, Jorge Icaza, Ciro Alegría, Güiraldes, both Arguedas, even Asturias after *El Señor Presidente*—which was still our model and which repeated, unwittingly, the themes and fashions of European naturalism imported half a century ago. (ibid. 388/132 [translation slightly modified—Tr.])

The specter of national mediocrity, the regional tone of its culture (which appeared to Vargas Llosa as a constant threat to his dreams of international recognition), the weight of indigenous themes, and the "naturalist" reference to vernacular elements that he perceived as limitations in the literature of his contemporaries constituted (as did his shift from Sartre to Camus) significant cultural gestures that denounced a particular understanding of the role of the intellectual and the relationship between truth and individuality. Those gestures also testify to an atmosphere accepted by certain segments of the Latin American intelligentsia of the era and the social consciousness that characterized them.

The 1950s generation, in which Vargas Llosa is usually situated, corresponds to a particularly oppressive moment in Peruvian national history. It coincides, at least in part, with the authoritarian government of Manuel Arturo Odría which began with the formation of a military junta in 1948 and then continued with his civilian presidency, which lasted from 1950 to 1956. This period combined the process of modernization, characterized by the massive construction of public works, and the growth of migratory movements from the Andean region to the capital, along with the repression of artists and communists and an exponential rise in corruption. Vargas Llosa thematizes this latter phenomenon in his 1969 novel *Conversación en La Catedral* [*Conversation in the Cathedral* (1974)]. Recalling the years of his adolescence, the frustration and disenchantment that Odría's repressive government managed to imbue in Peruvian society seeps into the writer's reflections, but he also reveals his disappointment with his own generation, which gave in to the crushing weight of power:

> The young *apristas* and communists that Odría imprisoned or exiled will [...] remember those years with both pride and rage. In contrast, we, the adolescents of that tepid middle class whom the dictatorship was content to debase, to make feel disgusted with Peru, with politics, with themselves, or to turn them into conformists or harmless tiger cubs, we can only say: we were a generation of sleepwalkers. (*Contra viento y marea* I 65)

Conformism and the necessity of reaction will become constant motives in Vargas Llosa's work. As is well-known, he proposed a model of the intellectual defined as a permanent rebel in constant opposition to the status quo, a position that, as Mario Benedetti points out, ends up functioning as an almost mechanical agitator of the ruling regime, whatever its politico-ideological character, as perhaps a form of payment of the outstanding debt for past somnambulism.

The social context of the Odría government (which, of course, in those years also affected the first stage of Arguedas's literary production) in the novel presents an urban setting that is both complex and anarchic as a consequence of the massive migration of indigenous and peasant populations to Lima and other cities that offered employment opportunities with the consequent development of slums or "*pueblos jóvenes*"[8] on the outskirts of urban centers. The marginalization that has resulted from the internal displacement and the endemic inequality of the Peruvian population, intensified by social and economic transformations as well as by the processes of technologization that began to impact the organization of work, transportation, mass communication, and consumption of goods, produced a profound change in the imaginaries and the various ways of life in Peruvian society, particularly in the coastal areas that received the heaviest influx of migration. Both Arguedas and Vargas Llosa thematically and compositionally incorporated these social and economic changes into their narrative work.

From a cultural and ideological point of view, Marxism and existentialism constituted the most influential currents within Latin America in those years, although aesthetically, orientations such as Italian neorealism, Faulkner's novelistic style, Anglo-Saxon modernism, and speculative fiction (e.g., Kafka and Borges) left an undeniable impression on artists and intellectuals of the time. Within national culture, the so-called generation of the 1950s followed the path of César Vallejo and José Carlos Mariátegui, promoting the project of a literature committed to social change that had already been represented by major figures for decades. Thus, the modernizing drives that were rapidly transforming the ethnic and cultural makeup of the country and generating conflicts associated with those transformations converged with transculturating processes. The impact of European and North American currents opened up the possibility of cosmopolitanism and, with this, a connection between national culture and a suitable international audience for the consumption of its symbolic products. When this cosmopolitanism was translated into the commercialized and technologized splendors of the Boom, this path (which Arguedas, notably, did not take) would be affirmed as the most promising and efficient line of flight for escaping the limitations and drawbacks of localism.

Toward the end of the 1950s, the Cuban Revolution would come to establish yet another more radical and uncertain alternative in this situation which, up to that point, had been seen as a variation of the traditionalism/modernity dualism that had characterized other historico-cultural conjunctures in Latin America. However, the perspective of socialism demanded other commitments and resignations and required at the same time specific spaces and methods of cultural and political action. Without being at odds with the avenues opened up by cosmopolitanism (which perseveres to this day as a characteristic and a desideratum of Latin American culture), the Leftist option incorporated ethical problems, utopian projections, forms of popular interpellation, principles and values (such as collectivism, internationalism, egalitarianism, social justice, anti-imperialism, decolonization, solidarity, and ideological discipline) into the individualistic backdrop of capitalist modernity. These ideas appeared to radically change the rules of the game as they had been understood up to that point. From the perspective opened up by the alternative of socialism, it became necessary to rethink the conceptual and geocultural limits of national cultures and the strategies of the transculturation of literary products in relation not only to the transformation of cultural production but also to the transformation of symbolic consumption by rapidly diversifying segments of society. In the 1970s, this question would come to constitute one of the most frequent topics of debate among intellectuals, artists, critics, and cultural administrators. It is from within this context that the concept of heterogeneity and the theory of transculturation were developed and the study of the processes of the internationalization of literature began. These new areas of focus opened new horizons regarding the production and comprehension of symbolic products.[9]

As we have seen, Vargas Llosa's work articulates some of the most salient features of the options mentioned above, negotiating the limits and degrees of each one within the new parameters of transnationalism. He carries out his methods of relating to national from the highest levels of the intellectual hierarchy, which allows him to avoid the risks of becoming reabsorbed by the limitations of his surroundings. From this flexible position within his national context, Vargas Llosa's narratives are woven like deep passages into a possible world (with numerous identifiable references to the real world) that palimpsestically manifest their materiality like the raw material of poetic creation. But it would be the process of textual production itself, the manufacture of the literary artifice, and its forms of relating to the reader that would appear to guard the secret of the triumph of Vargas Llosa's narrative. For his insertion into the globalized market, the superstar writer produces the materials which make up his literary thematic, submitting them to a treatment that conditions them for a vast, multicultural audience that, in the final instance, will legitimize his aesthetic choices. Attempting to avoid the most obvious risks of exoticization and the hackneyed options of magical realism, tellurism, or mimetic representation, Vargas Llosa's narrative is bolstered by hybrid materials in which the regional element is reshaped by narrative techniques that mediate the local and transform it into a symbolic commodity for mass consumption. His fiction is always supported by mechanisms of the universalization of the local; hence his appeal to evil and his melodramatic treatment of the ethical and social dynamics that his texts establish are essential to the accessibility achieved by his fictitious worlds, which are offered to readers from very diverse social backgrounds. This dynamic which oscillates between thematic particularism and aesthetic accessibility, between the production of distance and the creation of apparatuses for identifying with the symbolic world of his fiction, depends on a variety of formal devices as well as on a capacity for ideological flexibility that simultaneously makes Vargas Llosa's narrative universe both possible and vulnerable. Communicating vessels, conceptually nested arrangements, redoublings of characters, temporal, spatial, or narrative *shifts*, alternating points of view, flashbacks, discursive simultaneity, affective intensifications, appeals to thematics in which violence, eroticism, and class and race antagonisms constitute a varied and meticulous repertoire of methods appropriated from the great masters (Faulkner, Hugo, and especially Flaubert) and refashioned according to the expressive needs imposed by the themes Vargas Llosa addresses.

Nevertheless, if the exuberant technical array on which Vargas Llosa's work is supported reveals a careful and deliberate narrative plan crossed by multiple, expertly assimilated influences, the author's reflections on the creative process and the role of literature have persistently introduced very diverse (and particularly extra-rational) elements to the understanding of the creative process. Vargas Llosa's theorizations of literary production, although rife with commonplaces and psychologisms about the nature of literature and the instances that drive symbolic labor, were unquestioningly accepted by literary criticism—when not inflated to the point of being turned into a paradigmatic critical model opposed to that advocated by the Left in the context of the transformations that socialism appeared to have started.

Although the arguments that Vargas Llosa employs in defining the role and nature of the task of literature have varied over time, the leitmotiv of this elaboration rests on the capacity of art to compensate for the mediocrity of life, to express opposition to the real world, and to elevate the perception of aspects of everyday experience that would otherwise be overlooked by the common man. Thus, for example, in his speech on receiving the Rómulo Gallegos Prize in 1967, Vargas Llosa referred, as an introduction to the topic of the role of literature, to the almost mythic avant-garde poet Carlos Oquendo de Amat (1905–1936), whom he characterized as a "sorcerer," a "visionary," and a madman who sacrificed himself at the altar of literature. In the tradition of the *poètes maudits*, which reached its highest expression in the work of Charles Baudelaire, Vargas Llosa denounced the society that kills the poet "by hunger, indifference, or ridicule," and that condemns this "beautiful but [...] also absorbing and tyrannical" vocation to marginality. Within the ideological framework of his time, Vargas Llosa's proposition should have sounded more or less anachronistic. In an era of pure ideological commitment, a view which

Vargas Llosa himself shared during his period of adherence to Marxist thought, when, as we have seen in Arguedas's case, the role of the intellectual was rapidly incorporating the perspective of materialism and converting it into a form—one form, among many—of cultural work, the romantic and idealist conception of the artist as a little god who opens up fictional realities to substitute for the insufficiencies of the mundane world could not fail to appear as a somewhat outmoded and retrograde *petitio principii* that would give rise to multiple debates regarding the political role of the intellectual in Latin America.

In 1969, for example, Vargas Llosa participated in a polemic with Julio Cortázar and Óscar Collazos based on an article the latter wrote titled "La encrucijada del lenguaje" ["The Crossroads of Language"], published in the Uruguayan weekly *Marcha* at the end of that year. This debate, published later under the title of *Literatura en la revolución y revolución en la literatura* [Literature in Revolution and Revolution in Literature] (1970), addressed aspects connected to the problem of the role of literature in terms that were quite representative of the aesthetic and ideological criteria which characterized the cultural atmosphere of the era.[10] Collazos' article, which opened the debate, begins by establishing questions linked to the utilization by Latin American writers (principally those associated with the Boom) of literary techniques from European and Anglophone literature. Collazos also refers to what he calls the "mystification of the creative deed understood as verbal autonomy, as another world in dispute with reality, in 'competition with God.'" In this regard, he refers to Vargas Llosa's opinion that "literature cannot be evaluated in comparison with reality. It should be an autonomous reality that exists for itself." All creative activity channels the obsessions and fantasies of the artist, although as Vargas Llosa recognizes, "when novels are great they are great because they encompass the demons of society at large and not just those of the novelist" (Collazos et al. 9–10).[11] Behind these claims of literature's autonomy, Collazos identifies "the symptom of a crossroads"—which is to say, a dilemma, *a double bind*—that traps the revolutionary intellectual between the desire to strengthen art as an independent instance of symbolic expression and the necessity of recognizing the demands of social reality, that is, between the temptation to mystify the poetic act and the responsibility to recognize it as part of a world in the process of transformation that requires an art which contributes to clarifying and advancing social consciousness. This "rift between political being and literary being" (15) constitutes for Collazos an *ideological* (in the sense of false consciousness) way to define the role of the intellectual in Latin America. Such a conception is determined by the neocolonial condition and the dependence on metropolitan centers (the USA, Europe) that have incorporated representational models and forms of conceptualizing artistic work that were external to the needs of societies "on the path of (no longer only economic but cultural) development" (31). According to Collazos, the Latin American writer is torn between the legacies of colonialism assimilated by criollo society and the progressive products of the former colonial powers, bearers of the promise of modernity. In an anti-imperialist and *dependentista* approach expressed in the rhetoric of the era, Collazos thus summarizes the attitude of the Latin American intellectual faced with the techniques and literary canons of the developed world: "Fleeing the ghost of provincialism, we let ourselves be carried away by the cadaver of the metropolis and, weeping, we want to attend its funeral, even with the secret mission of being the authors of its resurrection" (22).

According to Collazos, the challenge in Latin America was rather not to try to emulate the "spectacle" of foreign culture but "to overcome *our own* barbarism" (31). From this perspective, literature would have an unavoidable, primary commitment to the world from which it emerges. Any language that has no connection with the world it represents will end up exploding because the meaning of literature, including its formal devices and aesthetic games, is achieved through the relationship of knowledge that it establishes with respect to the reality to which it belongs. In this way, language should be utilized as a means and not an end, thus avoiding the dangers and distractions of aestheticist escapism and literary games. The writer establishes a commitment with a concrete reality which demands that the symbolic product that emerges from that reality contribute to the effort to develop revolutionary forms of social consciousness.

Reacting against Collazos' restrictive and, to a certain degree, normative vision, Cortázar intervened, claiming for the revolutionary writer instead an opening toward a creative freedom that would make it possible to avoid the prescriptive dangers of socialist realism and, in general, of excessively immediatist conceptions of literature that end up subjecting it to the contingencies of the historical moment without allowing for any opening to new horizons for thought and imagination. Cortázar's proposal can be summarized as the idea that, in the historical moment which produced this debate, what was needed was more revolutionaries within literature than writers within revolution (Collazos et al. 76). The role of the intellectual should be based on moral responsibility, which each cultural worker will define within the parameters of his or her field of action, without escapism but also without prescriptions that limit the essential freedom of art.

In the intervention titled "Luzbel, Europa y otras conspiraciones" ["Lucifer, Europe, and other conspiracies"] Vargas Llosa emphasizes that literature is able to relate dimensions that history cannot tell. In this argument, he follows Balzac's idea that literature is the private history of nations, their intimate, affective, and often shameful trajectories. Always defending the irrational element, Vargas Llosa suggests that an eminently "rational" literature would have to find a way to stop permeating the writer's dark elements, his desires, instincts, and obsessions, his phantoms or demons[12]:

> I think that the vocation of literature establishes in those who take it up an inevitable duality or duplicity (I use this latter term, of course, without the pejorative charge it frequently carries), because the act of creation is simultaneously maintained, to different degrees in each case, of course, by the two sides of the writer's personality: the rational and the irrational, convictions and obsessions [...] I think that these unconscious, obsessive elements, which I have called "demons" (Goethe did it first, didn't he?), are those that almost always determine the "themes" of a work, and that the rational faculty that an author can exercise over them is fleeting or non-existent insofar as in the specific domain of form—the choice of a language, the conception of a structure in which those elements are embodied—the intellectual factor is predominant. (Collazos et al. 82–83)[13]

Similar concepts were also discussed at an April 1970 roundtable organized in Paris in which the participants included Rubén Bareiro Saguier, Roberto Schwarz, Julio Le Parc, Vargas Llosa, and Julio Cortázar, leading to the brief book this latter published later that same year under the title *Viaje alrededor de una mesa* [Voyage around a table]. On this occasion, Vargas Llosa returned to insisting on the difference between the intellectual *strictu sensu*, whose production is clearly headed in a deliberate politico-ideological direction, and the literary creator, who produces texts whose content can be only partially controlled, owing to the interference of irrational elements unleashed by the writer's own demons in the process of literary creation. Cortázar and Vargas Llosa agreed on the defense of an autonomous space—or at least a relatively autonomous one—for literary creation, protesting against the claims of accessibility, pragmatism, and ideological alignment for symbolic products. The distinction that Cortázar establishes between "a revolutionary creation" and a "creation within the revolution" is oriented in the same direction as Vargas Llosa's refutation of art as an activity in the service of predetermined ideological positions.

Obviously, the debate over the nature of the literary act was only the tip of the iceberg of a vast process of the redefinition of the intellectual field in the face of socialism's proposals—which is why the debate in Paris inevitably drifted onto properly political terrain. They discussed Hugo Blanco's protests from prison in Peru directed to "the revolutionary poets and to the poetic revolutionaries," asking that they return to writing literature for hire. The paradigms of this poetic option were César Vallejo and Javier Heraud, who, giving in to the requirements of their historical moment, had written poetry of supposedly popular extraction, distanced from the exquisite elitism of bourgeois humanism.[14] Reviewing this exchange of ideas confirms once more the multiplicity of dilemmas—*double binds*—that tormented literary creativity and intellectual reflection in those years and which we have seen function from other perspectives in the case of Arguedas, whose solidarity with Blanco's positions is well-known.

Against this backdrop, in 1972, a time when Vargas Llosa and other intellectuals had already registered their dissent regarding the cultural policies of the Cuban Revolution, the polemic Vargas Llosa maintained with Ángel Rama from the publication of *García Márquez: historia de un deicidio* [García Márquez: the history of a deicide] (1971) staged, even more radically than in the debate of 1969, two opposed views of the relation between literature and society, cultural production and political commitment, providing evidence of the existence of two starkly differentiated models of critical thought.[15] Vargas Llosa studies *Cien años de soledad* (1967) [*One Hundred Years of Solitude* (1970)] as a "total novel" which combines biographical, historical, and imaginary elements. Vargas Llosa analyzes the broad web of influences that left its imprint on García Márquez's work, from the imaginary Yoknapatawpha, whose map Faulkner included in the final pages of *Absalom! Absalom!* (1936), to Ernest Hemingway, without forgetting the marked influences of authors as disparate as François Rabelais, Jorge Luis Borges, Albert Camus, *One Thousand and One Nights*, Daniel Defoe, Virginia Woolf, and chivalric romances.[16] Studying García Márquez's literature, Vargas Llosa groups together the Colombian Nobel Laureate's "demons" into three categories: the personal, the historical, and the cultural. The first are those liked to the writer's private, family life, the second are epochal and are related to the time he happened to be alive and the events that mark his experience in society. Finally, cultural demons are those that continue to guide his intellectual interests and concerns, including the pursuit of style, thematic choice, and the processes of representation. The book analyzes the process that transforms experience into discourse, which is to say, the stages that correspond to the construction of fictitious universes from the materials that provide personal experiences and forms of socialization in a determinate historical moment. Literary creation thus would consist in the transformation of elements of subjectivity into aesthetic material, that is, into its symbolic materialization through language. For Vargas Llosa, more than an intervention, literary creation is a veritable "kidnapping" of reality and an arduous task for those who are absorbed by writing and elaborating their personal obsessions. In this schema, originality consists precisely in achieving the goal, which is an objective not an originary impulse. All work negates reality when it replaces it with the fictional world, and for this reason it must be convincing, to persuade the reader to leave the ordinary world behind in order to follow the creator into the intricacies of an alternative universe.[17]

What gave rise to this polemic with Ángel Rama was Vargas Llosa's conception of "demons" as an irrational element that takes hold of the writer's alienation from the surrounding world and organizes the fabrication of fictional universes. These worlds impose on the reader an imaginary web of spaces, relations, characters, and events that emerge from the writer's exceptional genius. This creative energy makes the writer a god, master, and maker of the fictional world that competes with the one in which our perceptions and rationality are revealed.

This setting, in which critical styles and approaches confront one another over the long-debated theme of poetic inspiration, transferred deeper antagonisms to the literary plane. This included the cultural politics of socialism, the relation between the intellectual and the State, and the connections between the diverse aspects of the superstructural level: aesthetic, ethical, and ideological elements related to the content of fiction, with its capacity for interpellation and with the forms of knowledge that can be extracted from art in a world in the process of transformation. From Vargas Llosa's perspective, "real reality" can be avoided, ignored, or left behind, in any case, overcome—displaced—through the manufactured and controlled universe of fiction, fabricated according to the creator's desire. The idea of demons as a primary force of the creative process, in itself an anodyne concept, often utilized as a reference to the emotional elements and recurring themes that appear in artistic work, was rapidly transformed for many into an irksome and provocative ideologeme. The appeal to irrationalism and the suggestion of a reality that can be transformed in an ephemeral and illusory way on the plane of the imagination, thus becoming independent from social determinations, unavoidable impositions of power, and economic and political demands, could not sit well with the ideological horizon of the era, especially taking into account Vargas Llosa's disagreements with socialist thought and the watershed moment that had given rise only a year earlier to his criticisms of the Cuban regime and his subsequent rupture with Fidel Castro's administration after the Padilla affair. Within this context, the constant reference to demons sounded like alienation, the substitution of reality seemed like an escapist negation of history, and the writer becoming a "god" suggested that Vargas Llosa was possessed of an uncontrollable individualism and a bourgeois *hubris* utterly foreign to the ethic of proletarian labor and the collectivist mentality of the new man.[18]

Rama's reaction to Vargas Llosa's scatological vision of literary creation is organized by dialectical materialism but also by historicism, opposing the logic of historical developments to the Peruvian author's much more improvised and sensationalist arguments, which Rama brands as *mauditiste* and negativist. In Vargas Llosa's conception, the writer is defined as a being dominated by anomalous forces that he cannot control; literature is in turn presented as the flipside of reality, as the articulation of the deficiencies and defects of the world we know. For Rama, Vargas Llosa's psychologistic impressionism and his vision of novelistic narrative as the materialization of obsessions and dark drives that dominate rationality bring the writer and literature closer to the world of madness than to the world of art. Imbued with the socio-historical focuses of Lukács and Goldmann, the Foucauldian episteme, the heterodox thought of Walter Benjamin, and a determination to refound critical thought as the *exercise of judgment*, as an instance of rationalization and analysis capable of exploring the deeper causes of the social and of redefining the functions and specificities of symbolic labor, Rama argues for a form of critical reflection that can keep pace with the transnationalized developments of Latin American literature. At the same time, he tries to reaffirm the condition of the literary text as a product able to satisfy both the expectations and needs of diverse audiences and the cultural programs of societies in the process of transformation. For Rama, art, including literature, must transmit knowledge of the real and drive decolonizing forms of critical thought. From this perspective, Vargas Llosa's irrationalist perspectives appear to be alienating insofar as they make literature into an *ideology*, into an apparatus able to generate false consciousness at the collective level. Ángel Rama points out the "shadowy archaism" of Vargas Llosa's thesis on deicide, arguing that the exhausted formula he uses to rescue the idea of the irrationalism of art betrays an antiquated concern for the genesis of the creative process (which ultimately turns the writer into a "chosen one") precisely at the same time that Marxism was attempting to promote the artistic ideal as human labor and social practice:

> The inspired writer, the writer protected by muses, the writer of terrible and sacred intimacy, the writer possessed by demons, the writer irresponsible for whatever, the child or crazy writer, as Jaspers says, all those formulas were definitively nothing other than ideologizations meant to preserve the "status" of a professional from whom the bourgeoisie, taking cues from the European world, withdrew its trust, as Benjamin saw with typical lucidity. (Rama and Vargas Llosa, *García Márquez y la problemática de la novela* 9)

In evaluating Rama's positions on Vargas Llosa's concepts, one should not forget that it was precisely at that time that Rama was beginning his systematic study of Andean literatures, particularly an evaluation of José María Arguedas's work. This latter provoked in Rama more than anything else a great sense of astonishment that lead to the elaboration of his theory of transculturating narrative processes.[19] It is not too much to suppose that Rama comparatively evaluated the work of both Peruvian authors, notoriously leaning toward Arguedas, whose originality, passion, and ideological positions seemed much more convincing as a whole than Vargas Llosa's highly regarded work, which constituted one of the most highly developed and effective technical repertoires in contemporary Spanish-language literature.[20]

It is also interesting to note that the supposed irrationalism transmitted by Vargas Llosa's conception of demons undertook the task of reestablishing the notion of the *aura* that modernity had seen fade away from art in the face of advancing cultural technologization.[21] Vargas Llosa's positions, marked by an individualism which insists on maintaining a zone of creative autonomy in the face of authority and the expansion of political discourse, seek to preserve a humanistic stronghold in which high culture could remain established in the myths of the artist's exceptionality, aesthetic superiority and creative liberty, principles that Vargas Llosa staunchly defends throughout his work, from "La literatura es fuego" ["Literature is

Fire"] to *La civilización del espectáculo* [The Civilization of the Spectacle]. In *Cartas a un joven novelista* (1997) [*Letters to a Young Novelist* (2002)], for example, he returns to the theme of the "productive lie" and the symbolic substitution of an insufficient reality through literature:

> Fiction is a lie covering up a deep truth: it is life as it wasn't, life as the men and women of a certain age wanted to live it and didn't and thus had to invent. It isn't the face of History but rather her reverse or flip side: what didn't happen and therefore had to be fabricated in the imagination and in words to fulfill the ambitions real life was unable to satisfy, to fill the voids women and men discovered around them and tried to populate with ghosts they conjured up themselves. (Vargas Llosa, *Cartas a un joven novelista* 16/*Letters to a Young Novelist* 8)

Rama's purpose is to consolidate critical discourse as a cultural practice that could go beyond impressionism as well as plain hermeneutics and that could contribute to the perception of historico-cultural developments, perspectives, and relationships between literary events and politico-economic processes. This purpose persisted and re-emerged in a confrontation with Vargas Llosa's opinions regarding the Boom and its meaning within Latin American culture.[22]

It is only fair to note that, from the beginning, Vargas Llosa's positions within the intellectual and commercial space of Boom literature were framed by his desire for public recognition. The writer's fears of becoming subsumed by the provincial mediocrity of national culture or absorbed by dominant ideologies always kept him on the defensive and caused him to maintain an attitude of constant self-promotion, hoping to enter the global market. In the previously mentioned Caracas speech, when he was awarded the Rómulo Gallegos Prize, Vargas Llosa detected the social transformation that now clearly, in the second half of the twentieth century, drove the professionalization of the writer and the commercialized and transnationalized circulation of symbolic products. On this occasion he thus indicated:

> it is true that in recent years things have begun to change. Slowly, a more hospitable climate for literature is creeping into our countries. The number of readers is beginning to grow, the bourgeoisie is discovering that books matter, that writers are rather more than gentle fools, that they have a function to fulfill in society. But then, when justice is finally beginning to be done to the Latin American writer or rather, when the injustice that has weighed

down on him is finally beginning to lift, another threat can arise, a diabolically subtle danger. Those same societies that once exiled and rejected the writer can now think that it is useful to assimilate him, integrate him, confer on him a kind of official status. ("La literatura es fuego" 1/"Literature is Fire," in *Making Waves* 71–72)

It is not necessary to highlight the fact that what Vargas Llosa interprets here as an effect of societal change regarding the recognition of Latin American literature's high value (a transformation that the writer considered an example of spontaneous social justice) is actually a response to a series of concrete factors that he never recognizes for some reason. Nor is it necessary to point out, a propos the final lines of the above quote, that Vargas Llosa had no reason to be in a passive position when it came to being coopted by officialdom. On the contrary, this indicates that his integration into the literary canon was the result of Vargas Llosa's complicity and even complacency with regard to a process that links him to centers of power. One could claim that Vargas Llosa himself willingly fell into the snares of the global market, no longer—or not only—on the strength of his ability as a *writer* [*escritor*] but in his capacity as *transcriber* [*escribidor*], in his role as a mass media intellectual, as firmly established on the platform of neoliberalism as he once was on the socialist platform. This would have nothing to do with passively assimilating the impositions of cultural globalization but rather with adopting a new conscious and militant stance in the face of a new form of officialdom which imposes strict professionalization on the creative world and makes the writer dependent on the vast commercial circuits of literary commodities, particularly considering the increasing privatization of the globalized culture industry. Nevertheless, in those years, Vargas Llosa's attitude was one of affected innocence meant, perhaps, to indicate modesty in the face of the upheavals of a tumultuous Latin America reality, taking refuge in literary production as if it were a more aseptic space, closed off from the tensions and demands of the moment. On the occasion of the *Coloquio del Libro* that took place in Caracas in 1972, he would reaffirm his basic "incomprehension" of the cultural context of the era, referring to the phenomenon of the literary Boom in the following terms:

> What is called the Boom (and no one knows exactly what it is—I don't particularly know what it is) is a grouping of writers (no one knows exactly who, although everyone has his or her own list) who at one time more or less simultaneously acquired a certain level of diffusion, a certain level of

recognition from the public and from critics. This can be called, perhaps, *a historical accident*. (Vargas Llosa, quoted in Rama, "El *boom* en perspectiva" 59, my emphasis)

Trying to get to the heart of Vargas Llosa's supposed candor, the candor of someone who was now being called one of the most outstanding representatives of the literary Boom, Ángel Rama, commenting on Vargas Llosa's opinions, not unimpatiently reviewed the cultural delimitations of the era in the following way:

> As such an accident of history it corresponds to transformative forces that continue to generate new situations: the aforementioned advance of communications media that not only were typified in the form of "magazines," but notably, one should also see the development of television, the visual media of advertising, and the new cinema in relation to those transformative forces generating its new audiences. Among them I should mention the impact of population growth, urban development, the notorious progress of primary and secondary education (thanks to the evolution of post-secondary education), and especially the post-war industrialization that in the Americas sealed off advanced positions that demanded ever more talented organization than before, all changes whose limitations and fragility are more than well-known. (Rama, ibid. 60)

Rama brings up social factors which, linked to economic changes, frame and found the emergence of the Boom, which constitutes, from his sociological perspective, one of the main transformative forces that impacted Latin American society in the 1960s.

Vargas Llosa's perspective avoids this sort of rationalization. Instead, he is interested in promoting a situation that would favor literature's importance as testimony of a reality that demonstrates on a daily basis (as is the case in Latin America, for "a true surfeit of reasons") that it is "imperfectly made" (Vargas Llosa, "La literatura es fuego" 2/"Literature is Fire" 73). Latin American reality, Vargas Llosa notes, is plagued by nightmares such as ignorance, injustice, exploitation, and inequality. In these objective conditions, fictional universes act, as we have seen, as mechanisms of symbolic denunciation and substitution. Fortunately, as Vargas Llosa indicated early in his career, the time of social justice was approaching since

> within ten, twenty, or fifty years the hour of social justice will arrive in our countries, as it has in Cuba, and the whole of Latin America will have freed

itself from the order that despoils it, from the castes that exploit it, from the forces that now insult and repress it. And I want this hour to arrive as soon as possible and for Latin America to enter, once and for all, a world of *dignity* and *modernity*, and for socialism to free us from our *anachronism* and our *horror*. (ibid., my emphasis)

The italicized terms in the quote point to a restless Manicheanism which we will see emerge and re-emerge in various ways throughout the length of Vargas Llosa's work. For him, the dignity—the panacea—of modernity is opposed to the horror of anachronism, as identity is to otherness. In Peru, he points out, "what is exceptional is to be loyal to [the vocation of writing] against all odds…to keep swimming against the current." What, Vargas Llosa asks, "does it mean to be a writer in Peru?" ("Sebastián Salazar Bondy" 93/62). It means being considered, as indicated previously in the present study, "a picturesque and eccentric individual, a sort of harmless madman who is allowed his freedom because, after all, madness is not contagious" (ibid., 93/61).

Seen as a temporality in which processes "happen" and in which social change is conceived of as "historical accident" or as divine intervention, history and its contradictions at all levels of peripheral Latin American societies will be interpreted as fate, as circumstantial, or as a manifestation of the inability of subjects to overcome their conditions of existence and incorporate themselves into diverse forms of social progress that liberalism could democratically put within everyone's reach.[23] From this perspective, it becomes unnecessary for Vargas Llosa to rationalize processes of change since they can be grasped solely through their effects and repercussions or through the aesthetic and ideological production derived from them. Not a single ethical demand torments his world, for which he nevertheless establishes a moral theme within the conventional parameters of an imaginarily liberal thought (to once again take up Lauer's estimation of Vargas Llosa as the "imaginary liberal") crossed by universal values of Occidentalism that make it possible to avoid the contingencies imposed by an uneven, exclusive, and unfinished modernity.

In this economy, intellectuals are by vocation "the professionals of dissatisfaction, the conscious or unconscious subversives of society, the rebels with a cause, the irredeemable insurgents of the world, the insufferable devil's advocates" (Vargas Llosa, "La literatura es fuego" 2/"Literature is Fire" 73). Subject to an irrationalist conception like the one outlined here, the function of the intellectual intrigued Vargas Llosa, who has appeared to be constantly reposing the question (for others but especially for himself) in multiple ways. What is the writer? Demiurge or victim of its own drives? What is the role of fiction? Does it always lie, instilling in the reader an unreality that definitively substitutes for one's surrounding circumstances? Where is the border between fiction and simulacrum? What separates and unites falsity and fantasy? And if we can, in fact, identify this limit, what dangers or benefits will emerge from transgressing it?

Vargas Llosa was situated at the crossroads—in the *double bind*—of his era, in which the demands of Latin American political and social transformation also implied entering the region of international markets and the recomposition of national cultures as primary (although not determinate) spaces of identity and praxis—subordinated, in other words, to the need to redefine symbolic representation in terms of the closely related notion of political/social/cultural representativity. At this crossroads, Vargas Llosa produced his literature as a negotiation between two opposing dimensions. On one side, the demands of representing local material provided by the multifaceted and contradictory culture of the Andes; on the other side, the globalized dimension that required the production of literature as a commodity designed for transnationalized consumption. His task was framed (although in a manner substantially different from the form this question assumed in Arguedas's work) by the problem of translation, or to put it in Rama's terms, of an inverse transculturation designed to insert regional content in the universalizing register of the technological reproducibility of literature, thus facilitating Latin American literature's access to the World Republic of Letters without having to cut ties with everything, especially not a simultaneously fertile and problematic national culture. Vargas Llosa found the secret to victory in the diversification and technological reproduction of the poetic product. The theory of creative demons allowed him to defend an intangible zone of the poetic process as the domain of individuality, a space of action that while it preserved the aura of the symbolic product also linked this peripheral creation to prestigious and renowned traditions of the Western world: Goethe, Baudelaire, Ducasse, Bataille.

Vargas Llosa's work abounds in representations of sub-spaces in which he reproduces, as in a microcosm, the interactions between subjects and segments of society that, although they are typologically recognizable in the real world, have been made artificial by the literary act that supports the creation and manipulation of the distance between reality and fictional worlds. The prison, the bordello, the convent, the school, the tavern all constitute institutionalized spaces that function according to highly differentiated regulations and hierarchical codes. These environments allow for the interaction of characters, cosmovisions, and discourses whose intersections and collisions organize the process of the production of meanings. They are interstitial, transitional, relational spaces: *non-places* that produce a *solitary contractuality* (Augé, *Los no lugares* 98), confluences ruled by their own regulations, which generate their own languages and position themselves according to their own particular teleology. They produce exchanges, symbolic transactions, transitory and ephemeral forms of recognition behind which, independently of individual and collective subjectivity, they continue to develop a reality that is in itself unattainable. The individual who interacts with others in these transitional spaces is always solitary; the individual's social existence is constructed in a situational, contingent way, subject to conditions and choices that continue to unfold and involve it in diverse social and political levels.

Always exposed to the mechanisms of authority and its disciplinary strategies, Vargas Llosa's narrative subject is almost always the victim of the *physical* or *symbolic violence* that Pierre Bourdieu discusses and which reinforces or acts as a counterweight to dominant power. Exercised like a physical restraint on the individual or collective body, or like the application of immobile hierarches that model the organization of society, Vargas Llosa's narrative elaborates on the degraded adventures of the world, exposing its contradictions as if it were a spectacle parodying a social epic whose greatness and transcendence have always been sacrificed, leaving intact only the domain of the contingent and circumstantial. Throughout the closed, microcosmic spaces in which fictional action unfolds, a symbolic capital circulates, linked to various alienated forms of identity that have been devalued by social friction. Social and ideological contradictions are taken in as data about the real world without giving rise to deeper investigation. Instead, only their effects are registered and understood as definite, concrete epiphenomena of forces that do not flourish at the surface level of consciousness. Seemingly as if they were dealing with an irrational (and because of that inexplicable) energy, the principal characters of Vargas Llosa's novels possess an element that distinguishes and defines them and that makes them the key to the processes of symbolic exchange through which their stories are articulated. This shows how exceptionality circulates through *the social*, leaving its imprint on the ordinary world. As Bourdieu reminds us:

Symbolic capital is an ordinary property (physical strength, wealth, warlike valor, etc.) which, perceived by social agents endowed with the categories of perception and appreciation permitting them to perceive, know and recognize it, becomes symbolically efficient, like a veritable magical power: a property which, because it responds to socially constituted "collective expectations" and beliefs, exercises a sort of action from a distance, without physical contact. (*Practical Reason: On the Theory of Action* 102)

This is obviously the case with Saúl Zuratas, the storyteller. It also represents the character of Bonifacia in *The Green House*, who is transferred from a convent to a brothel and prostituted in both places—which thus acquire a symbolic equivalence and an exchange value in the utilitarian economy dramatized by the text. It is also the case with Cuéllar, the castrated boy in *Los cachorros* (1967) ["The Cubs" (1979)], as well as the figure of Mayta, who circulates like a symbol of rebellion and evil in different contexts throughout his eponymous novel.[24]

In Vargas Llosa, reality can only be addressed and understood at the cost of a flagrant reduction of its complexity, translated into a parodic realism that represents the drama of history, the interminable struggle between good and evil, the inevitable degradation of the social, the inherent corruption of power, the deep cracks within human nature, as if they were unavoidable stops on the linear and progressive tour of history. If one can in fact speak of a more or less explicit "poetics of social change" in Vargas Llosa's work it would be as a collection of clichés which extol the spontaneous and enlightened condition of the artist as an irrational and privileged form of penetration into the arcane plans of history, as an emotional and visionary impulse to substitute a universe of fiction for the insufficient and defective reality in which we happen to live. This corresponds to the limited consciousness of many of his characters, whose incomprehension of the circumstances that surround them yields more narrative dividends than any illumination of their interior world or the representation of a project that transcends the immediate. The complexity of Vargas Llosa's fictional world must not be confused with a deeper complexity that corresponds to the real world. His disjointed plots, technical devices, and complicated narrative settings do not necessarily imply a profound grasp of social conflict. However, they certainly demonstrate the ability to construct an imaginary tapestry laid against the measureless background of the drama of history which continues to develop beyond the false consciousness of literature.

Evil pervades Vargas Llosa's work because its existence and resources confirm his conception of the universe as a space of forces that have been unleashed and drained of all transcendence, where what is truly aesthetic is the inequality of content and what is really seductive is the way in which negativity is confronted. To the extent that his work does not channel an alternative project or transmit certainties about the direction of historico-social processes that end up exhausted in their own tormented contingency (also, to the extent that his aesthetic and philosophical supports come from the most obvious canonical repertoire of European and Anglo-Saxon modernity, which always have in Latin America a spurious and fragmentary legitimacy), his literature's foundation lies rather in anecdote supported by texts and multiple strategies for manipulating time and space, in communicative modalities, and in thematic selection. From this basis, Vargas Llosa's literature conveys the impression of a complete and self-sufficient fictional universe along with an evacuation of sense, as if the reader were abandoned on the edge of an abyss, left only to contemplate the desolation of the surrounding landscape.

As Cornejo Polar has already pointed out ("Hipótesis"), Neil Larsen argues that it is Vargas Llosa's technique which acts as a substitute for the lack of coherence of the narrative fragments that make up his novels, or the equal incoherence of his multiple levels of representation and fictional *narrative action*. What is missing here, according to Larsen, is a minimal investigation into political reason in its function of making sense of the social totality beyond its innumerable particularities. In Vargas Llosa's narrative texts as well as in his essays and autobiographical writing, reality remains, Larsen notes, "un-described." Vargas Llosa's prose is thus a narrative saturated with anecdotes which are almost never deduced from the profound historical, ethical, or political sense of the social.

Julio Ortega, in turn, has detected a "perverse derivation" in Vargas Llosa's work which is supported by the discovery and revelation of the evil that resides in the very heart of the social. His technical and stylistic ability sustain this act of *concealing while seducing*, which allows the narrative to deploy its effects without penetrating into the nature of the individual or collective, the subjective or structural conflict of the world being portrayed and the values that sustain it (Ortega, "Vargas Llosa: el habla del mal" 169–77). As Ortega points out, Vargas Llosa avoids both allegory and didacticism; in his work, humanity "denigrates itself": "existence is intolerable, and literature feeds precisely on the decomposition of the social, favoring the unfolding of corruption and squalor, which is to say, the demonstration of evil in all its variables and degrees."[25] Vargas Llosa himself thus indicated in 1965: "The novelist is a little like a vulture: he feeds on decaying organisms. When societies are on the verge of crumbling they encounter their best contributions to the genre of the novel" (*Primer encuentro de narradores peruanos* 163).[26]

The narrator's function is *to expose*: to open the gates of meaning that underlie the representation of the real:

> I believe that this is the novelist's function: to demonstrate in an objective and impartial manner the world in which he lives; I believe that this is the greatest service the novelist can do for his contemporaries; and if his vision of the world and his transposition of it to his vision is authentic and profound, through this vision and this fiction other men will continue to discover their own faces, their own vices and defects, as well as the beauties and truths of this reality according to which they might transform it, will change it, will take control of it. (*Primer encuentro de narradores peruanos* 162)

Note that in this conception (written in the same year as "La literatura es fuego") the creative process is referred to as *transposition*, as an instance that communicates a knowledge that the individual will in no other way be able to perceive, making the word an inaugural and catalyzing form of social action. The artist thus relocates—resituates—the materials he or she encounters in reality itself; the artist's function is to carry out an exposé, that is, to serve as mediator between the world in which we live but can never ourselves grasp without the help of art and the level of consciousness it helps to develop. In addition, it assumes the impartiality and objectivity of the artist within the process of literary representation. What happens, then, with the irrational forces that supposedly guide him? With the demonic passions that traverse and mold subjectivity?

One does not detect in Vargas Llosa the same urgent need Arguedas's work demonstrated for finding modes of representing social agency or to discover in literature adequate spaces for developing utopian thought. Nor does one find the same perception of history as something more than the accumulation of fragments of temporality in which forces, beings, and discourses converge as if they were spontaneous, immanent developments in a desacralized and post-auratic world. As Vargas Llosa indicates in his study of *Tirant lo Blanc*, what he especially admires in the novel is its ambition, "that will to *deicide*, to recreate everything, to account for everything—from the most infinitesimal to the largest—available to human vision, imagination, and desire" (96, emphasis in original).

The theme of resistance does not form part of Vargas Llosa's repertoire outside the scope of the isolated individual in which it is possible to explore the forms of power conflicts produced at the subjective level. His intense, disjointed settings, both natural and institutional, as well as his ably dramatized plots, without a doubt have primacy over the psychological density of his characters and the exploration of historical and social coincidence, both of which tend to recede into the background of the story. This totalizing effort has to do with the arborescence of the text, which expands, encompassing multiple and disparate territories, proliferating in detail and wallowing in the overabundance of levels, perspectives, and temporalities. The hero's adventure is all-encompassing, at least at the anecdotal and thematic levels.

According to what some of his critics have observed, Vargas Llosa's polemic *ars poetica*, developed at various points over the last several decades, converges in more than one sense with the literature he writes, creating a significant articulation between theory and creative praxis. Some have seen a correlation between Vargas Llosa's distinct moments of theorizing about literary creation and his ideological positions. The irrational impulse that Vargas Llosa postulated as the generative matrix of literary creation, the refuge of alternative realities presented as a *deicide* in which the writer becomes Creator with absolute control and autonomy over the fictional world, later gives way to the idea of the allegorical struggle between angels and demons that pushes the individual to withdraw toward literary fantasy or eroticism in search of escape and symbolic and sensual compensation. Critics have interpreted these torsions within Vargas Llosa's poetics in relation to the writer's ideological variations. The moment of deicide thus connects to Vargas Llosa's period of adherence to socialist ideas (in which, nevertheless, the idealist conception of art never met its match) to the publication of *La ciudad y los perros*, *La casa verde*, and *Conversación in La Catedral*. These novels, which are among his most critically acclaimed, reveal a preoccupation with the social question that becomes diluted in the second stage of his narrative development (which we have been outlining here). Nonetheless, even in these novels, which are clearly framed by social concerns, anecdote dominates the narration, not only in the careful weaving together of discourses, themes, and narrative strategies but also in the characters' intricate vicissitudes. The reader sees him or herself as involved in a symbolic journey that passes over diverse social strata without asking too many in-depth questions of them.

For Gerald Martin, *La casa verde*, written at the apogee of the Cuban Revolution, represents the highest point of Vargas Llosa's political radicalism, for its critique of patriarchy, capitalism, and imperialism, which were inescapable themes of the era (30). According to Martin, the novel "mythologizes, simultaneously, the nation, the continent and, more secretly, the author's own autobiographical experience" (ibid.). The act of creating the text denotes vitalism and sensuality in the way that it covers natural spaces, integrates characters with diverse traits and backgrounds, and makes the plot evolve between the settings of the jungle, the Santa María de Nieva mission, and the city of Piura.[27]

Carlos Fuentes defined this novel as "the story of a pilgrimage from a convent to a brothel," replete with escapades and adventures that never fail to invoke the author's passion for chivalric romances (44). But Vargas Llosa's world is not based, as those narratives were, on an epic inspiration or on an adherence to fixed values capable of sustaining the world being portrayed. Nor does it succumb to the easy pleasure of the journey as the possible framework for a modern picaresque, although the preeminence of visual and auditory elements convert these adventures into a kind of exoticist film that eludes interiority every step of the way (Martin, 32). The journey undertaken in *La casa verde* is instead presented as a movement toward the degradation affecting all levels of the world represented in the novel. Through an intense process in which spaces, bodies, and languages inevitably continue to contaminate one another, the narrative draws the reader in with the spectacle of the growing decadence of the characters and the social space they inhabit. The perception of evil *à la* Bataille (which Ortega observed as one of the characteristics of Vargas Llosa's work) manifests itself here in all its overwhelming negativity.[28] Violence is not glorified, nor are the characters presented as flat, formulaic projections of social roles, as in the chivalric model. In Vargas Llosa, the characters and the situations in which they find themselves maintain instead a density and opacity that (although they do not lead to a profound exploration of the interiority of the characters, emphasizing instead the intricacies of the plot) are able to communicate the *pathos* of a reality that hopelessly self-destructs as a result of its own dynamic.

A good illustration is *La Historia de Mayta* (1984) [*The Real Life of Alejandro Mayta* (1986)], a novel in which intertwined sequences unfold on two levels. One level constructs a narrative present (1983) in which a writer investigates the story of Alejandro Mayta, a Trotskyist imprisoned in Lima, through interviews, testimonies, and so on. The other level explores Mayta's past, which corresponds to the end of the 1950s, when the ill-fated socialist revolution the protagonist led in Juaja was developing. Following a Chinese-box procedure in which one narrative contains and frames the unfolding of the next, the notions of evil, corruption, and ideological failure are articulated in order to transmit a disenchanted version of revolutionary thought and action. This without a doubt constitutes an autobiographical reference to Vargas Llosa himself and fits with his ever-present desire to represent the creative process in its distinct stages of processing, expansion, and re-elaboration of the real. His appeal to journalistic discourse, investigating and registering sources, together with his more poetic use of literary language, his alternation of testimonial and fictional sequences, as well as his manipulation of the borders between the political and the poetic, truth and invention, all highlight the simulacral aspect that unfolds throughout the text. The farcical character of literary constructs in the novel are, in fact, notorious. By breaking reality into multiple fragments, the ultimate meaning of the story is dispersed, and its (pseudo-) historical dimension and all its pretensions to reality are squandered. All that remains standing is the far from minor theme of the impossibility of representing the world and its conflicts. In this sense, the novel makes what was originally tragedy return as farce. Experience is confused with history, and all the reader possesses are impossibly verifiable visions/versions.[29]

In its own register, the dialogism of *Conversación in La Catedral* conducts (as does *La ciudad y los perros*) an exploration of the intricacies of power and the contradictions and perversions that flourish within the project of modernity in different spaces and frequencies. William Rowe has noted that this entire period of Vargas Llosa's narrative sets out to analyze "the failure of liberal individualism in Peru," a project he abandoned when the military government of Velasco Alvarado began to implement its social reforms:

> This historical failure of the middle classes, who showed themselves to be incapable of achieving social modernization, is, in Vargas Llosa's stories and novels, the abandonment of criticism of the bourgeoisie, and a growing impatience with the lack of liberal institutions and behaviors, which was first blamed on the military and then increasingly on the supposed fanaticism and immorality of the Left. (*Hacia una poética radical* 66–67)

The 1970s correspond, in fact, to the second moment of the development of Vargas Llosa's narrative, which Efraín Kristal characterizes as the period of struggle between good and evil, when the writer distanced himself from the Left and increased his political skepticism after the prolonged and symptomatic debate unleashed by the Padilla affair. Texts such as *Pantaleón y las visitadoras* and *La tía Julia y el escribidor* frame this transitional period in which Vargas Llosa also published *La orgía perpetua: Flaubert y Madame Bovary* (1975) [*The Perpetual Orgy: Flaubert and Madame Bovary* (1986)], one of the key texts in which Vargas Llosa elaborates his conception of art and literary creation. Following his analysis of Vargas Llosa's aesthetico-ideological positions, Rowe notes: "The novels of the 1970s are oriented toward the comedy of manners, in which the failure of liberalism is compensated by a consensual and superior irony that emerges out of middle-class values, from which individualism (in a now even more modernized society) can more confidently function as an ideology" (*Hacia una poética radical* 67). The third moment, which, according to Kristal, is characterized by the representation of evil in all its forms (corruption, violence, crime, obsession, fanaticism, degradation, self-destruction, etc.) and by the expression of historical and social pessimism, would coincide with Vargas Llosa's period of neoliberal militancy. Moreover, it is this decade that produced the most radical confrontations between the Shining Path and the national armed forces, as well as the murders of Uchuraccay. The change in direction Vargas Llosa's literature underwent in the 1980s is expressed above all in works like *La guerra del fin del mundo* (1981), *La Historia de Mayta* (1984), *¿Quién mató a Palomino Molero?* (1986) [*Who Killed Palomino Molero?* (1987)], *El hablador* (1987), and *Elogio de la madrastra* (1988) [*In Praise of the Stepmother* (1990)], although this grouping obviously includes texts with a very diverse range of themes and literary achievements.

Published at the beginning of this period, in 1981, *La guerra del fin del mundo* undoubtedly constitutes one of Vargas Llosa's most ambitious (and most heavily criticized) literary projects. Conceived as an allegorical formulation of the conflicts opened up by the initial moments of modernization and development in Latin America, the novel focuses on the paradoxes and risks of utopian thought in peripheral regions in a context that sheds light on the radicalization of class antagonisms, belief, and race within postcolonial society. The narrative is presented as a totalizing, apocalyptic, and in large measure Manichean reinterpretation of a historical uprising that took place in Brazil at the end of the nineteenth century. *La guerra del fin del mundo* deals with the uprising and destruction of the holy city of Canudos and is a rewriting of Euclides da Cunha's impressive

Os Sertões (1902) [*Rebellion in the Backlands* (1944)], which detailed the same events. The narrative portrays a popular rebellion against the modernizing measures taken by the new Brazilian Republic, which implemented the separation of Church and State as well as other efforts to establish civil government and which part of the population saw as evil. Desperate and hungry in the face of looming chaos, the inhabitants of the region were ultimately devastated by military forces. This genocide occurred against an ideological backdrop that was shaped by new scientific theories, anti-clericalism, literary naturalism, and the struggles surrounding the foundation of the republic in 1889, one year after slavery was belatedly abolished.

In its ambition as a totalizing novel, *La guerra del fin del mundo* unfolds against the backdrop of the anonymous indigenous masses in Canudos, a complex socio-political frieze made up of individual and collective characters, republicans, monarchs, and soldiers. It portrays, above all, the story of a sublime and uneven struggle waged by the inhabitants of a remote and isolated territory in northeastern Brazil, a region which is today covered by water as a result of the damming of the Vaza-Barris river, which overflowed and flooded the villages. The massacre, which brought the Canudos uprising to an end, wiped out around 30,000 people, primarily former slaves, indigenous, and mestizos, in a conflict that is regarded as one of the most barbaric human slaughters to have ever taken place in the Western world. Of primary importance is the figure of Antônio Conselheiro, founder of the holy city, a charismatic man, "fierce and extravagant," as Da Cunha describes him, who embodied mystical force but also esotericism, primitivism, and magic. What also stands out in the novel is the Scottish anarchist character Galileo Gall, who represents European ideology and is linked to the social and political advances of modernity.

Vargas Llosa's novelized version (which necessarily confronts both the historical record of the War of Canudos and Da Cunha's monumental work) reinserts the events into his own aesthetic and ideological register, imparting to them a fragmentarism and irrationality visible in Vargas Llosa's other texts. In this register, organicity and deep exploration of the more complex strata of the events of the narrative are sacrificed in favor of a technical flair that, among other things, assists in visualizing what is being narrated. Antonio Cornejo Polar consistently points out in his analysis of this novel that the opposition of the worlds confronting one another in Canudos to the point of collective extermination is not, in Vargas Llosa's version, derived from any idea of totality but is rather, at best, an antithetical, mechanically represented dynamic. If in Da Cunha's account the War of Canudos refers to a unique but divided and suffering universe, in Vargas Llosa's novel the conflict is posited as the record of a disconcerting and practically inexplicable opposition. This interpretation of the novel is influenced by Vargas Llosa's use of a compositional form he had already used in other narratives: alternating "hinge" chapters which portray the confrontation between both universes as connected to the cosmovision of the characters leading the opposing groups. Also, the story is written from a fragmented enunciative position which impedes the articulation of a point of view capable of guiding the comprehension of a world represented on its multiple levels of meaning. As Cornejo Polar indicates, "the narrator is instrumentalized like a kind of transcriber of what [the characters] perceive, feel, or think without making it possible to detect any inflections that would betray his individuality: he is an objective and distant narrator" (*La novela peruana* 236).

This configuration of narrative perspective and alternating chapters reduces the characters, cultures, and situations to the traits assigned to them. This contributes to the narrative's inorganic quality, which transmits to the reader a sense of disconnection and an impression of irrational, absurd relationships between the different levels of the text.[30] According to Cornejo Polar, in Vargas Llosa's work, "the senselessness that permeates the entire history of Canudos seems to be absolute" (*La novela peruana* 237). This senselessness, derived from Vargas Llosa's narrative composition, disarticulates the history of the destruction of Canudos, a fortress of anti-modernity, in which the collapse of the modernizing project of rationalization (in the name of which the genocide is eventually carried out) was clearly announced (Larsen 166).

With regard to this novel, Rowe echoes the idea put forth by other critics that a "narrative paralysis [...] prevents the two sides from interrelating historically, given that the allegory of fanaticism immobilizes them" ("Vargas Llosa y el lugar de enunciación" 73–74). Here we see Vargas Llosa fascinated, in typical fashion, by the farcical moment in which the story ceases to be a tragedy and is transformed into a *performance* parodying its initial *ethos*, stereotyping its own contours. This produces an emptying-out derived from the perspective of the narrator of *La guerra del fin del mundo* who renounces all personal influence and presents himself as definitively external to the reality represented in the text. By means of an artificial and *ideological* narrative, Vargas Llosa's version of the Canudos tragedy conceals more than it reveals. In the end, the novel is a devastated battlefield in which the only one left standing is the writer, alone in his freedom, foreigner in the universe he created out of his own fantasies.

But if *La guerra del fin del mundo* constitutes for many a paradigmatic example which exposes the most salient features of Vargas Llosa's narrative, perhaps it is *El hablador* which best illustrates the idea of the simulacrum: the identities that the individual forges for him or herself as strategies of (self-)recognition and connection to the real and as a way of redefining this category until it dissolves in the intricacies of individual and collective subjectivity. Jean Franco has called attention to the duality of the search for the Other that organizes the story. The *double bind* that unfolds in the text is established around the hybrid figure of Saúl Zuratas and is supported by the interspersion of the storyteller's dialog with autobiographical fragments, a form of pastiche through which the plot is assembled. No less important, as Franco notes, is the mediating element of Catholic and Protestant missionaries which connects to a fundamental theme in the novel: that of the recycling of events that the narrative material undergoes in the process of its construction. The story covers diverse registers and discursive strategies, from orality and memory, where the proximity between the storyteller and his audience is essential, to the distancing of the storyteller from his audience, without forgetting the intervention of modern mass media technologies in the realm of cultural reproduction.[31] The television program to which Vargas Llosa refers in the novel, significantly titled "The Tower of Babel," is also suggested as one of the keys to the text. Thus, the novel addresses the question of multiculturality and multilingualism from different perspectives and leads toward a reflection on the mediation of writing and, more specifically, of fiction as an example of the encounter and conflicting articulation of communicative cultures and technologies. Of course, the core of the novel, however, is otherness in its multiple forms, from the stage of the elaboration of the I and the recognition of individual identity to the integration of *difference* as a constitutive quality of the social and as a line of flight from the uneven and exclusive modernity of Latin America.

At this point it is necessary to dedicate a couple more words to the theme of pastiche, which is one of the devices Vargas Llosa uses to link together modern and premodern elements as a representation of cultural conflict in *El hablador*. According to Jean Franco, in this novel pastiche has the function of channeling, more than the contrast between primitivism and modernity per se, the conflict between modern writing in search of raw material and the storyteller's mythico-legendary tale, linked to orality and tradition (*Critical Passions* 396–400). As Franco, citing Jameson, reminds us, the use of pastiche reveals the exhaustion of high culture, at least in some of its expressive aspects, and occurs when artists facing a crisis of representation return to older, stereotypical forms of literary expression (ibid. 393). From a Bakhtinian perspective, this device is considered a form of "double voicing," a stylization that expresses two different discourses of semantic intentionality without necessarily appealing to the distance that characterizes parody (in which two voices oppose each other and pursue different objectives). Franco points out that in peripheral cultures, this *double voice* (double discourse, double language, double culture) is linked to *mimicry*, in accordance with Bhabha's analysis of postcolonial contexts. Mimicry produces a displacement of hierarchies, a parodic appropriation or cannibalization of *other* positions it incorporates into its own discourse. In *El hablador*, the present of criollo culture and the individuality of the writer appear as juxtaposed to the community relation that surrounds the practice of mythico-legendary discourse, which, making use of orality, transmits ancestral content. As Franco points out, pastiche primarily channels curiosity and nostalgia without at all modifying the author's or the reader's experience. What intrigues the narrator of Vargas Llosa's novel is not the real history of indigenous populations, or their destiny within the modern nation-state, but rather Zuratas's regression toward primitivism and the possibility of documenting the storyteller's practice in the very process of its disappearance. Finally, in a vein similar to what Rowe has elaborated, Franco argues that Vargas Llosa's culturalist preoccupation with representing indigenous populations never surpasses his concern for his aesthetically oriented literary project:

> Although it is possible to read Vargas Llosa's pastiche as a response to the movement known as "indigenismo" and the representation of the Indian by urban and nonindigenous writers, the novel does not register the contemporary indigenous movements in any way. There is no reference to contemporary battles and antagonisms, the political protests, or the international network of indigenous organizations which have sprung up over the last few years. (*Critical Passions* 399)

Pastiche serves the function of inserting Machiguenga culture into the bourgeois genre of the novel in a decontextualized way, as if an image were taken from an archive in order to include it in a more prestigious one. In an implicit way, this procedure rests, albeit precariously, on an unstable equilibrium of intercultural struggle, incorporating a nostalgic and condescending tone toward the irreversible erasure of indigenous culture as it continues to disappear from Western cartography.

Vargas Llosa presents a form distinct from narrative and cultural collage in *Lituma en los Andes*, in which the classical myth of Ariadne and Dionysius is articulated as the Andean myth of *pishtacos*, which serves as a metaphor for the irrational forces Vargas Llosa associates with the activity of the Shining Path in the 1980s.[32] In this novel the gruesomeness of violence, concentrated in the fictional city of Naccos, takes demonic flight. The story explores the aesthetics of excess and fragmentation, introducing the reader to a cosmovision in which reality appears to be disarticulated into different registers—political, military, mythic, juridical, detective, sentimental—and interwoven throughout by an intertextuality with the fictional universes developed in other works by the same author (*La casa verde*, *¿Quién mató a Palomino Molero?*, *La Chunga*), thus increasing the sensation that the world the novel represents is overflowing. An anthropological perspective, which recovers the figure of the *pishtacos* as mysterious and cruel beings who steal fat from the bodies of Indians and practice cannibalism, combines with allusions to characters from classical mythology, references to pagan rites like the bacchanal and human sacrifice, and an appeal to historical memory related to recent events, such as those that took place at Uchuraccay. The novel thus gives way to an ensemble which, although it presents some accomplished narrative moments (the story of Pedro Tinoco, e.g.), creates a saturated aesthetic that dissolves the fictional world into an exhausting multiplicity of effects, references, and connotations.

Finally, completing a cycle that goes "from utopia to reconciliation," according to Kristal, the most recent stage of Vargas Llosa's narrative output would be the result of a more tolerant attitude toward the contradictions and insufficiencies of the real, exemplified in books such as *La fiesta del chivo* (2000) [*The Feast of the Goat* (2001)], *El paraíso en la otra esquina* (2003) [*The Way to Paradise* (2003)], *Travesuras de la niña mala* (2006) [*The Bad Girl* (2007)], and *El sueño del celta* (2010) [*The Dream of the Celt* (2012)].[33] According to Kristal, ever since his failure to be elected president in 1990, Vargas Llosa's perspective has become less optimistic and increased its moralizing tone. These novels issue from a dark and disillusioned point of view on human nature, an attitude that Kristal finds to be exemplified very well in the words of the character of Dr. Herbert Spencer Dickey, directed to Roger Casement in *El sueño del celta*:

We carry wickedness in our souls, my friend [...] We won't be rid of it so easily. In the countries of Europe, and in mine, it is more disguised and reveals itself only when there's a war, a revolution, a riot. It needs pretexts to become public and collective. In Amazonia, on the other hand, it can reveal itself openly and perpetrate the worst monstrosities without the justifications of patriotism or religion. Only pure, hard greed. The evil that poisons us is everywhere human beings are, its roots buried deep in our hearts. (Vargas Llosa, *El sueño del celta* 293/*The Dream of the Celt* 233–34)

Many of the themes explored in this period have appeared in Vargas Llosa's work since the very beginning of his career: sexuality (incest, homosexuality, bisexuality, all related to violence, prostitution, etc.), political utopianism, the search for artistic perfection, the relation between imagination and eroticism, and ideological fanaticism. *El sueño del celta* articulates all of these in a forced synthesis.

El sueño del celta is the fictionalized reconstruction of the multifaceted life of the Irish diplomat and activist Roger Casement (1864–1916). This character with an intriguing and seductive historical, political, and social profile, worked for many years in support of human rights in Congo and Peru (Putumayo), missions for which he received, among other recognitions, a knighthood in the Order of the British Empire. In spite of these honors and the weight of his denunciations of the human rights situation in Africa and in the Amazon region controlled by rubber extraction companies, Casement was accused of treason for his nationalist mobilizations in support of Irish autonomy and subsequently executed by the English government.[34] According to some versions, his connections to the Easter Rising (considered a crucial point in the process of Irish independence) were wrongly interpreted by British authorities, leading to his immediate conviction. Also, according to certain sources, some of his personal documents were falsified in order to bring about his downfall.

As has been pointed out elsewhere, *El sueño del celta*'s anecdotal frame and the configuration of its characters are points of contact with Jorge Luis Borges' story "Tema del traidor y del héroe" ["Theme of the Traitor and the Hero"]. Thus, this novel is also familiar with the notion of simulacrum, which we see functioning as part of Vargas Llosa's poetics throughout all of his narrative work, although his use of the device intensifies during the later period of his novelistic production. Vargas Llosa seems to portray Casement, like Paul Gaugin, Flora Tristán, and other figures of the era, as an inhabitant of his own delirium. All of these characters take on roles they clearly cannot fulfill, giving way to a narrative tension between the desired and the attained, between the initial conditions that drove the dynamic of the characters and what these latter were effectively able to achieve throughout their lives.

In his review of *El sueño del celta*, the Irish writer John Banville emphasizes the naïveté of Vargas Llosa's approach, a quality which the writer himself projects onto his character. Won over by Casement's romantic aura, Vargas Llosa loosely develops the life story of the "incorrigible Irishman"—incorrigible both on the public stage and in his private affairs. The result is a text in which biographical elements and general historical information seem to function, as Banville notes, as an exoskeleton that supports the work's exterior without completely holding together the narrative body. In particular, Casement's secret life as a homosexual, confirmed in his personal diaries, is minimized in the novel, which relates details of his relationships with natives from Congo and Peru so reluctantly that this angle of Casement's life loses all relevance. Nevertheless, this aspect of Casement's life would be thoroughly exploited by the British government after his execution as a way of soiling his reputation and reducing the importance of his denunciations of the horrors of colonialism.[35] Thus, in this fictionalized biographical account Casement is simultaneously recovered and diluted. *El sueño del celta* makes its protagonist a kind of shadow of the historical individual, whose personality is absorbed in the process of being made into literature, yielding a more polite, less intense version of the original who inspired the character.

The direction Vargas Llosa's narrative work followed in this period thus continued to develop around procedures which have loosely supported literature throughout history. He has used these procedures as a basis for a re-elaboration of his literature that, while adding some definition, ultimately blurs certain primary features of the models being used. The rape that occurs at the beginning of *La fiesta del Chivo* as an allegory for a nation subjected to dictatorship, Vargas Llosa's modification of Casement's *Black Diaries*, the Irishman's alleged betrayal of the political cause, vague allusions to his homosexuality, as well as Flora Tristán's political passion, Paul Gaugin's sexual experimentation, or the appeal to Mexican cinema as a source for the sentimentalism and kitsch of *Travesuras de la niña mala*—these are all instances in which Vargas Llosa introduces a *tour de force* designed to place the character in extreme situations which dramatize and amplify the narrative. He thus creates a moment of excess in the story in which an *additional element* provokes the dissolution or downfall of narrative processes and the story becomes a *performance* through parodic affectation.[36]

However, beyond periodizations and thematic characterizations, having arrived at this point of the analysis, we must ask: Where does one find the main key to Vargas Llosa's narrative work? What angle does this writer offer to the representation of such a varied thematic, thus allowing him to combine it with his fluctuating ideological positions? How can we understand his work as, before anything else, a *cultural and ideological practice* from which he outlines a *model of intellectual action* that, for half a century, traversed the most volatile stages of contemporary Latin American history? How can we interpret such a contradictory and sensationalist poetics, which Vargas Llosa has used as a way to export (as part of but also beyond the Boom's historical and stylistic parameters) a commodifiable image of Latin America for international markets?

I think that the responses to these questions have to do, in a broad sense, with the *farcical treatment* that Vargas Llosa incorporates into his narrative works. This farcical element should be understood as a carnivalized (at times parodic, at other times satirical, and often simply dramatized) approach to a social reality that is itself also *constructed*, ideologized, in the process of its fictionalization.

In her study of farce (a term we will use loosely here), Priscilla Meléndez recognizes that, although it is difficult to define and categorize, in broad strokes, farce is characterized by the excessive complexity of its plot, the improbability of its situations, and the utilization of prototypes (Meléndez 24–34). All these features indicate the presence of a farcical "situation" and appear, with their own characteristics and to varying degrees, in Vargas Llosa's narrative work, especially in texts from the 1970s (*Pantaleón y las visitadoras*, *La tía Julia y el escribidor*) and more recently in novels published after 2000 (*El paraíso en la otra esquina*, *Travesuras de la niña mala*). As a *narrative tone*, however, this stylistic tendency appears in other, more serious and socially oriented works. For our purposes, we are interested in the idea of farce as a *lesser genre* (lesser than tragedy and drama, which are at the top of the hierarchy of genres) that lends itself to *light* compositions, like many of the titles that make up Vargas Llosa's body of work. In these works, farce effectuates a dramatization of the social that, while recognizing the deeper dimensions of its principal themes, is in any case able to *decenter them* through a ludic exposition, a "pseudo-comicality," that primarily aims to distract and entertain. Meléndez insists on the duality of farce and on its ability to penetrate the tensions between global centers and the Latin American periphery as well as the level of the *split identities* that characterize postcolonial society:

> It is indeed accurate to say that Spanish American farce takes from its Western counterpart its dual nature. But this duality reflects not so much the subjection to the center by the marginalized other as the split identity of Spanish America's art and its past and present political reality. [...] The relative power of farce in Spanish America to distort, destroy, dismantle, expose, attack, re-write, and erase lies in its experience as a victim of such acts and in its desire to redefine a discourse traditionally associated with an oppressive culture and region such as the West. (Meléndez 32–33)

The notion of farce that we will adopt in this study has to do (in addition to the points already covered) with the concept of deception that Vargas Llosa postulates as part of his poetic art. In fact, his idea that "one must lie knowingly," his recurrent references to "the truth of lies," his conception of art as concealment, inversion of the real world, subterfuge, simulacrum, disguise, all point in this direction. Vargas Llosa's narrative work also supports itself technically on the constant use of devices that manipulate the narrative material to the point at which the story begins to function as a kind of kaleidoscope whose fleeting images can only have an aleatory, fluctuating, unpredictable meaning. His narrative world thus goes on to create a scenario in which levels of plot development are constructed and anecdotes and events are interlaced among them without the characters' deeper dimension coming to interfere with its principally fragmentary and palimpsestic nature. Vargas Llosa's narrative work emphasizes the idea of the simulacrum in which a caricaturized appearance definitively replaces the reality which gave rise to it: the given and the invented maintain a farcical coexistence, an unstable but enduring equilibrium.

The simulation that sustains farce is closer to mimicry than mimesis because it includes hyperbolized, burlesque, intentionally artificial features that expose and exploit the distance between original and copy, between desire and the object of desire. Farce above all emphasizes non-being, incompleteness, and anxiety about completing an unrealized moment that is thwarted time and again. Farce's raw material is, as such, failure, lack, decline, and ruin, and its principal dynamic is the exhibition of a void filled only with the semblance of the object of desire, with the watered-down, nostalgic version, which can never be possessed: the sexual act for a castrated youth, revolution occurring in the wrong time and place, the brothel consumed by fire, the country that irreversibly "fucked itself," the Presidency never attained. Fiction, even biographical fiction, is organized as the textual framework which structures those voids: being what is not, coming to be, ceasing to be, imagining what is, being and non-being, all moments that feed the simulacrum as an aesthetics of carnivalization and parody, in which dramatic elements constantly rub up against, on one side, the grotesque, the sordid, and the corrupt, and on the other side coming close to kitsch affectations, to a baroque game of masks which opens up to pretense and pathos.[37]

Let us recall just a few central characters and situations from Vargas Llosa's narrative work. In *La ciudad y los perros* (a novel which the author at one point considered titling *Los impostores* [The imposters]), fraud and denunciation constitute the instigating elements of the narrative action. With the core of the plot consisting precisely of deception (the theft of the answers to an exam in the Leoncio Prado Military College), the narrative weaves a dynamic of betrayal and confrontations in which violence and sexuality create lines of tension that develop in different spaces and temporalities following the trajectories of the cadets' lives. But what is essential is precisely that violation of the moral norm, that initial transgression which precipitated the tearing of the social fabric that decomposes bit by bit in the novel, beginning with the act of fraud, the decisive factor of the narrative action. In *Los cachorros*, Cuéllar's castration functions as an alienating apparatus that makes it possible to explore reality from an anomalous point of view, to delve into resources that compensate for loss but above all verify its devastating mechanisms and allegorize the condition of a truncated youth in a relentless and mean-spirited social milieu. In *El hablador*, a story assembled around the problematic of *difference*, "Mascarita" describes himself as "half Jewish and half monster," referring to the mark that deforms his face and to his *impure* background, features which make him his own alter ego, a redoubled character in whom alterity and identity are two sides of the same coin. Pedro Camacho, the scriptwriter who creates fantasies to be broadcast on the radio in *La tía Julia y el escribidor*, constructs in his delirious parallel worlds, where falsity operates as the counterpoint to the anxiety experienced by Varguitas, who wants to become a writer, a respectable member of the *lettered city*—a project that Camacho seems to parody with his own literary snobbery. The character of Zavalita (without a doubt one of the most accomplished in Vargas Llosa's narrative work) in *Conversación en La Catedral* guides the exploration of the individual and collective repercussions of national disaster and the challenge of mediocrity and vulgarity that plagues criollo society. The text's arborescent structure, in which discourses constantly multiply, intermix, and (con)fuse, illustrates the vastness of a reality that does not seem to have any more dimension than the proliferation of frustration and anomaly, as if a malignant tumor had rooted itself in different levels of the social and reached the forms of perception of the world and the social consciousness that registers it. Simulation and the absurd define Pantaleón Pantoja and his false orders, in the same way that Mayta pursues his eccentric revolutionary project. In *El paraíso en la otra esquina*, the thwarted stories of Paul Gauguin and Flora Tristán appear as another form of pursuing a utopian horizon that will never be achieved and which is based in a view of the world that gets mistaken for reality. Similar mechanisms are also present in Vargas Llosa's theatrical works, for instance in *Kathie y el hipopótamo* (1983) [*Kathie and the Hippopotamus* (1990)], which the author describes as a farce in the preface. Meléndez chooses precisely this work to illustrate the theme of farce in Latin American literature and particularly in Vargas Llosa's work, especially for the way in which the work seems to dramatize the themes of communication and literary creation.

In *Kathie y el hipopótamo*, the protagonist hires a university professor to help her give shape to a book made up of material recorded during her exotic travels in Africa and Asia. The play moves through different registers, from the orality of the dialog and Kathie's recordings to the literary form she wants to construct. The work explores the process of textual construction and the forms of (un)reality from which it is composed, from orality to writing, from sub- or pre-literary forms to literature properly speaking, insofar as it is an instance of refinement and consolidation of discourse, a movement perceptible in several of Vargas Llosa's texts. Literary writing is thus preceded by farcical instances (scriptwriters, directors, transcribers [*escribidores, guionistas, transcriptores*]) which prepare the way for the text to emerge (illustrated well by the rewrite that the professor produces on transforming Kathie's elementary diction into aesthetic content). According to Meléndez:

> The farcical dimensions in *Kathie y el hipopótamo*—mainly the clash between the ludic nature of reality and fiction's capacity to reflect on and parody life—are portrayed through the transgression of the play's structures of communication, particularly as they characterize representational-theatrical language and textual literary discourse. *Kathie*'s complex understanding of

language and communication is underscored by its diverse manifestations: language in the form of informal, oral communication; in its written form, with literary or poetic overtones; in its physical and theatrical expressions; as a vehicle of seduction; as an expression of the inner self; in its rhetorical dimensions; and language as a misleading mask. But more important is to recognize that in *Kathie* these contradictory manifestations interact with each other in the context of farce, itself an aggressive and transgressive theatrical language. (149-150)

In this way, as Meléndez notes, themes Vargas Llosa deals with in other works are approached in a different register, such as the problematization of the authorship/authority narrative explored in *El hablador* and the alternation of voices in *Conversación en La Catedral*, *La tía Julia y el escribidor*, and other novels, and focuses in *Kathie* on a tone that parodies earlier efforts. In this way, farce permits an implicit intertextual unfolding and nuancing of certain things that, through being approached in different narrative styles, reveal new formal and thematic angles.

But if farcical modulation is what gives Vargas Llosa's narratives their artificial character, it will be the appeal to the *melodramatic matrix* that will impress upon his literature its distinctive quality with regard to the tone of this narrative itself as well as the aesthetic and ideological configuration of the universe portrayed in it. Farce explains his conception of fiction as a lie, a construction, a simulacrum. Melodrama affects the composition of his characters and situations, their chiaroscuros, their excesses, and helps in comprehending his persistent irrationalism and his perception of reality as a setting in which narrative technique reigns over the exploration of the deep structures to which the fictitious world refers in a mediated way.

Vargas Llosa's literature, thus established in the "politics of farce," is elaborated as a negotiation between realist techniques and melodramatic strategies, alternating the representation of the degraded world and its parody, the presence of the social problematic and its affected, fictional entanglement. To varying extents, these counterpoints make the themes and conflicts in Vargas Llosa's work less dense while at the same time they fulfill the role of maintaining nimble and accessible plots, producing a literature that is conceived as a happy medium between entertainment and a dramatized exposé of social antagonisms.

In *La nueva novela hispanoamericana* (1969) [The new Hispano-American novel], Carlos Fuentes discovered early on this crucial feature of Vargas Llosa's narrative:

One of the keys to *La casa verde* [...] and one of its riskiest and most attractive aspects [is] its embrace of melodrama as one of the axes of Latin American life [...] Vargas Llosa has not been able to avoid the problem of the melodramatic content of lives that would know no other way to affirm their being [...] When tragic consciousness, historical reason, or personal affirmation are lacking, melodrama supplements them: it is a substitute, an imitation, an illusion of being. (*La nueva novela hispanoamericana* 47)

This critical intuition should be developed further.

As Peter Brooks has pointed out in his foundational study of melodrama, this latter expresses the anxiety of a world where traditional moral models no longer reign, making the drama *legible* in a desacralized universe in which passions are released with neither restraint nor direction. According to Brooks, melodrama is moralistic in the sense that it is the "drama of morality," that is, the dramatization of the profound ethical crisis of a world without God. Hence, it prefers to feed on evil, just as psychoanalytical notions (trauma, conflict, repression, the disintegration of the self) constitute an essential factor of modern sensibility. The "melodramatic imagination" is thus for Brooks a form of (re)cognizing reality and approaching the ethical dilemmas that the problem of evil poses to reason, without the help of transcendent planes that would make it possible to project the conflict and resolve it at an extra-human level.

If melodrama fundamentally expresses the anxiety produced by the generalized crisis of morality and the lack of stable parameters from which one can comprehend and represent ethical conflict without turning to religion, it is not surprising that the main components of the genre belong to the universe of affect and activate the level of desire and instinctive drives within the individual and the community. Melodrama represents these aspects in an aggravated way, as an excess that invades and disarticulates the habitual forms of knowledge of the real. Melodrama thus comes closer to the unrepresentable, staging the distance between the sense of the real and its literary dramatization, that is, between the level of experience and its symbolic performance. This staging of distance, on which melodrama is based, highlights the moral dilemma debated by the characters of the fictional world.

As we have seen, in this way the notion of melodrama does not only refer to a style or a particular aesthetic but also to a sensibility, a form of knowledge, and a communicational strategy (a rhetoric) that responds to the will to make the real intelligible, aesthetically and ideologically intervening in it through devices that hyperbolize what is being represented (Mercer and Shingler). "Melodramatic rhetoric" (Brooks) is thus eminently a *mise en scène*: the exaggerated unfolding of the sign that invades consciousness, turning social behaviors into an intense, ritualized, and at times farcical gesturality from which *the social* manifests in its spontaneous, dispersed, and inorganic form.

Melodrama insists on the signifying capacity of the ordinary as the source of polarities which cannot accept any form of articulation, let alone any dialectical synthesis that resolves conflict by subsuming its constituent terms. Light and shadow, salvation and condemnation, good and evil, modernity and barbarism, identity and otherness, Eros and Thanatos, the Apollonian and the Dionysian, all constitute antagonistic effects of the real, extremes of a spectrum that in the process of its own intensification has ended up reducing itself to its most salient and stereotypical features.

Extreme emotionality and the suffering (individual, social) body are the last redoubts in which melodramatic energy can take refuge: the lines of flight through which this energy, which derives from unresolved conflict and the immanent ethics it contains, escapes. For this reason, the body is the great protagonist of melodrama: the tortured, mutilated, prostituted, imprisoned body, consumed by passion or devastated by violence. As a repository of pleasure and pain, the body is the space of desire and transgression, hence it gives rise to instances of ritualization, sacrifice, and martyrdom in which the symbolic component is provocatively situated between materiality and subjectivity, releasing messages that cover the entire ideological, affective, aesthetic, and moral spectrum. Otherness, which has its most obvious support in the body, is thus the great metaphor of the disintegration of the self and of the fragmentation of individual and collective identity discourses that sustain it. The Other does not only exist as exteriority: it is the self, divided between the observing gaze and the image that appears in the mirror, a primary—substitutive—way of objectifying an always unique and unrepresentable trauma. The individual body and the social body, as Alonso Cueto has pointed out with regard to Vargas Llosa's work, are possessed bodies, which the Peruvian writer represents as if he were trying to turn them into animals. The titles of several of his works (*Los cachorros*, *La ciudad y los perros*, *La fiesta del chivo*), as well as the names that he gives to many of his characters (Boa, Jaguar, Becerrita [Heifer]), express this idea, as if instinct were progressively taking the place of rationality and the body had become the space in which these transformations exposed their provocative reality (Cueto 17–19).

Situated at the limit of the social, Vargas Llosa's characters are simultaneously ordinary and exceptional, singular and representative of specific forms of socialization and collective experience. Subject as they are to historical circumstances and interior forces that drive and control their interactions, the behaviors they exhibit are almost always reactive, the result of contingency in an immanently desacralized world.

The melodramatic model is visible at all levels of Vargas Llosa's work. As a rough approximation of the theme, one can begin by noting that, in the first place, at the autobiographical level, the melodramatic paradigm is utilized as a strategy of (self-)recognition and a dramatization of interiority through the selection of facts and the language used to channel it. *El pez en el agua* is in this sense a clear example of a subjective world that unfolds before our very eyes as a presumably selective memory, as an attenuation of the real which makes lived experience coincide with what has been recorded and what is recorded with what is narrated. This biographical exercise puts the subjectivization machine into play, and all writing, literature, and its related genres (speeches, essays, journalism) are assumed as apparatuses for producing and reproducing (false) consciousness. The autobiographical narrative thus operates not just as a production of the spectacle of an imagined identity—which the subject produces as his or her own image and as a projection toward others—but also as a construction of otherness, that constitutive outside of identity that endows it with sense and defines it on the basis of its most notable features. *El pez en el agua*, as critics have previously noted, in no way limits itself to being a mere testimony of the process of Vargas Llosa's political campaign as a candidate of the Frente Democrático [Democratic Front] at the end of the 1980s.[38] It also brings together elements of the *Bildungsroman* (a narrative of the trajectory that takes the author/narrator/protagonist from infancy to adulthood) with a political line, another *coming of age*[39] story that almost seems like an epiphenomenon of the first, as if the writer identified maturity with leadership, bringing the intimate into the public, the individual into the collective, the imagined and the desired into the witnessed.

El pez en el agua proposes the convergence of author and nation, personal biography and collective history, attempting to construct at this crossroads the platform for a politico-literary narrative that would sustain the intellectual's singularity over and above the failure of his political narrative. Saturated with anecdotes and bereft of any deep reflection on the Peruvian political process and the factors which effectively led to Alberto

Fujimori's triumph, *El pez en el agua* demonstrates Vargas Llosa's anxiety over controlling the most minute details of how his individual story, as well as the story of his political candidacy, will be read. Melodramatic *mood* makes it possible to interweave characters and levels, the private sphere and the public sphere, as if they were serial installments whose capricious sequentialization further emphasized their fragmentary nature, faithfully pursuing the primary goal of constructing one's own image and of fixing a strict interpretation of the circumstances that influenced its development. Additive and documentarist, the memoir's style is supported throughout by an excess of double perspective—individual and collective, private and public. Even with its undeniable narrative and ideological heft, Vargas Llosa's individualism is unable to compensate for the lack of *necessary* relations between both registers, which proceed in a precarious and unstable union, as if the background music from a Mexican soap opera were playing as it unfolded.

Reflecting on Vargas Llosa's work, Julio Ortega's interpretation correctly brings together the "perverse derivations" that he perceives in the Peruvian writer's work on the subculture of the grotesque "as revelatory information about the individual deprived of a normative world" ("Vargas Llosa: el habla del mal" 172). Many episodes in *El pez en el agua* shed light on this feature: the distribution of toys among poor children in Puerto Maldonado, Cuzco, and Andahuaylas, the middle classes gathered in the San Martín plaza demanding his candidacy, the angry mob in Piura, all of which we have already mentioned.

In the second place, on the level of fictional plot (to which we have already referred in the present study), melodrama is the matrix from which the world is thought and represented, not in order to implement a form of rational knowledge of reality, but to communicate a different knowledge by means of the "sad collisions" of affect and desire. The melodramatic imagination is an obsessive form of thinking and feeling: a mode of sensibility that circulates socially before its narrative even exists. For this reason it is considered a communicational technique that pushes the limits of the *lettered city*, which disassembles and exceeds the hierarchies of reality.[40] In a melodramatic key it is possible to emphasize the ritualized aspects that social behaviors assume and which attract Vargas Llosa through their capacity for dramatization and his (generally vain) enthusiasm for regulation and control. Social conflict can thus reveal itself in hidden connections with desire, passion, irrational drives, and prejudice, demonstrating the effects of these antagonisms as if it were all an atavistic performance that exists in the memory of the species and which therefore requires neither explanation nor investigation. Sexuality, violent tendencies, survival instincts, various forms of belief (myth, taboo, religion, or superstition), and internal history are all taken up by melodrama as proper materials for the carnivalized display of its interior tensions. Melodrama thus appears as a modern form of orality that reclaims modes of subjectivity which move through the codified borders of official cultures and manifest as transgression and exceptionality. It is from this melodramatic structure assumed by the social being that one can rethink heterogeneity and the popular and perceive the tearing of the fabric of modernity through which impure forms of collective sensibility are filtered. Melodrama is an apt form of representation for the residual or marginal elements that exist of the edges of bourgeois sociality, middle-class morality, and capitalist productivity. Melodrama prefers non-places, those transitional and provisional territories where many of Vargas Llosa's narratives develop, hierarchical and formalized spaces in which "the moral occult" Peter Brooks discusses exists, as does the hidden logic of the non-rational and the particular ethics that sustain it. Melodrama accommodates *difference* as an imaginary and transgressive alternative, charged with particularism. It thus serves as a representative example of ethnic and class alterity, gender difference, and cultural diversity, since, in the melodramatic context, the conflicts and affinities of different social groups and the passionate dynamics that connect them (sexuality, violence) can be exhibited without the solemn requirements of the epic or the exoticism of magical realism, allowing interactions and the unique dimension of individual personality to provide the elements necessary for the narrative to unfold.

Julio Ortega has argued that Vargas Llosa's creative spectrum can be determined between two poles whose logics are concentrated in long-established models of literary composition: on one hand, the chivalric romance, which would constitute the paradigm of harmony and totalization; and on the other hand, the model of the melodramatic serial, a universe of emotional excess and hyperbolic action in which "existence becomes an involuntary parody." If the chivalric romance exemplified by Joanot Martorell's *Tirant lo blanc* (1490) represents a self-sufficient and carefully regulated universe, melodrama confronts us with the "world of heroic misfortune" (Ortega, "Vargas Llosa: el habla del mal" 172).[41]

As a proponent of understanding social regulations as an attempt to contain the natural chaos of both the individual and society, and as the narrator of the deregulation and disintegration of the social (as the storyteller, in Larsen's words, of *demodernity* [*desmodernidad*]), Vargas Llosa finds in the representation of otherness his most fertile narrative field. *Otherness*—that which exists as the objectification of what *the modern* would like to expel from its register, which exists as the space of the repressed which always returns, of the fearsome and the atavistic, of that which simultaneously underlies and contextualizes identity—constitutes the abstract place in which time and again the failure of the liberal republic and the need to reinvent it are confirmed. It is this (melo)drama of the folding and refolding of the social that Vargas Llosa explores in his writing, neither as deep investigations that aim to develop a utopian project nor as an inquiry into the limits of the spiritual alternatives for both individuals and the nation, but as a tour of the textures and accidents of the cultural terrain, as an exploration of the ruins that mark the landscape and which document what could have been and what now definitively will not be. The Peru of *demodernity* in which everything is always "fucked," in which everything rots, the country which insists, nonetheless, on regulating, ritualizing, institutionalizing, prescribing, and mutilating (in order to reinscribe it afterward on the residue of the social) the adventure of the degraded hero—this Peru is the raw material of Vargas Llosa's literature, which through melodrama is able to be exhibited in all its *pathos*.

In his reflections on Vargas Llosa's literary themes, Alonso Cueto notes that his compatriot's work expresses a natural predilection for transgression: Alberto Fonchito, in *El elogio de la madrastra* and *Los cuadernos de Don Rigoberto*, Antonio Imbert in *La fiesta del chivo*, Flora Tristán in *El paraíso en la otra esquina*. His preference for authors such as Sade and Bataille, or for characters from universal literature like Madame Bovary and Jean Valjean, should be understood in the same register (Cueto 13). It is a matter of the critical and literary development of the topic of rebellion—indiscriminate, *glamorized* more as a gesture than as a concrete position—that Vargas Llosa would absorb in his own way within the revolutionary climate of the 1960s and which persisted as part of the melodramatic model of the writer persecuted by inner demons, handed over to his obsessions, and tormented by the "vice of truth." Cueto also notes that the language of rebellion always supports itself on the strength of orality, a flexible, evasive presence opposed to the written word. Potential rebellion is the specter haunting the peripheral and uneven modernity of the Andes, exposing the ridiculous precarity of the *status quo*. Vargas Llosa lends artificial and melodramatic elements to this rebellious drive, hypertrophied by the perspective that he often assumes as the authoritarian organizer of the narrative, as an Author definitively situated on a plane over and outside that of his characters and the situations he invents for them.

In the third place, on the level of political discourse properly speaking, the melodramatic matrix is also expressed, with an intensity that is exacerbated by the public *mise en scène* of self-postulating individuality through the (imagined) messianic message of liberal ideology. Vargas Llosa does not spare any melodramatic element, neither on the discursive level nor on the plane of mediated performativity. Some examples include his sharp opposition between good and evil as ancient forces that dominate the world of life and his carnivalized presentation of collective characters (the people, marginalized segments of society, the Left, the middle class, intellectuals) as a strategy for identifying social actors destined to fulfill roles forever marked (in a more or less distant way) by irrational and atavistic forces. The devastating violence of the Shining Path, the people who encouraged his presidential candidacy, the masses that attacked him during his campaign, even the demons that drive his literary work, all respond to forces that, according to Vargas Llosa, exceed or escape rationality. From this perspective, social action cannot be considered the exercise of a political or social *agency*. The symbolic constructions to which it refers thus constitute the spontaneous development of the sign liberated from meaning.

Other critics have also discerned this tendency toward simulacra that characterizes Vargas Llosa's work. As we have already seen in the present study, Alberto Flores Galindo has drawn attention to the spectrality of the political in Vargas Llosa's discourse and in the mode in which the Movimiento Libertad mobilized elements present in the national imaginary in order to launch a commodifiable image of the writer-turned-presidential candidate. Neil Larsen has noted Vargas Llosa's tendency to fictionalize the ideological, effectuating, as Rowe also points out, "the impoverishment of the political." Beatriz Sarlo refers to the dramatization and simulacrum Vargas Llosa draws on as a way of producing a mediated image capable of articulating popular fantasy by using slogans from his political campaign and creating theatrical scenarios in which to stage the fiction of empathy with his fellow citizens.

In this way, within a poetics in which reality has lost its status to invention and in which lies and truth compete in an uneven struggle for the definition of the space of representation, the act of simulation, as an anti-utopian gesture, ends up erasing the borders between false consciousness and real consciousness, thereby making the pressures of ethics and politics irrelevant. As Baudrillard has pointed out:

> Conversely, simulation starts from the *utopia* of this principle of equivalence, *from the radical negation of the sign as value*, from the sign as reversion and death sentence of every reference. Whereas representation tries to absorb simulation by interpreting it as false representation, simulation envelopes the whole edifice of representation as itself a simulacrum. (*Simulations* 11)

NOTES

1. The Peruvian generation of the 1950s, of which Vargas Llosa was a member, generally also included authors like Sebastián Salazar Bondy, Julio Ramón Ribeyro, Francisco Bendezú, Carlos Eduardo Zavaleta, Luis Loayza, Alejandro Romualdo, Pablo Guevara, Eleodoro Vargas Vicuña, Javier Sologuren, Jorge Eduardo Eielson y Blanca Varela, among others. On this generation, see Miguel Gutiérrez's controversial book, *La generación del 50: un mundo dividido*, in which he studies intellectuals born in Peru between 1921 and 1936, including figures like Abimael Guzmán.
2. The notion of "world literature," long-established in the European context, was coined, significantly, as a geocultural reference to the space in which literary texts and authors receive transnational recognition and attention. This concept, which has been debated in the academic world for its undeniable ideologico-cultural connotations, constitutes another form of referring to the topic of the recognition, promotion, and consumption of a literary product in the global market of symbolic goods that capitalism consolidates and redefines in the second half of the twentieth century. On the concept of world literature, see Casanova and Moretti. For a critical perspective on this topic, see the texts in Sánchez Prado's book.
3. The perceived mediocrity of the Peruvian cultural milieu continued to torment Vargas Llosa even after he had achieved widespread recognition. He writes, for example, in *La utopía arcaica*, published in 1996: "Inequality, discrimination, backwardness, the concentration of wealth in the hands of an infinitesimal minority surrounded by an ocean of misery affect not only workers, peasants, and the unemployed. They are also obstacles to the practice of intellectual or artistic activity. In what kind of conditions can a writer survive in societies where half the population is illiterate? How can literature flourish in countries with no publishing houses or literary journals, where, in order to not just up and die, authors often must cover the publishing costs of their own books? What kind of literary life can be mustered in

societies where material conditions—lack of education, miserable salaries, chronic unemployment—have established a veritable cultural apartheid that segregates books from the vast majority? And if, on top of it all, the state has imposed systems of control on the press, television, radio, and universities, places where literature might find refuge and support, how could any writer remain blind and deaf to social problems?" (26).
4. On Vargas Llosa's ideological profile and his contradictory political positions, see Juan E. de Castro, "Mr. Vargas Llosa goes to Washington."
5. Following Larsen's critique, Vargas Llosa interprets the project of modernity from this position of ideological *inanity* that converts reality and political thought into simulacra—a tendency that makes him "the Pantaleón Pantoja of neoliberalism" (147)—thus turning it into a modernity that, according to Larsen, seems to reveal itself more easily to those who, although they have the ability to represent it aesthetically, are poorly equipped to understand it theoretically (168).
6. Thus, Vargas Llosa admits: "These are individualistic values by definition, resistant to any purely social conception of man, in which Camus saw two forms of redemption for the species, a way of regenerating society and a superior and privileged type of human relationship" ("Albert Camus y la moral de los límites," in *Contra viento y marea* I 237/"Albert Camus and the Morality of Limits," in *Making Waves: Essays* 111).
7. Vargas Llosa dedicated a series of articles to Sartre's work. One may consult, for example, in *Contra viento y marea*, I, in addition to "El mandarín," "Los otros contra Sartre," "Sartre y el Nobel," "Sartre y el marxismo," and "Sartre veinte años después." On Sartre and Camus' relationship and the polemics between the two, see, in the same volume, "Revisión de Albert Camus" and "Albert Camus y la moral de los límites." In this latter article, originally published in *Plural* in 1975, Vargas Llosa appeals to Camus' moral questioning of every ideology and the author's obsession with State terrorism and the sacrifice of liberty in order to make his shift to a neoliberal position, leaving behind both Sartre's thought and the socialism that had previously seduced him, focusing on the real root of all of his intellectual and political preoccupations: "the relationship between the creator and the principles that govern societies," which is to say, the relationship between power, the role of the intellectual, and the relative autonomy of the cultural sphere ("Albert Camus y la moral de los límites," in *Contra viento y marea* I 231-52/"Albert Camus and the Morality of Limits" in *Making Waves: Essays* 107–16). Rowe has pointed out "the impoverishment of political discourse" in this essay on Camus, a quality that will impact all of Vargas Llosa's political discourse in subsequent years ("Vargas Llosa y el lugar de enunciación autoritario" 68).

8. [This term refers to the large shanty towns—literally "young towns"—that have developed around Lima and other cities in Peru as a result of massive migration (largely of black, indigenous, and mestizo peasants) from the countryside since the 1940s.—Tr.]
9. On this topic see Cornejo Polar, Rama (*Writing Across Cultures*), and Losada.
10. The debate includes articles entitled "Literatura en la revolución y revolución en la literatura: algunos malentendidos a liquidar," by Cortázar; "Contrarrespuesta para armar," Collazos' January 1970 response to the Argentine writer; and Vargas Llosa's reply, "Luzbel, Europa y otras conspiraciones," which dates from April 1970.
11. The article by Vargas Llosa that provoked Collazos to respond was "La cultura en México," published in *Siempre!* on 16 April 1969.
12. To confirm the use of the idea of "creative demons" among writers of the Boom era, including the concepts that they continued to support up to the present, see Collazos' response to José Carvajal, in which the Colombian writer addresses ideas about creative demons, the disconformity of the writer, and literature as an escape from reality:
    JC: Do you still believe that "literary creation is a kind of exorcism of our inner demons"?
    OC: If this were not the case, the writer would constantly be exposed to madness. Literary creation is his "escape route," as Graham Greene confirms in his autobiography.
    JC: Does that mean that the writer's inner demons have always been exile, eroticism, and politics?
    OC: In a certain sense, yes: those are the dominant themes in my narrative. And they respond to a nomadic experience, assumed from a very young age. A dangerous experience: I never pushed it away, I assumed it. Exile as an autobiographical experience, eroticism as an expression of character, the pleasure principle that has ruled my life; politics, in the broadest sense, as an ethical response to a world or a social order I despise (Carvajal, "Oscar Collazos: la inconformidad irremediable").
13. On the theme of demons in Vargas Llosa, see Raymond Williams, particularly Chap. 2, in which he summarizes Vargas Llosa's ideas and connects them to Freud's theory of the unconscious, Nietzsche's irrationalism, etc.
14. It remains obvious that, in its pure revolutionary intentionality, this idea overlooked, for example, Vallejo's thematic and linguistic complexity, a feature that inevitably distanced him from any direct relationship with the popular subject with whom he ideologically identified.
15. The texts that make up the polemic which took place in the pages of *Marcha* are, in order of publication: (1) Ángel Rama: "Vade Retro" (no. 1591); (2) Mario Vargas Llosa: "El regreso de Satán" (no. 1602); (3) Rama: "El fin de

los demonios" (no. 1603); (4) Vargas Llosa: "Resurrección de Belcebú o la disidencia creadora" (no 1609); (5) Rama: "Nuevo escritor para nueva sociedad" (no. 1610); and (6) Rama: "Un arma llamada novela" (no. 1612). The articles that correspond to Vargas Llosa's interventions have been reproduced in *Contra viento y marea*. All the interventions also appear in the book co-edited by Rama and Vargas Llosa, *García Márquez y la problemática de la novela*.

16. Vargas Llosa's book on García Márquez, never republished owing to the enmity that later emerged between the two writers, originally constituted Vargas Llosa's doctoral thesis at the Universidad Complutense de Madrid, where he obtained the title of Bachelor of Literature in the Faculty of Philosophy and Letters, Romantic Philology department. The academic courses he took for the degree were completed between 1958 and 1960. His doctoral thesis was directed by Alonso Zamora Vicente.
17. On the polemic between Rama and Vargas Llosa, consult Sánchez Lopez, Mariaca, L. Castañeda, and Perilli.
18. Goethe has been cited as one of the forerunners of the idea of the demons of creation, as has Georges Bataille, both establishing in different contexts the notion of evil and satanic disorder as one of the driving forces behind understanding creation as both rebellion against the established order and the uncovering of occult, prohibited aspects of reality. For example, see Kristal, *Temptation of the Word* (3–5). In the national context of Peru, the influence of César Moro—from whom Vargas Llosa takes a text as an epigraph for *El elogio de la madrastra*—has also been established. Vargas Llosa says of Moro: "The extreme case of the exiled Peruvian creator is certainly that of the poet César Moro. Very few have so completely and desperately felt the demon of creation, very few have served solitude with such passion and sacrifice" (*Contra viento y marea* I 98). The idea of an association between the satanic or demonic and the creative process has a metaphoric value that criticism has at times exaggerated. In general, it is a figurative way of discussing the transgressive or subversive impulse that literature can yield. In Vargas Llosa it is a commonplace appropriated from different contexts, repeated in order to reaffirm the "rebel" and exceptional quality of the writer as well as the experience of his literature. With Moro (who was, together with Emilio Adolfo Westphalen, one of the most interesting representatives of surrealism in Latin America) Vargas Llosa shares the idea of literature as a domain separate from the real, completely autonomous, defined by arbitrariness, and which does not admit of any specific agenda or program linked to social poetry, indigenist art, etc. Pragmatics and poetics are thus separate domains of action and thought. On Moro's influence on Vargas Llosa, see Castro-Klarén, *Mario Vargas Llosa* 95–96, and Kristal, *Temptation of the Word* 12–19.

19. Regarding the essays that make up *Writing Across Cultures: Narrative Transculturation in Latin America*, originally published in Spanish in 1982: "The Andean Cultural Area" first saw the light of day in 1974; "The Saga of the Mestizo" was published in 1975 as the prologue to *Fundación de una cultura nacional indoamericana*, in which were gathered disparate and unpublished works by Arguedas; and "Mythic Intelligence" was published in 1976 as an introduction to the collection of essays Arguedas published as *Señores e indios*. All this critical material is evidence of Rama's tastes and preferences, which have already been analyzed in previous chapters of the present study.
20. Rama and Vargas Llosa worked together at the Casa de las Américas and were also aligned (with Rama being more moderate) on certain critiques of Castro's cultural policies. In spite of the passionate and rigorous tone of the polemic, Rama always recognizes the merits of Vargas Llosa's narrative work. A good example is his admiring review of *La guerra del fin del mundo*, published in 1982. Vargas Llosa also recognized Rama's contributions in "Ángel Rama: la pasión y la crítica," a note he wrote as a biographical sketch on the occasion of Rama's death in 1983.
21. According to Franco, in *García Márquez: historia de un deicidio* the conception Vargas Llosa presents of the artist as Lucifer rebelling against society to create his own reality is another version of the writer-hero (Jean Franco, "From Modernization to Resistance," in *Critical Passions* 295).
22. All of Rama's work can be read as the most significant Latin American attempt to clarify the process of cultural institutionalization in the region as well as to contribute to it, demonstrating the tensions, contradictions, and paradoxes of the intellectual field in general and the literary field in particular. As I have shown elsewhere, the theory of transculturation is situated at the crossroads established in the 1970s between national culture and foreign ideological influences, not only liberal modernizing influences but also Marxist influences, whose "foreign" character constituted one of the bases for Right-wing repression of Leftist theory and praxis. Rama attempts to reflect on these convergences which necessarily and productively sustain postcolonial cultures in Latin America and combine with vernacular currents which *cannibalize*, that is, incorporate their contents, reformulate, and convert them into a constitutive part of ideology and social practice. A book like *The Lettered City*, designed to offer a cartography of the processes of cultural institutionalization that at one time demonstrated the relative autonomy of the cultural field and of the multiple systems that tensely coexist within it, must not be seen in any other way. In this regard, see Moraña, "Ideología de la Transculturación" and other essays on these themes included in *Ángel Rama y los estudios latinoamericanos*, as well as Poblete, "Trayectoria crítica de Ángel Rama." For a critique of *The Lettered City*, see Perus.

23. With regard to this subject, one may consult Van Delden's (in my opinion, oversimplified) opinions on the almost always Manichean dualisms that affect Vargas Llosa's thought. Mentioned in his text are oppositions which include fiction/reality, private/public, literature/politics, conformity/transgression, democracy/dictatorship, which become more fluid, Van Delden recognizes, in a fictional world (214). Also, according to Van Delden, Vargas Llosa's anti-utopian vision of society as a whole nonetheless admits of the possibility of individual or symbolic utopias. Although Van Delden understands that "[Vargas Llosa's] itinerary is rich in situations and in intellectual dilemmas" (196), his study never explores the ideological baggage or the aesthetic connections that these intersections establish for the Peruvian author on the level of politics and art.
24. Oviedo has highlighted the similarities between both spaces and the fact that these institutions constitute closed, marginal, and hierarchical nuclei around which the characters circulate, adopting or retaking new names (La Selvática, Lituma) according to the settings and roles they happen to be portraying in each case ("Historia de un libertino," *Dossier Vargas Llosa* 33–48).
25. "The system of images in Mario Vargas Llosa's novels illustrates a central intuition of evil and distortion. This intuition responds to itself in the critical commentary on his novels, in their systematic denunciation. But even in criticism Vargas Llosa's work preserves its drama and its irresolute condition. This drama makes existence show itself in its intolerable modality, in its perverse and poorly configured spectacle. This condition, which reveals existence to be incomplete and even imperfectible, annihilating itself in its lack of a genuine rule, making destruction its ultimate horizon" (Ortega, ibid., 177).
26. For more on this topic, see Cano Gaviria.
27. Several critics sort and classify Vargas Llosa's work according to diverse criteria beyond the period in which they were written. Thus, for example, O'Bryan-Knight studies *La tía Julia y el escribidor*, *La historia de Mayta*, and *El hablador* as a trilogy, in spite of the fact that the works are not contiguous and the author has never indicated that they belong to the same novelistic cycle. For O'Bryan-Knight, the three works become stronger together as they focus on, respectively, different spaces or phases of Peru: the Capital and the coastal region, the mountains, and the jungle, although this distribution of Vargas Llosa's work is hardly radical since, for example, *La historia de Mayta* develops partly in the Lurigancho prison in Lima, and other novels, like some sections of *La casa verde* and *Pantaleón y las visitadoras*, also venture into the space of the Amazon jungle.
28. In "¿Quién mató a Mario Vargas Llosa?" Ortega calls attention to the behaviorist nature of narratives that develop characters as products of social

circumstances and that put more importance on the plot than on the treatment of intimacy.
29. O'Bryan-Knight notes, along with other critics, the metafictional character of *La historia de Mayta* and the consequent objectivization of the ideological (68–71). See also Dunkerley.
30. In one of his books, John King cites Anthony Burgess's review of *The War of the End of the World*. This opinion is illustrative of the way in which Latin American literature is still perceived in certain international media, in spite of the efforts of many award-winning authors from the region. Burgess notes: "There is a danger that the Great Contemporary Latin American novel will soon be laying down (if it has not done so already) rigid rules in respect of its content, length and style. Apparently it has to be bulky, baroque, full of freaks and cripples with names hard to fix in one's mind, crammed with wrongs done to peasants by the state or the land owners, seasoned with grotesque atrocities, given to apocalyptic visions, ending up with resignation at the impossibility of anything ever going right for South America" ("Latin Freakshow," *Observer*, 19 May 1985, qtd. in King, *On Modern Latin American Fiction* ix).
31. On this theme, see Sergio R. Franco, "Tecnologías de la representación."
32. Enrique Mayer has referred to the belief in *pishtacos* as an element that on a popular level thematizes the fear caused by violence and the oppression of indigenous culture and which serves to localize, in an irrational zone of the collective imaginary, collective feelings of terror, hatred, vengeance, etc. It is interesting to note following Mayer's suggestions that the figure of the *pishtaco* also serves as a vehicle for a critique of capitalism understood as social vampirism, especially regarding the most dispossessed segments of society. Supposedly, the fat that the *pishtacos* extract from the bodies of Indians serves as a lubricant for industrial machinery or is utilized as a way to pay Peru's foreign debt. Here, belief articulates economic aspects signaling the biopolitical implications of capitalist exploitation. See Mayer, "Peru in Deep Trouble" 472–73.
33. Of course, this periodization is not definitive, and it is only partially complete since some works from one period present the characteristics of works from others. In any case, the stages Kristal recognizes provide one idea of how to organize Vargas Llosa's writing according to the changes in his political thought. In this regard, see Kristal's "Introduction" to *The Cambridge Companion to Vargas Llosa* as well as "From Utopia to Reconciliation" and *Temptation of the Word*.
34. Casement was accused of having sympathized with the so-called Easter Rising, which took place in Dublin 23–30 April 1916 with the objective of liberating the Irish people from the domination of the UK. However, Casement seems to have been convinced that these actions were going to fail

and had returned to Ireland to persuade the insurgents that the situation would not turn out well. The uprising, stifled six days after it began, was led by James Connolly, chief of the Irish Citizen Army, who was also executed.
35. For a detailed account of Casement's life, see Reid and Mitchell.
36. "The primary obligation of a novel is to become independent of the real world, to impose on the reader an autonomous reality, valid in and of itself, capable of persuading the reader of its truth through its internal coherence and its intimate verisimilitude rather than through its subordination to the real world. What authorizes a fiction's sovereignty, what emancipates it from worldly affairs, from 'history,' is the *additional element*, that sum of thematic and formal ingredients that the author did not take from reality, that he did not steal from his own life or the lives of his contemporaries, that was born from his intuition, his madness, his dreams, and which his intelligence and skill blended together with everything else that every novelist takes from experience, whether his own of that of others" (Vargas Llosa, *Carta de batalla por Tirant lo Blanc* 102, emphasis in the original).
37. M. Keith Booker has seen in these features reason to categorize Vargas Llosa as a postmodernist writer, particularly because of his parodic treatment of social conflict and political history.
38. See Sergio R. Franco, "The Recovered Childhood," as well as Kelly Austin, and Larsen.
39. [In English in the original.—Tr.]
40. See Herlinghaus, "La imaginación melodramática," in *Narraciones anacrónicas* 21–59.
41. Ortega argues that Vargas Llosa is not interested in "popular exoticism" or in the hybrid forms of popular culture, but rather in the possibilities that those spaces can offer for parodying society's rules and exploring the grotesque in a world in which moral norms and principals are in crisis. This is the Peruvian author's "perverse derivation."

CHAPTER 9

Endpoint? Death/The Nobel Prize

Based on the preceding analysis, it is clear that the intellectual and life trajectories of José María Arguedas and Mario Vargas Llosa could not have been more disparate. Both inhabitants of the coveted and unstable territory of the literary canon, they are very dissimilar in their use of language and the paraphernalia of discursive strategies of modernity. Creators of fictional worlds adjacent (although in many senses also antagonistic) to one another and representatives of opposed models of intellectuality and political conduct, each of these authors' work has achieved an undoubtedly significant point of culmination, with the death of the former and the international recognition of the latter. On the ideological level, Vargas Llosa's conspicuous figure has become practically inseparable from the rightward turn in international politics that expanded after the end of the Cold War as well as the controversial politics of neoliberalism, both in its economic applications and in its cultural impact. For his part, Arguedas's work and persona are associated with indigenous movements, the failure of the Latin American Left, the reclamation of languages disappearing before the predatory advance of hegemonic cultures, archaism, emancipatory utopianism, and "narratives of failure." If Arguedas's death has come to constitute a paradigmatic moment of the representation of the struggle for decolonization by peoples in Latin America subjected first to colonialism and then to the project of nation-building, then the high point of Vargas Llosa's international recognition—namely, the Nobel Prize in Literature in 2010—constitutes the establishment not only of a major

© The Editor(s) (if applicable) and The Author(s) 2016
M. Moraña, *Arguedas / Vargas Llosa*,
DOI 10.1057/978-1-137-57187-8_9

body of work in Hispanic letters but also of the model of the *superstar* writer and the "imaginarily liberal" ideology that informs it.[1] While Vargas Llosa aligned himself with the transnationalized flows of subjects, commodities, and symbolic products, embodied in an exemplary form of cultural circulation and self-promotion in the Western world, Arguedas and his cultural practices reclaimed instead the knowledges and practices of marginalized communities, subjectivity, tradition, and memory, opening onto desire and affect as modes of consciousness and action. Death and the Nobel Prize thus constitute comparable forms of entering posterity: modes of transcendence through the art that they involve, each one in its own register, a singular mode of inscribing oneself in history and conquering one's time. Both moments are in their own way performative insofar as they articulate the individual and the community, as Arguedas shows in his careful attention to the details of his burial, the musical selection that would accompany the closing of his life cycle, and the delegation of pre-planned roles, scenarios, and ceremonies to carry out the disposal of his corpse and to assure the continuity of his work. In Vargas Llosa's case, the Nobel ceremony established both his physical and textual body within the international community and assured him a place in the literary canon. Both moments constitute landmarks that will always indicate the reception of these two literary bodies: writing now brushes up against the absolute.

Nevertheless, this transcendent dimension of literary textuality can only be fully apprehended on the basis of knowing the contingencies of its elaboration and its reception. It is intrahistory—the vicissitudes of the interpersonal and the intertextual—that contributes otherwise imperceptible nuance to literary interpretation. As we have seen, the comparative exploration of the poetics of Arguedas and Vargas Llosa brings us face-to-face with an aesthetico-ideological framework which expresses a national culture strongly impacted by the dilemmas modernization establishes in postcolonial societies, creating unavoidable conditions for symbolic production and reception. Keeping this in mind, we can ask ourselves how to evaluate (beyond its formal effectivity and its communicational efficacy) Vargas Llosa's literature and cultural activity, his ability to conquer global spaces, and his international omnipresence in contradistinction to Arguedas's rather peculiar and defiantly localist writing. Furthermore, how can we connect both projects with the broader space of globality and with the ideological challenges that exist in a world in which the spatiotemporal coordinates, the construction of affectivity, and the experience of the social and the political are rapidly changing? Some lines of reflection on these questions have to do with the definition of the intellectual field and with the function of the practice of lettered culture [*la práctica letrada*] and the dissemination of the symbolic product in the context of neoliberalism.[2]

It would be impossible not to see in Vargas Llosa's literary canonization an identification of literary institutionality with the fluctuating ideological paradigm of the intellectual the author embodies in *La ciudad y los perros*, a model which confers a *sufficient* amount of attention to cultural diversity, allowing the writer to create a dialog between the particularism of the Andean region and central discourses—exposing their *difference*—without passing judgment on the social and political mechanisms that hide behind the ideologeme of the *radical inequality* of the society that produces them. The Nobel Prize (which, as we have previously noted, confirms and documents a level of recognition that Vargas Llosa had already been enjoying for a long time) also effectively functions as documentation of citizenship in the World Republic of Letters, that transnationalized space in which the specificity and even exceptionality of national cultures is reabsorbed as an exotic and decorative note that feeds and exalts the literary world. The social criticism that runs throughout Vargas Llosa's texts almost always has (as the present study has noted) a *functional* dimension: it is applied to the representation of corruption, to the recording of decay, to the verification of the presence and extreme cruelty of evil as forms of decomposition that corrode the social body and submit it to inevitably (self-)destructive processes. Social injustice, considered a *datum* of the reality represented in the text, is perhaps in Vargas Llosa's narrative work the element which produces the greatest poetic yield, as it supports his entire fictional edifice. Hierarchies, structures of domination, power struggles, cultural differences, or class, race, and gender discrimination feed the literary machine without ever destabilizing the precarious ideological equilibrium of the text. Vargas Llosa's work is thus a narrative that explores and exposes modernity without impugning it and that assumes it as a war of position whose intricate mesh can be penetrated in miniscule and even implacable ways without its hidden supports coming to the surface of the story. It is not possible to extract from such a universe anything conclusive about the origins of a systemic problem that seems to reside within the heart of the real and that manifests itself without any further ado as irrationality, corruption, and the inevitable and definitive rupture of the social fabric.

In Arguedas's literature, in turn, structures of domination act as a retaining wall for the representation of the conflicts that trouble the Andean region as it is always against that historical, political, economic, and social horizon that the characters' profiles are outlined and an *other* world is conceived as both possible and improbable. In Arguedas's work, the narrative is organized as a form of historical imagination in which the particularities of characters and anecdotes are less important than the way in which they clearly show, through the textual body, the tense world of capitalist modernity, and the mythical and poetic contents that survive as a repository of resistance and vital force in Andean society. Arguedas's narrative is in this sense the murky water through which one can perceive the internal movement of collective subjectivity, its emotional infrastructure, and the surviving forms of intuition of nature and communitarian rationality. Arguedas's literary proposition is based on a *relational* conception of otherness that affirmatively responds to the question of whether there can be an anthropology without exoticism, in which alterity and ultimately its representation are conceived as fluid moments—not static or situated in a neutral and ahistorical space/time, as in traditional anthropology. This concept of alterity emphasizes cultural interactions that constantly modify not only the object of study but also our own point of view and the critic-theoretical categories utilized in approaching it.[3]

The contrast between both narratives has been elaborated on thematic, linguistic, technical, and ideological levels at multiple points, but it has been the ideological coincidences and contrasts that have received particular attention from literary criticism. The concepts that Vargas Llosa applies to his compatriot in *La utopía arcaica* (to cite one of the more obvious instances of textual contact between both writers), instead of shedding light on the aesthetics or ideology of the subject of the biography, help to characterize the aesthetic and representational model that the biographer constructs to illuminate the merits of his own literary style, contrasting it with that of his object of study. For Vargas Llosa, Arguedas's literature reveals an inferiority complex and a vulnerable and insecure will to victimhood, which, beginning with the disadvantages and misfortunes that accompanied the Quechua-speaking writer throughout his entire life, are relentlessly projected onto his literary work (*La utopía arcaica* 310). According to Vargas Llosa, Arguedas's use of a language that can be classified as aphasic, alienated, and erratic, a language which expresses madness and contributes to the configuration of a fictional world that, like the Tower of Babel, harbors characters who speak to each other without communicating [*se (in)comunican*] in an indecipherable, artificial, caricaturesque jargon correlative to a grotesque and incongruous reality (ibid. 320–21).

Vargas Llosa's work seems to be based on his choice to situate himself at the opposite end of the poetic spectrum. In fact, Vargas Llosa integrates (as we have shown) *difference* into identity, *domesticates* conflict, and makes it intelligible and thus assimilable for dominant sensibilities and international audiences. If Arguedas evokes "deep Peru," Vargas Llosa represents "official Peru," which encourages the path of capitalist modernity as an authoritarian and exclusive model for the Andean nation, and which simplifies the social, cultural, and political reality of the region to such an extent that it even exceeds the parameters of fiction.[4] Both instances are allegories of the possible modes of situating oneself before the *double bind* established by dualisms such as centrality/periphery, hegemony/marginality, dominant culture/dominated cultures, Spanish/Quechua, ideology/politics, and ethics/aesthetics in postcolonial societies.

Thus, there is no doubt that the ideological factor plays a fundamental role in evaluating these authors, turning into a differential element from which there arises a watershed point which is not only foreseeable but also indispensable when the time comes to evaluate the contributions and limitations of intellectual projects that, from the very beginning, use politics to support a literary edifice. Vargas Llosa's work and persona are given, along with the practically unanimous recognition of the high quality of his narrative, to heated polemic, while Arguedas's work has instead, through a slow but steady process, stimulated enthusiastic support and enduring loyalties. In Vargas Llosa's case, the Nobel Prize has not silenced adverse criticism of his ideology or his self-representation as a public intellectual both inside and outside Peru. At the same time, there has been no shortage of interpretations of his Nobel recognition as a homage to Latin American culture as a whole and to Spanish-language literatures more generally, thereby making Vargas Llosa into a kind of ambassador of the values and potential of the periphery in the hallowed spaces of World Culture. However, the public performance of Vargas Llosa's rejection of the Left in the 1970s, the shadow of Uchuraccay, his failed presidential candidacy, and his adherence to neoliberal ideology all continue to cast a shadow over his image—the image of someone who was nevertheless (paradoxically) recognized by the Swedish Academy for his contributions to clarifying the themes of power and resistance in Latin America.[5] The Nobel committee hit the nail on the head with this explanation of the merits that earned Vargas Llosa the Swedish cultural award, bringing to collective memory the ex-presidential candidate's interventions not only in the political affairs of his own country but also those of other nations, as well as interviews, opinion pieces, and diplomatic efforts that have not improved his in any case unstable public image.

To cite only one example, in 2010, a little before the Nobel Prize was announced, in an article titled "Vargas Llosa: un militante de la impunidad" ["Vargas Llosa: militant of impunity"], the Argentine jurist Alejandro Teitelbaum protested against sending Vargas Llosa as a representative of the Peruvian government to the inauguration of the Museum of Memory and Human Rights in Chile.[6] This was directly linked to Vargas Llosa's actions as chairman of a High-Level Commission named by Peruvian President Alan García for the establishment of a similar museum with a similar name in Peru, dedicated to those killed in the armed conflict of the 1980s. Vargas Llosa's presence in Chile began with his repudiation by a group of Peruvian immigrants belonging to the Movimiento Tierra y Libertad (Land and Freedom Movement) led by ex-priest Marco Arana. Teitelbaum recalls Vargas Llosa's attempt to intervene in Argentina's internal affairs through the publication of an article that appeared in *Le Monde* on 18 May 1995 under the title "Jugando con el fuego" ["Playing with fire"], in which the Peruvian writer suggested that it was time to "bury the past" in that country with regard to the assassinations and disappearances carried out by the military dictatorship of the 1970s and early 1980s. According to Vargas Llosa, these actions involved a large segment of the population and not only those directly responsible for the crimes or the military hierarchy that ordered them. Teitelbaum himself, as well as sociologist Silvia Sigal and writer Juan José Saer, responded to this article, considered an insolent intrusion into a delicate and heated issue in Argentina, in texts published in a subsequent issue of *Le Monde* on 26 May 1995. Saer explains that he will not polemicize with Vargas Llosa in spite of the truncated information and mythomania his article contains because the Peruvian writer "does not have the intellectual significance or the moral convictions that would make him not just an adversary but also a valid interlocutor" (Teitelbaum). A little while later Vargas Llosa decided to withdraw his participation as chairman of the commission in Peru, indicating in his letter of resignation "his disagreement with the passing of Legislative Decree 1097 that permits the archival of cases of human rights violations when processing them would exceed legal deadlines."[7] However, as in the case of Uchuraccay, the damage had already been done, and his belated resignation did not erase from memory certain facts which speak volumes about the insistent, prolific, and in many cases needless public activity of the ex-candidate, as well as his inconsistent ethico-idoelogical positions.

As several critics have shown, the ideological dimension that clearly manifests itself in Vargas Llosa's activity as a public intellectual has more complex and sophisticated manifestations at the literary level, having given rise to important international debates and to themes that exceed the limits of politics in Peru or even in the Andean region. In fact, Vargas Llosa's work has come to occupy international literary criticism both ideologically and aesthetically, and one sees in it an example of cultural cosmopolitanism—not only for its variety of themes and cultural references but also for its approaches to contemporary problems such as nationalism, the representation of otherness, and the construction of postcolonial subjectivity in peripheral societies.

Perhaps the most profound and nuanced analysis of Vargas Llosa's work is that which has focused on *El hablador*, a novel whose thematic and ideological features the present study has already addressed. Nonetheless, it will be useful to review the effects of a final contrast between the poetics of Arguedas and Vargas Llosa that connects to current debates. In particular, it is important to acknowledge the reach achieved by Vargas Llosa's literature in the diverse contexts in which it has been received as well as the complexity that has been discovered in his stories, particularly those that deal with the relation between nation and transnational spaces, aesthetics and politics, and otherness and identity in multicultural societies. Above all, it concerns taking note of the interpretative results that emanate from the cultural criticism projected onto Vargas Llosa's texts and the themes that this criticism privileges, with an eye to the theoretical horizons of our time.

Responding to the famed political scientist Benedict Anderson, who analyzed *El hablador* as an eminently national(ist) novel (i.e., as an allegory of the conflictive fragmentation of the Andean region and of the coexistence of diverse, and historically antagonistic, socio-cultural registers within the nation of Peru), Jonathan Culler has instead highlighted its status as a commodity primarily designed for a reader who generally accesses the Peruvian writer's work in translation. Following Timothy Brennan, Culler indicates that the genre of the novel has become a cosmopolitan form through which *the national* can fully manifest itself outside its natural context. Culler argues national culture has been to a large extent, but not completely, replaced by the globalized domain of culture which transcends borders, diluting the proximity between the producer, the product, and the consumer of symbolic commodities. This particularly affects cultural production in what used to be called the Third World, in which the function of literature (which served as a fundamental element of national identities) is being substantially transformed.[8] What particular approach to these central themes of contemporary comparative literary study does Vargas Llosa's work offer?

We must begin by emphasizing at this point that the problem of communication addressed by the main narrator of *El hablador* recalls, in more than one sense, Arguedas's dilemma in which the dominant language constitutes an obstacle for the communication of elements outside official culture. These elements require their own classification, neither *ideological* nor derived from the conqueror's epistemology. *El hablador* enters into close combat with dominant language in order to express elements from a different episteme that has been relegated to the margins of modern rationality:

> Why, in the course of all those years, had I been unable to write my story about storytellers? The answer I used to offer myself, each time I threw the half-finished manuscript of that elusive story into the wastebasket, was *the difficulty of inventing, in Spanish and within a logically consistent intellectual framework, a literary form that would suggest, with any reasonable degree of credibility, how a primitive man with a magico-religious mentality would go about telling a story.* All my attempts led each time to the impasse of a style that struck me as glaringly false, as implausible as the various ways in which philosophers and novelists of the Enlightenment had put words into the mouths of their exotic characters in the eighteenth century, when the theme of the "noble savage" was fashionable in Europe. (*El hablador* 152/*The Storyteller* 157–58, my emphasis)

The narrator confronts the contradictions and restrictions of a linguistic regime that incorporates the marks of domination through which it perpetuates the stereotypes imposed by colonialism. Once again, as we have seen before, literature confronts anthropology and reveals the foreignness—the fraudulence—of a literary elaboration that confirms, in the terrain of fiction, the hegemony of the imaginaries of the conqueror over the cosmogony of the conquered. González Echeverría recognizes Arguedas as the most dramatic representative of the narrative model that emerges from anthropology. According to his analysis, Arguedas constantly moves between the ethnographic register and literary creation: "Arguedas's extreme solution is a literal version of the reduction of the self, inherent in the process of rewriting Latin American history in the context of anthropological mediation. Method, discourse, and writing occupy the place of life" (41). For González Echeverría, Arguedas's narrative thus accomplishes a process of "de-writing" [*desescritura*] that is a necessary preliminary step for any attempt to rewrite Latin American history from a decolonizing perspective (41–42). Grand narratives (Enlightenment discourses based in the dominance of Reason) and myths that idealize Otherness in order to neutralize its difference (the "noble savage") share with literature (an eminently Westernized product) a duplicitous and fallacious mode of representing the world. In the final instance, this ends up providing evidence of the unrepresentable character and the irreducible mystery of that which has been condemned to invisibility and nonknowledge. Like anthropology, literature must begin by recognizing the crisis of discourse representing the *other* since the linguistic and epistemological model that should have revealed its specificity actually ended up obscuring it. Whether anthropological or literary, the discursive formation betrays its object of desire in the attempt to represent it, turning it into an ideological image of the self, in a reflection of the gaze of the observer. Incapable of managing the distance between subject and object, the representational operation is plunged into the same process of simulation and can only be resolved as *pastiche*: the tragedy of colonialism returns as farce.

Following Anderson's reflections regarding the mode in which *El hablador* approaches the thorny thematic of *the national* as the space in which the struggle between archaism and modernization is resolved, Culler points to a crucial issue linked to the principal dilemma the present study has been analyzing: the *double bind* that the writer confronts with respect to language and the processes of symbolic construction in the attempt to represent postcolonial otherness. Paradoxically, Culler indicates, any effort to preserve otherness (the primitive, indigenous, archaic, or vernacular) seems inevitably to be integrated as an inclusion of the Other in the Same, as a subtraction of the anomaly that alterity entails, and as an assimilation of its *difference* into the dominant identity. The intervention of modernization is thus presented, also paradoxically, as the only adequate mechanism for saving the Other from the processes of dissolution and invisibilization wrought by this same modernity. The preservation and erasure of alterity appear as two sides of the same representational operation. The discourses that intersect in *El hablador*, the coincidence and divergence of speakers, the discordance between the stylized language of the Western narrator and the Babelic speech of the Other that reveals the existence of *radically* different models of thought, all establish a postcolonial duality in the novel understood as the dissociation of consciousness[9]:

> The impossible relation between the novel's parts dramatizes the unsolvable problem of the position of the Indians in Peru, where inclusion means assimilation, transformation, and destruction of their world, just as surely as exclusion will bring their destruction. [...] preservation occurs through the intervention of an outsider; culture is preserved through imitation, repetition, and adulteration (for instance, the assimilation to Machiguenga culture of tales from Kafka and from the history of the Jews). Moreover, and this is especially pertinent to the novel's performance, from the point of view of the reader, it is precisely the "dubious," "compromised" representation, in Spanish, of the Machiguenga world that earns support for the idea of preserving this world in its purity and autonomy. (Culler, "Anderson and the Novel" 32)

The modern nation is supported precisely by the unstable and unequal coexistence of both registers, and Vargas Llosa's novel consists precisely in dramatizing the interactions between these registers. In *El hablador*, lettered mediation [*la mediación letrada*] has a deceptive, ideological function in which the bearer of the word who brings the community together and makes it cohere is based on mimicry and simulacrum. The place of the community, usurped by the logics of the global market, constitutes another line of flight for the narrator, whose aura is blurred before the experience of the inertial, cacophonous repetition of Western grand narratives. As a thematization of loss, *El hablador* could not be a more nostalgic story; nevertheless, it avoids becoming a prisoner of melancholia. Mourning for what has been lost is in Vargas Llosa's narrative not an apocalypse, nor does it end (as in Arguedas's *Zorros*) in the dissolution of the world and in the belligerent identification of the global dynamics which precipitated that downfall. Instead, loss is presented as fate, almost as a natural cycle that in a Darwinian fashion condemns the weakest to marginalization, diaspora, and disappearance. In Arguedas, the vampirism of capital maintains its diabolical rationality to the very end: the war machine of modernity not only destroys communities but also radically disarticulates Western narratives.

Throughout their work, Vargas Llosa and Arguedas sustain rather different theses about the elaboration and impact of the idea of national culture. Arguedas works to expand the concept's range, understanding it as an all-encompassing and inclusive field of daily practices and intellectual action within which cultures decimated by colonialism and marginalized by the criollo republic should converge, assuming and elaborating on their heterogeneity, with the project of modifying the structures of domination that control the national totality. The author of *Todas las sangres* understands culture as the confluence of criollo and indigenous production, technology, mass media, transculturated European contributions from the Conquest, and the massive influences from the metropolitan centers of global capitalism. His posture is not characterized by the exclusion of any cultural fields articulated by modernity in the space of the criollo nation. However, in this confluence, Arguedas always radically warns against and problematizes hierarchies and privileges, understanding the intrinsic relation between capitalism, modernity, and nation from which derive the specific forms of domination and their effects on subjectivity and collective imaginaries. He thus pushes the limits of *the traditional, the national, the popular*, but also *the modern*, attempting to elaborate a possible basis for an alternative modernity where *the local* is constituted on a platform of communitarian reclamation and affirmation beyond empty and essentialized national identities, which in Arguedas's work acquire a subversive and poetic fluidity. Arguedas's literature, along with the writing of Inca Garcilaso, is confirmed as one of the most authentically hybridized voices of the Andean region and interpellates the different segments of society that make up the Peruvian nation and the Andean region more generally. As a product of lettered culture [*producto letrado*], his work's immediate recipient is necessarily one who is literate in the dominant language. However, Arguedas's diverse work, which extends to musical, performative, and artisanal manifestations, which is concerned with the reclamation of local customs and community traditions, and which is based on the study of social phenomena like migration, economic development, and the problem of multiculturality, reaches a dimension that extends even further. In the broad intellectual field in which he circulated, Arguedas incessantly redefined and re-signified *the national* and democratized cultural practice itself, connecting to education, ethnography, cultural diffusion, collecting, practices that presuppose direct contact with indigenous and *cholo* communities and with diverse segments of criollo culture.

Thus, the theme of the nation is re-signified, moving from salvific connotations established in the background of modernity as a primary category of social analysis to the critical postulation that it presents as one of the ideological moments that is decaying along with late capitalism and its globalized and phantom forms of domination. It is interesting to see the ways in which the theme of the national approaches the question of the public and connects with strategies of literary representation.

As we have seen, Anderson, a theorist of nationalism, identifies in the paradigmatic text *El hablador* a central aspect that, with some variations, can also be detected in other works by Vargas Llosa. Anderson emphasizes the importance assumed by the *"performance of nationalism"* (*The Specter of Comparisons* 356) which *El hablador* establishes as the *mise en scène* where the different actors of the modern nation, in the context of peripheral and dependent capitalism, are inserted into the "empty and homogeneous" space/time of the novel's discourse. If in Latin America the nineteenth-century novel represented (as Sommer has established in *Foundational Fictions*) the project of national reconciliation on top of the plurality of voices and positions dramatized by fiction, the novel of the final decades of the twentieth century going into the twenty-first century can only represent the fragmentation of the nation and the unfulfilled promises that liberalism sustained on the basis of (nowadays largely considered obsolete) notions of the State, national culture, and modernity. Before the decline of the integrationist model that sought to assimilate the different cultures and social formations of the Andes to the comprehensive paradigm of the criollo nation, what persists in Vargas Llosa's "imaginarily liberal" vision is the aestheticization of the strongly divided and polarized modern world. The extremes of the social spectrum correspond, on the one hand, to the Westernized world of the modern nation and, on the other hand, to the pre-Hispanic remains represented by the decimated Machiguenga population. In the novel, the Machiguenga accept as authentic the simulacrum of their own cultural memory which is returned to them as a game of masks through the storyteller's ventriloquism. The function of the mediator is marked, as the narrator indicates to us, by melancholia and solitude. His role with respect to the community has ceased to be primordial and has become, in being spatiotemporally recycled, a form of *management* that registers an unchangeable, incommensurable reality. In the unusual and remote contexts that the novel establishes, the storyteller's tale circulates like symbolic capital, following the laws of a cultural economy that knows no limits. They are present in the expansive space of the market of competing discourses and communicational practices, the mechanisms of consumption, and the diversified audiences that demand generic and accessible content that is also, however, touched by the magic of exceptionalism and *difference*. The novel metaphorizes all these levels, which coexist as a result of narrative carnivalization. The

Tower of Babel as the place in which dissimilar stories are articulated for the broad audiences that use communication technology is a clear example of the *pastiche* brought on by the market as well as of the modifications that the role of the narrator has undergone.

For Anderson, *El hablador* is directed to an immediate audience of national readers, a notion that Culler disputes, leaning more toward a profile of Vargas Llosa as a transnationalized author inscribed in the broad space of world literature. The theme of the reader is of the utmost importance since defining the text's intended recipient makes it possible to clarify to whom the representational strategies deployed on the symbolic level are primarily being directed and to explain, therefore, some of the compositional decisions Vargas Llosa made in writing this novel. For Culler, *El hablador* reveals its deliberately cosmopolitan effects not just through an abundance of European cultural references: Dante, Kafka, the Bible, the city of Florence (as an artistic showcase whose classicism contrasts with the bows and arrows that frame a storefront display that attracts the narrator's attention and initiates the story). In addition to these allusions, Culler notes the use of a language in which proper names and technical terms are avoided in order to make reference to the objects exhibited as part of an ethnographic display. According to Culler, the choice of generic names, less precise but more comprehensible outside the cultural contexts that the novel portrays, points to a cosmopolitan reader at the international level who consumes the exoticism of the periphery as an *added value* in the literary text conceived as an apparatus of entertainment and an aestheticization of the primitive. Culler brings into focus the theme of multi/interculturalism and the impact that colonialism and modernization have had on indigenous populations, a theme whose critical political connotations are patiently presented to the foreign reader. In this regard, Culler cites Sommer, who allows the "defense of difference" as one possible interpretation of *El hablador*, a theme in the novel that, according to Sommer, can be read against Vargas Llosa's own politics, which have on many occasions expressed the idea that Peru should strive toward a "modernity without the Indian" (Culler, "Anderson and the Novel" 34).

Sommer is not alone in identifying in some of Vargas Llosa's texts a movement from politics to poetics, from ideology to aesthetics, which in literature operates as a line of flight. In his polemic with Vargas Llosa, Mario Benedetti had already indicated that Vargas Llosa's literature is situated to the left of the writer himself, allowing one to read in the composition of his fictional world an exploration of and a sensitivity toward social and political problems that the same author's essayistic work would not allow to emerge.[10] Along the same lines, James Dunkerley ends his article on *La historia de Mayta* with an observation that, although it focuses on the representation of the Shining Path in Vargas Llosa's novel, is generally valuable for its relation to the national and international political climate of the time. Dunkerley observes that the repercussions of the Shining Path, their expansion throughout the Andes, and their social and political establishment in Peru in large measure exceed Vargas Llosa's capacity for historical comprehension. According to Dunkerley, the Peruvian writer is unable to capture the full dimension of the facts:

> Even Vargas Llosa's formidable imagination cannot face the enormity of this phenomenon. Oscillating between fury, incomprehension and resignation, he has penned us a parable of great promise that terminates as a paltry conceit. *He hears his enemy but understands only the words.* (122, my emphasis)

The problem with language(s) that Arguedas and Vargas Llosa (in *El hablador*) discern and elaborate thus has to do with social conflict in a symbolic register: that of writing as a background for the dramatization of the encounter between ancestral and modern forces which split the subject and the language it represents. However, while Arguedas radicalized the representation of these dynamics through the apocalyptic Babelization that appears in *El zorro de arriba y el zorro de abajo*, Vargas Llosa limits his fiction to the representation of discursive fragmentation. This is the feature that captures the perverse yet intelligible rationality of his imaginary world. The poetic effect of this strategy is diluted in the kaleidoscopic game of Chinese boxes, also depicted in *La historia de Mayta*, converting the characters' identity into a minor epic, a micro-story in which the meaning of historical drama is metonymically submerged.

As other critics have alleged, Arguedas's death, announced and textually elaborated as an inevitable progression in *El zorro de arriba y el zorro de abajo*, constitutes a self-erasure that metaphorizes the theoretical theme of "the death of the author" with an unforeseeable and surprising materiality.[11] If it is true that by bringing about his own demise Arguedas dramatically subtracted himself from the *double bind* that tormented his own individual history and the history of the Peruvian nation, it is also true that his suicide constitutes a "portentous form of self-inscription" (Moreiras, *The Exhaustion of Difference* 200) in the body of his posthumous text, in that of the nation of Peru, and in that of the Latin American literary canon, assuring an unavoidably allegorical conclusion for the entirety of his life and work. Neither the author's life nor his work can be read without the text that announced and sealed his end, nor can this latter be separated from that event which interrupted and intervened in his writing, converting it into a symbolic instance of great illocutionary intensity.

Arguedas's death, which obviously consummates the definitive silence of his narrative voice and which can be interpreted as the allegorical cancellation of the transculturating project (Moreiras), constitutes an emblematic instance, planned as such by the author who, throughout his entire life, traversed different stages of public recognition: marginal intellectual, educator, bureaucrat, public intellectual, cultural hero, and finally martyr to the cause of indigenous resistance in the face of marginalization and inequality. If it is true (as has been pointed out numerous times) that the lines of the ethical, the aesthetic, and the political all converged in his act of self-elimination, it is also true that at this final, definitive turning point, the climactic instants of the process of (self-)recognition of the subject in all its variations were articulated. In fact, Arguedas's death sutured his imaginary to different levels, both for the writer himself and for his audience: as self-consciousness and as alienated subjectivity; as individuality marked by the sign of singularity and exceptionalism and as representation of the community; as concretion of the peculiar mode in which personal and historical determinants are configured in the *social being*; and as affective emanation of a split and paradigmatic intimacy. According to González Echeverría:

> When he committed suicide in 1969, Arguedas not only expressed the extent of his desperation but also perhaps his remorse for having used the instrument of anthropology to study a part of himself, a process that was already a kind of suicide. Feeling, perhaps, that having silenced one of his interior voices through inscription, he thought the correct thing to do would be to annihilate the Other. (223)

Vargas Llosa would develop the idea, also held by other critics, that starting from his suicide Arguedas's work could no longer be read apart from the author's biography and his tragic ending. According to Vargas Llosa, Arguedas's dead body thus interpellates—blackmails—the reader, obliging a sympathetic reading of the text in which the author's disappearance crosses the border between literature and reality with impunity.[12]

With his commentaries on Arguedas's suicide, as on many other occasions, Vargas Llosa tried to absorb the impact and significance of Arguedas's work and practice into his own discourse, offering an interpretation that appropriates the death of the Other and dissolves it in the perspective of the individual gaze. Vargas Llosa's insistent proposition that Arguedas's aesthetics can be characterized by their morbid inclinations does not disguise his rejection of the radical presentation Arguedas offers of the biopolitical dimension of peripheral capitalism, an avenue that Vargas Llosa has chosen not to travel, at least not in the expanded form one finds in Arguedas's work. The wager Vargas Llosa makes for an aesthetic inclined toward cosmopolitanism and favorable to the politics of neoliberalism is based in the *superstar* writer's individualist triumphalism in which the avatars of private life can be thematized in literature—although only in the melodramatic or farcical register, which are much more commodifiable for international markets than Arguedas's belligerent and beseeching poetics. Nevertheless, in Vargas Llosa's own work (particularly in *El hablador*, a novel that articulates some of the most potent lines of force in his literature) death is also a significant nucleus of unavoidable poetic repercussions. Anderson notes, for example, in examining the relation between Walter Benjamin's notion of the *Erzähler* and the character of Mascarita, how death, story, and narrative authority are inextricably linked, resulting in the production of melancholia as a prolonged and torturous state in the face of the inevitable disappearance of a culture. In the final pages of the *Zorros*, Arguedas, seeing his life pass before his eyes, shares these images with the reader in a hybrid biography/fiction construction that abbreviates the limit experience of the assumed death.

The other aspect Vargas Llosa emphasizes is that of Arguedas's exhibitionism which is expressed through his use of obscene language, his preference for a grotesque and absurd vision of the Andean world, his presentation of abject situations, or in Vargas Llosa's words, his "fascination with the disgusting," his "compulsive use of vulgar words," and his "excremental obsession"—almost pornographic forms of representation of the social that emerge out of a psychology altered by childhood traumas and the marginalization of the indigenous people with whom Arguedas identified. This latter's taste for abjection is combined with "the mysticism of nature," irrationalism, linguistic chaos, and an archaicizing tendency. In this way, if from Vargas Llosa's perspective the ideological aspects of Arguedas's work can be dismissed as a product resentment and of a sensibility exacerbated by trauma, the persistent "attraction to mud" that Vargas Llosa discovers in Arguedas aligns the latter with the *poètes maudits* (an advantageous aesthetic niche for containing the challenging force of Arguedas's texts), thus relegating him to the space of strangeness and anomaly (*La utopía arcaica* 325). According to Vargas Llosa, Arguedas's ideal is "arcadian, hostile to industrial development, anti-urban, nostalgic [*pasadista*]" (ibid. 307). The complexity and contradictions of his world are reduced to spectacle, a dimension which Vargas Llosa somehow seems not to know. He does, however, continue to take notice of the presence of persistent dualisms in Arguedas's work, which he calls *dilemmas—double binds*—that torment his thought and his fictional universe. One of his fundamental dilemmas is the one that established the paradoxical identification of modernization with social justice. Vargas Llosa states that the Arguedas who came from Quechua culture resisted progress out of fear for the annihilation of indigenous culture:

> However, at the same time, the Arguedas who resided in Lima, intellectual of advanced social ideas, realized there was no escape: justice would mean modernization, and that would mean the Hispanicization and Westernization of the Indian, even when this process was carried out by socialism. This dilemma could not be resolved because it simply had no solution. (ibid. 306)

In Vargas Llosa's reading, Arguedas's literature constructs "a fresco of evil" in which the systematic perversion of modernity, which builds progress on the annihilation of otherness, is read in ethico-aesthetic code as the inevitable corruption that it unleashes onto humanity. The demonic world of Chimbote is presented as an orgiastic explosion of irrationalities. The logic of capital suspends reason and replaces it with the incessant machine of productivity in which the subject is consumed by the magical and destructive force of the object.

All these irresolvable tensions necessarily lead to death, which cancels the dilemma—at least for the subjectivity who perceives it. Thus, all possibility of consensus or negotiation is eliminated. The "impossible harmony" of the Andean world, which Cornejo Polar so expertly analyzes in *Escribir en el aire* (1994) [*Writing in the Air: Heterogeneity and the Persistence of Oral Tradition in Andean Literatures* (2013)] and in his articles on cultural heterogeneity, has definitively given way to the emergence of contradictions that do not accept dialectical synthesis.

Alberto Moreiras has seen in the maintenance of the antagonisms of the Andean region that Arguedas's narrative symbolically represents a rejection and a final, definitive renunciation of the conciliatory spirit of transculturation that Arguedas's work—and life/death—would carry to its conclusion. According to Moreiras:

> Arguedas's demon is the uncanny will to speak two languages, to live in two cultures, to feel with two souls: a double demon, demon of doubling, perhaps happy but also mischievous, as we shall see. In his affirmation of doubledness, Arguedas makes manifest his forceful rejection of the ideology of cultural conciliation, indeed stating his final conviction that, at the cultural level, there can be no conciliation without forced subordination. (*The Exhaustion of Difference* 196)

Among all of Arguedas's texts, it is surely the *Zorros* that most forcefully and without a doubt most dramatically portrays the dilemma—the *double bind*—of the postcolonial condition and the consequences of late capitalism in peripheral regions. Overflowing with affects and desires that no longer express the subject's humanity so much as its out-of-control dehumanization, *El zorro de arriba y el zorro de abajo* is an exercise in abjection and poetry, dis-identity, and the reaffirmation of the fundamental ground of the *Andean being*. This latter is defined not by means of essentialisms or universalisms but in relation to the contingent and precise crossroads of the diachronic processes and the inescapable politico-economic synchronies that place the subject before the horror of the non-knowledge of the self and of its urban and natural environment. If any proof is needed of the novel's extreme denunciation and its interpellative value, its end, that is, its ends, both real and fictional, are there to corroborate the terms on which *the writing of the limit* is performed and in what way one could imagine the possible return of life after the cataclysm of individual and collective death, that is to say, on "the edge of time" (Cornejo Polar, *Los universos narrativos* 300).

Additionally, according to some critics, within the Quechua cosmovision, death does not have the character of an inevitable and definitive closing but is associated instead with the idea of the renewal and continuity of various cycles of life. In this sense, as Carlos Huamán has argued:

> [t]he suicide that the "end" of the work announces is not in itself a final death for Arguedas or for the Quechua world; it is above all a path to renewal and continuity linked to the Quechua-Andean cosmic reality. [...] Death— as Cornejo Polar says—"is occasionally a sign of redemption: a change in the negativity of the world, through the heroic act, in an affirmative plenitude." (Huamán 77–78)

Fernando Rivera has also emphasized the importance of affect and the Andean notions of *reciprocity* and *donation* as fundamental elements for *reading* Arguedas's death within the parameters of Quechua culture:

> This limit where the author is taken to the extreme point of removing himself from the world of experience (committing suicide) to let writing become possible in this world as well, to make himself into writing and leave himself written in a sort of silent and infinite writing, which says without saying, and which makes fiction or this new form of fiction the only way to write the world of experience: erasing oneself from it so that others' voices may be restored. (312)

Along these same lines, Rowe has called attention to the idea of the continuity of the subject according to the conception of *Dioses y hombres de Huarochirí* [Gods and men of Huarochirí], in which death is understood as regeneration and resurgence, not as the disintegration and annihilation of what exists ("El lugar de la muerte"). The primary message consists, more than in the existential reemergence of the subject, in the renewed continuity of the social bonds which contain him or her and exceed the limits of the individual and contingent. The constant presence of death, which constitutes the subject from his or her early, formative stages ("death has made itself present to me since I was a child"), intensifies the experience of life and the desire to denounce the destructive forces that attack humanity, the environment, and the community's values and dreams of redemption and social emancipation. At the same time, the childhood/death relation in Arguedas links trauma to the "full body of death" (Deleuze and Guattari, *Anti-Oedipus* 8, qtd. in Rowe, "El lugar de la muerte" 171), an ecstatic body that exists to die (a body without an image or that is losing its image), and the incessant movement of desire.

Death and writing are thus closely intertwined in *El zorro de arriba y el zorro de abajo* and linked by an *agonic* process, related at once to struggle and the nearness of death, with action and the end of life (Rowe, "El lugar de la muerte" 168), as if it had to do with inseparable and mutually conditioned moments in the search for an enunciative position from which to cover the trajectory of life and meaning. Indeed, the relation between death and literature, as has been established by extension between literature and silence (this latter as the death of language) is inscribed in a long poetic tradition which connects to Maurice Blanchot, whom Jacques Rancière evokes in his studies of mute speech. According to Blanchot, as a radical experience of language, literature is an imaginary Tibet in which the sacred aspect of the sign resides; through it one approaches the experience of the night, of the desert, of suicide, forming a version of the Absolute. The poetic text is a production of silence, a confrontation with the unrepresentability of the human experience, a limit experience: "A literary work is, for one who knows how to penetrate it, a rich resting place of silence, a firm defense and a high wall against this eloquent immensity that addresses itself to us by turning us sway from ourselves" (Blanchot, qtd. in Rancière, *Mute Speech* 32).

Arguedas's suicide emblematically ties all these significations together, thus converting his final text into an epitaph, a text engraved on the author's tombstone, thus sealing with mute words the real body's disappearance. More than simply as *writing*, the *Zorros* are read from this perspective as an *elegiac inscription*. The work's final silence is thus neither reticent nor elliptical, neither hiatus nor omission nor absence of sense; it is a mute, explosive language charged with connotations and suggestions, saturated by silenced voices, repressions, calls, and unrepresentable contents. Exploitation, abjection, and marginality "have no name": they resist being signified and reduced to the conventionality of the sign.

Sartre has indicated that "silence is a moment of language; being silent is not being mute; it is to refuse to speak, and therefore to keep on speaking" ("What is Literature?" 38). If, in the *Zorros*, language expressed proliferation but also anomaly ("el Mudo," "La Muda," and *el tartamudo*/Stut as instances in which meaning recedes, subtracting itself from fluid and rationalized circulation) and integrated, along with the discourse of the Diaries, interlinguistic contaminations, vulgar, archaic, judgmental, and enigmatic forms, including neologisms, omens, prophecies, obscenities, or simply different sounds and music, then silence is also a *boiling* [*hervor*] that is indefinitely prolonged, not only toward the future. It also goes back into the past—as Edmundo Gómez Mango's reading suggests—on a search for the mother tongue and the mother, lost before time:

> To invent a new language in order to resuscitate, reanimate a dead mother tongue: perhaps (it cannot be established any other way) that absent fantasy is the empty and blind point of view of Arguedas's poetics. Even in his suicide, his writing, the invention of a new polyphonic and multi-linguistic poem, he never stopped questioning the origin and the death of the poetic word. His initiating, inexhaustible search for a language, the journey through the linguistic hell of "los *Zorros*" allowed him to discern an originary silence, an

original lack of the word, the muteness of a mother tongue that prematurely and permanently went quiet. (368)

If in the final instance individual death has a revitalizing sense insofar as it can be seen not only as personal redemption but as fertilization and renewal of life, it is also true that its unrepresentable reality has multiple aesthetic, ethical, and political effects.[13] Lienhard remarks, for example:

> With a gunshot as a final period, *El zorro* abandons the terrain of literature practiced as a game and opens an interrogation of the possibility and opportunity of writing a novel in a country like Peru.
> [...]
> The sequel to *El zorro* will not be literary but political: it will make the collective reader who grows bit by bit throughout the novel become at the end, somewhat mythically, an actor in history. (*La voz y su huella* 169, 171)

In this way, literature convokes life, invites action like resistance to the dynamics the *Zorros* expose through a simultaneously supplicating and exasperated denunciation. Inorganic, dispersed, and fragmented, *the social* summons *the political*; like an ancient tragedy, it aims, through sympathy and terror, at a catharsis that can only activate the indigenous political subject and social actor through an agenda of collective emancipation.[14] The literary text is thus outlined against the turbulent backdrop of history, an iconic, unavoidable, and provocative image in which guilt and sacrifice, martyrdom and punishment, delirium and painful rationality mix. On the tragic proscenium lies the author's cadaver, the dead body the writer has attached to himself and with his own hand, using literature as the apparatus for this attachment, like the pin that pierces the body of the butterfly to put it on display forever in the permanent collection of modernity. While the cadaver conquers immortality, the poetic, alienated word continues to float like a void full of meaning in the rarefied space of ideology, a story in search of *listening* that would give sense to the literary gesture and the social experience that sustains it.

The chilling details included in the final pages of "Último diario?" ["Last Diary?"] (with which *El zorro de arriba* closes) demonstrate a final desire to intermix reality and fiction, to model an image of the self that is completed in death and with which it acquires a final significance, a communitary dimension.[15] As is widely known, Arguedas gave instructions in this final text for his funeral, attempting to assure that it would not be "bullshit" but rather constitute a "palpitation," that is, a performance felt and represented by friends, according to his highlander tastes and with the values that guided his existence and intellectual work.[16]

Together with this final appeal to the affective, he also communicates the self-recognition of his exemplary value with which his individuality acquires historical resonance:

> Perhaps with me one historical cycle draws to a close and another begins in Peru, with all that this represents. It means the closing of the cycle of the consoling calender lark, of the whip, of being driven like beasts of burden, of impotent hatred, of mournful funeral "uprisings," of the fear of God and of the predominance of that God and his protégées, his fabricators. It signifies the opening of the cycle of light and of the indomitable, liberating strength of Vietnamese man, of the fiery calender lark, of the liberator God. That God who is coming back into action. Vallejo was the beginning and the end.
> [...]
> In me bid farewell to a Peruvian era... (Arguedas, *El zorro de arriba* 245–46 / *The Fox from Up Above* 259)

This final phrase, which is later repeated, creating a kind of recurring motif in the text, points to an aesthetico-ideological objective that underlies the lyricism and emotional intensity of Arguedas's writing and is perhaps the key to his poetic art: construction from culture, from a national-popular subject articulated not just from the point of view of class but also ethnically. It is from this subject that it would be possible to *elaborate* the social conflict that troubles the Andean region and to achieve the implementation of a modernity *with* the indigenous, that integrates culture without denaturalizing it, that maintains *difference*, overcoming antagonism and that does not reduce the drama of inequality to the performance of *difference*.[17]

What limits and limitations do communications technologies nevertheless recognize? How do we liberate the contents of the prison of language? To what extent does the sign negotiate over the background of the signified? As Spivak argues, "recognition begins as differentiation" (244). Nevertheless, recognition only exists as a relational, socialized process that only acquires its full meaning in the context of the community. Arguedas, who knew the games and traps of language and practiced translation as a semiotic bridge between classes, cultures, and temporalities, brought his life and his work to an end in Spanish, allowing the dissociated and kaleidoscopic writing of his *Zorros* to realize its full communicative potential. His writing thus passed from chaos to "order," from Babelic (mythic, legendary, ritualized, local) composition to national language, the language of consensus and of citizenship, the language of oppression, exclusion, and modernity. Thus ended the long and torturous journey marked by the mediation of the writer who managed and administrated intercultural contacts through translation (understood as the traffic of not only linguistic but also cultural and epistemological meaning), the discourse of the subaltern who exists as a specter established in the Peruvian nation, and, metonymically, in the lettered city that discursively organizes it. That which goes from "dirty" (contaminated, hybrid, impure) saying to the communicative "cleanness" with which the "¿Último diario?" (to refer only to the evolution registered in his final work) is the consciousness that the intellectual acquires as translator/intercultural producer of his own endeavor and of the limits that condition it. Arguedas is conscious that cultural translation can be reduced to a monological exercise if it does not account for the active participation of the recipient who makes sense of the communicative strategy. As Spivak has argued, returning to the theme of the intelligibility of the message of the *Other* in subaltern conditions, communication depends on that *hearing* as much as it depends on the linguistic code that it utilizes in each case: "The founding task of translation does not disappear by fetishizing the native languages [...] Sometimes I read and hear that the subaltern can speak in their native languages [...] No speech is speech if it is not heard. It is this act of hearing-to-respond that may be called the imperative to translate" (Spivak 252–253).

It is in the indeterminate and perhaps indeterminable zone created by the *double bind* of postcolonial consciousness where Arguedas's discourse is inscribed (at least according to some readings): in that space in which the word resounds even without being heard, conquering an existence that obtains no response and that never constitutes that *imperative to translate* Spivak discusses, thus allowing for the parallel and always conflictive existence of existential and cultural registers. Homi Bhabha calls attention to the peculiar type of subjectivity that is situated at the crucial point of this *splitting* of the subject and that is related more generally to the construction of authority (whether social, cultural, or political) and to the possibility of disarticulating the voice of power. For Bhabha, as for Spivak, the postcolonial subject is part of that problematic process of identification and self-recognition, and its imaginaries are intertwined with that historical, political, and social (as well as epistemological and representational) circumstance. Learning how to exist in this conjuncture constitutes a survival strategy that implies constant reaccommodations and negotiations, such as those that dramatically unfold in Arguedas's work. Bhabha takes from Walter Benjamin the idea of the disjunction of temporalities in which a historical event or situation occurs, an idea which can also be seen in Arguedas. This is the *third space* understood as the interval or place in which diverse and even antagonistic temporal registers coexist. The *third space* is that form of contemporaneity in which different histories develop, that gives rise to the simultaneity to which Enrique Lihn refers and which, not coincidentally, Cornejo Polar and Enrique Mayer take up again in their studies of the works we have addressed here.

Arguedas's work constitutes a complex and agonic process of intercultural negotiation that is not exempt from contradictions, concessions, or failures. In his very difference, Arguedas left behind the transnationalized canonical register subject to the commodification and the symbolic and mass media exchange of our era. The symbolic register of language in his work crosses through diverse forms of diglossia, hybridization, and lexical and morphological "simulacra." This process of exploration and communicative experimentation completes a journey that goes from attempts at inverse transculturation (Moreiras, Legrás) to the refuge of Spanish, the language in which he transmitted the definitive and crucial experience of the termination of his life and his work—an iconic moment the individual and collective significance of which the author was certainly conscious. It is in this language, Spanish, and not in the emotional and intimate register of Quechua, that the writer bid farewell to the world and gave precise instructions for his burial. It is from this dominant register, which assures that his voice would be heard and his message would spread, reaffirming the desire for the recognition of the ideological and aesthetic significance of a work from which a new phase in national culture can begin: "Perhaps with me one historical cycle draws to a close and another begins in Peru, with all that this represents..." (Arguedas, *El zorro de arriba* 245/*The Fox from Up Above* 259).

Does this final concession to the dominant language constitute an inevitable end for "narratives of failure"? Is it a pragmatic and irreproachable solution to the *double bind* imposed by colonization and reaffirmed by the criollo republic? Is it an Orwellian form of "doublethink" that the dominant cultural registers have been able to establish in the subject's consciousness? Is it a form of cooptation of marginality or a symbolic survival strategy? Is it a form of being "peripheral at the top" (Spivak 2) that makes it possible to participate simultaneously in the epistemological privileges of marginality and in the visibility of the dominant registers? Is identity in fact a commodity (a construct produced for exchange in the cultural market) whose use value and exchange value oscillate and are negotiated depending on the context, circumstance, and proposal? Is translation in the final instance, as Spivak argues, a "necessary impossibility" (270) which we inevitably place before the ultimate void of meaning and find ourselves situated (at least with Arguedas's work) on the edge of that abyss? These questions constitute a far-from-minor inheritance left to us by José María Arguedas's work as an opening onto decolonizing horizons in Latin America.

Like in an arrangement of Chinese boxes, Arguedas's writing contains multiple expressions of aesthetic performativity that attempt to represent the cultural plurality of the Andean region in all its nuance. From this multiplicity emerges the idea of abundance and complexity as much as the idea of chaos and disruption of the dominant order. It would be erroneous to look for some sign of harmony or equilibrium in the fracturing of this literature, whose powerful and unstable framework is testimony to the profound ruptures in the social and cultural fabric of the region, to its proliferating diversity, and to its inexhaustible symbolic productivity. Framed by the myths of modernity (identity, nation) which he challenged from their deepest foundations, besieged by the phantoms of an inescapable premodernity that resides in popular belief and in the never-defeated structures of power and domination, Arguedas's poetics anticipates postmodernity through its irreverent performativity of *difference* and through its reclamation of marginal discourses and positions in a world characterized by fragmentation and desperation. In an era of globalization, Arguedas's work, precisely for its unresolved tensions, for the figurative and unstable world it represents, and for the *difference* it introduces, situates us in a place where it is possible to question the new processes of hegemonic affirmation and cultural marginalization that globality drives and legitimizes. As Spivak suggests, facing the dynamics of cultural homogenization driven by globalization, "the Tower of Babel is our refuge." The diversity of languages and the plurality of intractable imaginaries that it sustains constitute some of the most effective and seductive challenges of our time. In this sense, Arguedas's work should be located, as the author himself informed us in his "¿Último diario?," in the iconic place in which he began to close one cycle and open another, and not only in the Andean region.

Notes

1. In Fredric Jameson's terms, Arguedas would have accomplished the allegorical act *par excellence* because of the method, location, and record of his suicide and because of the way in which it seemed carefully articulated to his literary project. In his now-classic text "Third World Literature in the Era of Multinational Capitalism," Jameson refers to what he calls "national allegories" in relation to certain basic models of fiction that come from so-called third-world cultures. Jameson says that these texts project "a political dimension in the form of national allegory: the story of the private individual destiny is always an allegory of the embattled situation of the public third-world culture and society" (69). As is well-known, this conception of Third World literature has been widely debated. In this regard, see Ahmad, for example.
2. This theme (an exhaustive treatment of which would exceed the limits of the present study) refers to the mode in which the literary institution functions, both within the parameters of national culture and in the wider context of globality. The theme is also linked to the already mentioned notion of "world literature."
3. In this regard, see Augé.
4. Degregori asks, for example, how the author who was able to portray a world full of social and cultural nuances and complexities in works such as *La casa verde* could be the same person who, in his electoral campaign, handled the theme of modernity in such a naïve and extremely simplistic way. One response to this question can be found in the behavior characteristic of a generation that began to involve Peru in new international circuits in the attempt to achieve thereby an alliance with the working classes (Degregori 74–75).
5. The Swedish Academy indicated that they conferred the ward on Vargas Llosa "for his cartography of the structures of power and his trenchant images of individual resistance, revolt, and defeat" (http://www.nobelprize.org/nobel_prizes/literature/laureates/2010/).
6. An attorney and jurist, Teitelbaum is the author of, among other books, *La armadura del capitalismo*, *Ética y derechos humanos en la cooperación internacional*, and *La crisis actual del derecho al desarrollo*.
7. This resignation letter was published in *El Comercio* on 13 September 2010 and is reproduced in http://elcomercio.pe/noticia/638568/mario-vargas-llosa-renuncio-presidencia-comision-lugar-memoria.
8. According to Culler (citing Brennan): "In particular, there has emerged an important strain of third-world writing: 'the lament for the necessary and regrettable insistence of nation-forming, in which the writer proclaims his identity with a country whose artificiality and exclusiveness have driven him

into a kind of exile—a simultaneous recognition of nationhood and alienation from it.'"
9. See note 3 of the "Opening" of the present study.
10. Referring to Vargas Llosa's comments on Left-wing intellectuals, Benedetti points out, "For some time now we have resigned ourselves to the fact that [Vargas Llosa] is not with us, not on our side but with them on the opposite side; however, we cannot resign ourselves, because of ideological differences or perhaps due to the privileges derived from fame, to stoop to low blows or dirty tricks that would reinforce their respectable arguments. Fortunately, Vargas Llosa's work is located to the left of its author, and will continue to be read with enthusiasm by zombies, robots, and Pavlov's dogs" (48).
11. In this regard, see the Forges's and Moreiras's interpretations.
12. Without giving in to the temptation of critical generosity, Vargas Llosa points out: "Without that body, offered as a pledge of sincerity, the narrator's consternation, preaching, and last will and testament would be seen as insolence, a lot of hot air, a not very entertaining game, due to the clumsy craftsmanship of many pages. The author's cadaver retroactively fills in the story's blank spaces, gives reason to unreason, and order to the chaos that threatens to frustrate the novel and make it into a fiction (which it also is), into a shocking document" (*La utopía arcaica* 300).
13. Cornejo Polar notes that Arguedas has a peculiar conception of death as the renewal of vital and cosmic energies and as a moment that makes the cyclical continuity of cultures split apart (*Los universos narrativos*). He pursues this idea in *Los ríos profundos*, "La agonía de Rasu-Ñiti," *Todas las sangres*, and, of course, in *El zorro de arriba y el zorro de abajo*. Vargas Llosa also deals with the theme of suicide in "Literatura y suicidio" ["Literature and suicide"], as does Rowe in "El lugar de la muerte." Moreiras takes it up as an allegorical moment that connects to the debate on transculturation.
14. On the theme of tragedy in Arguedas, see Forges, *José María Arguedas: del pensamiento dialéctico al pensamiento trágico* and Legrás, "*Yawar fiesta*: el retorno de la tragedia." The latter is applied to the theme of social antagonism and the dialectic with interesting theoretical effects connected to almost all of Arguedas's work.
15. Rowe has referred (as have others) to "the removal of the border between the empirical author and the implicit author, between life and writing" in Arguedas ("El lugar de la muerte" 167). In this article, Rowe also refers to "the incidence of death in the formation of the subject" and to the different types of death that are represented in Arguedas's narrative work: social death, the expulsion of discourse (which caused a kind of "narcissistic wound"), the ritualized death of Rasu-Ñitu, spiritual death, and so on.
16. Maruja Martínez has left a testimony of Arguedas's funeral, in which the cadaver attracted a multitude and ritual sutured the wound left by death:

"They say that Arguedas asked that there be speeches, that they be delivered by his students, his friends. Skinny 'Manzana,' president of the Federation of Students of the Agrarian University, was in charge of his teacher's final farewell. But I didn't understand very well what he said because his tears didn't allow him to clearly enunciate. Many of us were crying. And I could see Chepo, the brave mill organizer, 'Ojos,' 'Cabezón,' and other students, comrades, and party leaders, shedding the most beautiful tears one could ever imagine. At the moment in which the casket was placed into the tomb, on top of the pavilion appeared the figure of an Indian dressed for a feast; my myopia did not allow me to see him well, and I was also pretty far away. But I heard him shouting in Quechua. The eulogies and the militant farewells suddenly stopped, out of respect for this sad clamor which, in spite of not understanding it, I felt was a desperate and hopeless good-bye."

17. Legrás points to this question when he states that "an important point of contention focused on the definition of the popular subject in the Andes: is the subject an Indian or a peasant?" The Marxist formulation of this problem comes from the thought of Mariátegui, whose reflections in this regard served as a guide for Quijano, Cornejo Polar, and others.

WORKS CITED

Ahmad, Aijaz. 1986. Jameson's rhetoric of Otherness and the 'national allegory'. *Social Text* 15: 65–88.
Anderson, Benedict. 1998. *The specter of comparisons. Nationalism, Southeast Asia, and the world.* London: Verso.
Appadurai, Arjun (ed.). 1988. *The social life of things: Commodities in cultural perspective.* Cambridge: Cambridge University Press.
Archibald, Priscilla. 1998. Andean anthropology in the era of development theory. In *José María Arguedas: Reconsiderations for Latin American cultural studies*, ed. Ciro A. Sandoval and Sandra M. Boschetto-Sandoval, 3–34. Athens: Ohio University Center for International Studies.
Archibald, Priscilla. 2003. Overcoming science in the Andes. *Revista Canadiense de Estudios Hispánicos* 27.3(Spring): 407–434.
Archibald, Priscilla. 2011. *Imagining modernity in the Andes.* Lewisburg: Bucknell University Press.
Arguedas, José María. 1935. *Agua. Los escoleros. Warma kuyay.* Lima: Cía. de Impresiones y Publicidad.
Arguedas, José María. 1941. *Yawar fiesta.* Lima: Editorial Horizonte.
Arguedas, José María. 1954. *Diamantes y pedernales. Agua.* Lima: Juan Mejía Baca y P.L. Villanueva.
Arguedas, José María. 1958. *Los ríos profundos.* Ed. Ricardo González Vigil. Madrid: Editorial Cátedra.
Arguedas, José María. 1960–1961. *Cuentos religioso-mágicos quechuas de Lucanamarca,* 142–216. Lima: Folklore Americano.
Arguedas, José María. 1961. *El Sexto.* Lima: Editorial Mejía Baca.
Arguedas, José María. 1964. *Todas las sangres.* Buenos Aires: Editorial Losada.

Arguedas, José María. 1969. *El sueño del pongo: Cuento quechua.* Santiago de Chile: Editorial Universitaria.
Arguedas, José María. 1975. *Formación de una cultura nacional indoamericana. Selección y prólogo de Ángel Rama.* México: Siglo XXI.
Arguedas, José María. 1976. *Señores e indios.* Buenos Aires: Calicanto.
Arguedas, José María. 1978. *Deep Rivers.* Trans. Frances Horning Barraclough. Austin: University of Texas Press.
Arguedas, José María. 1980. *Between Quechua and Spanish.* Trans. Luis Harss. *Review* 25/26: 15–16.
Arguedas, José María. 1983. La novela y el problema de la expresión literaria en el Perú. *Obras completas*, 193–198. Lima: Editorial Horizonte.
Arguedas, José María. 1990. *El zorro de arriba y el zorro de abajo.* Madrid: Editorial Archivos.
Arguedas, José María. 1992. No soy un aculturado. In *El zorro de arriba y el zorro de abajo*, 256–258. México: Colección Archivos.
Arguedas, José María. 2000. I am not an acculturated man.... In *The fox from up above and the fox from down below*, 268–270. Trans. Frances Horning Barraclough. Pittsburgh: University of Pittsburgh Press.
Arguedas, José María. 2009. Entre el kechwa y el castellano, la angustia del mestizo. *Qepa Wiñaq...Siempre. Literatura y antropología*, 141–144. Madrid: Iberoamericana-Vervuert.
Arguedas, José María, et al. 1985. *¿He vivido en vano? Mesa Redonda sobre Todas las sangres. 23 de junio de 1965.* Lima: Instituto de Estudios Peruanos.
Augé, Marc. 1996. *El sentido de los otros. Actualidad de la antropología.* Buenos Aires: Paidós.
Augé, Marc. 1998. *Los no lugares. Espacios del anonimato. Una antropología de la sobremodernidad.* Barcelona: Gedisa Editorial.
Ávila, Francisco de (ed.). 1966. *Dioses y hombres de Huarochirí.* Bilingual edition. Trans. José María Arguedas. Lima: Universidad Antonio Ruiz de Montoya.
Ballón Aguirre, Enrique. 2006. *Tradición oral peruana. Literaturas ancestrales y populares.* Lima: Fondo Editorial de la Pontificia Universidad Católica del Perú.
Banville, John. 2012. Rebel, Hero, Martyr. *The New York Review of Books*, October 25. http://www.nybooks.com/articles/archives/2012/oct/25/rebel-hero-martyr/?pagination=false. Accessed 7 Nov 2012.
Barrenechea, Alfredo. 1998. Mario Vargas Llosa. In *Peregrinos de la lengua. Confesiones de los grandes autores latinoamericanos*, 263–305. Madrid: Alfaguara.
Bateson, Gregory. 1972. *Steps to an ecology of mind: Collected essays in anthropology, psychiatry, evolution, and epistemology.* Chicago: University Of Chicago Press.
Baudrillard, Jean. 1975. *The mirror of production.* New York: Telos Press.
Baudrillard, Jean. 1978. *Cultura y simulacro.* Barcelona: Editorial Kairós.
Baudrillard, Jean. 1981. *For a critique of the political economy of the sign.* St. Louis: Telos Press.

Baudrillard, Jean. 1996. *The system of objects*. London: Verso.
Baudrillard, Jean. 1998. *The consumer society*. London: Sage Publications.
Beasley-Murray, Jon. 2008. Arguedasmachine: Modernity and affect in the Andes. *Iberoamericana* 8(30): 113–128.
Benedetti, Mario. 1984. Ni corruptos ni contentos. *Vuelta* 8(92): 47–48.
Bernabé, Mónica. 2006. José María Arguedas traductor. In *José María Arguedas: Hacia una poética migrante*, ed. Segio R. Franco, 379–396. Pittsburgh: Instituto Internacional de Literatura Iberoamericana.
Bhabha, Homi. 1994. *The location of culture*. London/New York: Routledge.
Blanchot, Maurice. 2003. *The book to come*. Stanford: Stanford University Press.
Boff, Leonardo. 1989. *Desde el lugar del pobre*. Bogotá: Ediciones Paulinas.
Booker, M. Keith. 1994. *Vargas Llosa among the postmodernists*. Gainesville: University Press of Florida.
Bourdieu, Pierre. 1998. *Practical Reason: On the Theory of Action*. Trans. Randal Johnson et al. Stanford: Stanford University Press.
Brennan, Timothy. 1990. The national longing for form. In *Nation and narration*, ed. Homi Bhabha, 44–70. New York: Routledge.
Brooks, Peter. 1995. *The melodramatic imagination. Balzac, Henry James, Melodrama, and mode of excess*. New Haven: Yale University Press.
Bueno Chávez, Raúl. 1984. Relato oral y visión del mundo andino: "'El lagarto' y otros cuentos de Lucanamarca". *Revista de Crítica Literaria Latinoamericana* 10(20): 9–28.
Cardoso, Fernando H. 1973. *Problemas del subdesarrollo latinoamericano*. México: Nuestro Tiempo.
Cardoso, Fernando H., and Enzo Faletto. 1969. *Dependencia y desarrollo en América Latina*. México: Siglo XXI.
Carvajal, José. Oscar Collazos: la inconformidad irremediable. *Centro Virtual Isaacs*. S.f. http://dintev.univalle.edu.co/cvisaacs/collazos/la%20incoformidad.htm. Accessed 10 Oct 2012.
Casanova, Pascale. 2001. *La república mundial de las letras*. Barcelona: Anagrama.
Casanova, Pascale. 2005. Literature as world. *New Left Review* 31: 71–90.
Castañeda, Belén S. 1990. Mario Vargas Llosa: el novelista como crítico. *Hispanic Review* 58(3): 347–359.
Castañeda, Luis Hernan. La seduccion de las ruinas: *El hablador* de Mario Vargas Llosa y la transculturacion narrativa de Angel Rama. http://www.elhablador.com/especial18_castaneda.html. Accessed 8 Oct 2012.
Castro, Dante. *La fiesta del chivo* y el Premio Nobel. 8 Oct 2010. http://cercadoajeno.blogspot.com/2010/10/la-fiesta-del-chivo-y-el-premio-nobel.html. Accessed 8 Oct 2012.
Castro-Klarén, Sara. 1973. *El mundo mágico de José María Arguedas*. Lima: Instituto de Estudios Peruanos.
Castro-Klarén, Sara. 1988. *Mario Vargas Llosa. Análisis introductorio*. Lima: Latinoamericana Editores.

Castro-Klarén, Sara. 1990. *Understanding Mario Vargas Llosa*. Columbia: University of South Carolina Press.
Castro-Klarén, Sara. 1996. Monuments and scribes: *El hablador* Addresses ethnography. In *Structures of power: Essays on twentieth-century Spanish-American fiction*, ed. Terry J. Peavler and Peter Standish, 39–59. Albany: SUNY Press.
Castro-Klarén, Sara. 2000. 'Like a pig, when he's thinkin: Arguedas on affect and on becoming an animal. In *The fox from up above and the fox from down below*, ed. José María Arguedas. Pittsburgh: University of Pittsburgh Press.
Castro-Klarén, Sara. 2001–2002. 'Como chancho cuando piensa'. El afecto cognitivo en Arguedas y el con-vertir animal. *Revista canadiense de estudios hispánicos* XXVI, 1–2 (Fall–Winter): 25–39.
Castro-Klarén, Sara. 2003. The nation in ruins: Archaeology and the rise of the nation. In *Beyond imagined communities. Reading and writing the nation in nineteenth-century Latin America*, ed. Sara Castro-Klarén and John Charles Chasteen, 161–195. Baltimore: Johns Hopkins University.
Castro Urioste, José. 2000. Mario Vargas Llosa's *El hablador* as a discourse of conquest. *Studies in Twentieth Century Literature* 24: 241–255.
Clifford, James, and George Marcus (eds.). 1986. *Writing culture. The poetics and politics of ethnography*. Berkeley: University of California Press.
Collazos, Oscar, Julio Cortázar, et al. 1977. *Literatura en la revolución y revolución en la literatura*. México: Siglo XXI.
Cornejo Polar, Antonio. 1974. *Los universos narrativos de José María Arguedas*. Losada: Buenos Aires.
Cornejo Polar, Antonio. 1977. *La novela peruana: siete estudios*. Lima: Horizonte.
Cornejo Polar, Antonio. 1978. El indigenismo y las literaturas heterogéneas: Su doble estatuto sociocultural. *Revista de Crítica Literaria Latinoamericana* 7–8: 7–21.
Cornejo Polar, Antonio. 1980. *Literatura y sociedad en el Perú: la novela indigenista*. Lima: Lasontay.
Cornejo Polar, Antonio. 1981. *La cultura nacional, problema y posibilidad*. Lima: Lluvia.
Cornejo Polar, Antonio. 1982. *Sobre literatura y crítica latinoamericanas*. Caracas: Universidad Central de Venezuela.
Cornejo Polar, Antonio. 1984. *Vigencia y universalidad de José María Arguedas*. Lima: Horizonte.
Cornejo Polar, Antonio. 1989a. *La formación de la tradición literaria en el Perú*. Lima: CEP.
Cornejo Polar, Antonio. 1989b. Hipótesis sobre la narrativa peruana última. *La novela peruana*, 241–258. Lima: Editorial Horizonte.
Cornejo Polar, Antonio. 1994a. *Escribir en el aire. Ensayo sobre la heterogeneidad socio-cultural en las literaturas andinas*. Lima: Editorial Horizonte.

Cornejo Polar, Antonio. 1994b. *The multiple voices of Latin American literature.* Berkeley: University of California.
Cornejo Polar, Antonio. 1995. La literatura hispanoamericana del siglo XIX: continuidad y ruptura (Hipótesis a partir del caso andino). In *Esplendores y miserias del siglo XIX. Cultura y sociedad en América Latina*, ed. Beatriz González-Stephan, Javier Lasarte, Graciela Montaldo and María Julia Daroqui, 11–23. Caracas: Monte Ávila Ediciones.
Cornejo Polar, Antonio. 1996. Una heterogeneidad no-dialéctica. Sujeto y discurso migrantes en el Perú moderno. *Revista Iberoamericana* LXII, 176/177 (Julio–Diciembre): 837–844.
Cornejo Polar, Antonio. 1997. *Mestizaje e hibridez: los riesgos de las metáforas.* La Paz: Universidad Mayor de San Andrés.
Cornejo Polar, Antonio. 1999. Para una teoría literaria hispanoamericana: A veinte años de un debate decisivo (1992). *Revista de crítica literaria latinoamericana* 15.50: 5–12.
Cornejo Polar, Antonio. 2004. *Indigenismo* and heterogeneous literatures: Their double sociocultural statute. Trans. Christopher Dennis. In *The Latin American cultural studies reader*, ed. Ana Del Sarto, Alicia Ríos, and Abril Trigo. Durham: Duke University Press.
Corral, Wilfrido H. Vargas Llosa and the history of ideas: Avatars of a dictionary. In *Mario Vargas Llosa and Latin American politics*, ed. Juan E. De Castro and Nicholas Birns, 189–211. New York: Palgrave.
Cortázar, Julio. 1970. *Viaje alrededor de una mesa.* Buenos Aires: Editorial Rayuela.
Cortés, Enrique. 2009. Writing the mestizo: José María Arguedas as ethnographer. *Latin American and Caribbean Ethnic Studies* 4(2): 171–189.
Cueto, Alonso. Reality and rebellion. An overview of Mario Vargas Llosa's literary themes. In *The Cambridge companion to Mario Vargas Llosa*, ed. Efraín Kristal and John King, 9–21. Cambridge: Cambridge University Press.
Culler, Jonathan. 1999. Anderson and the novel. *Diacritics.* 29.4. *Grounds of comparison: around the work of Benedict Anderson*: 19–39.
Culler, Jonathan. 2007. *The literary in theory.* Stanford: Stanford University Press.
de Castro, Juan E. 2010. Mr. Vargas Llosa goes to Washington. In *Mario Vargas Llosa and Latin American politics*, ed. Juan E. de Castro, y Nicholas Birns, 21–27. New York: Palgrave.
de Castro, Juan E. 2011. *Mario Vargas Llosa: Public intellectual in neoliberal Latin America.* Tucson: University of Arizona Press.
de Castro, Juan E., and Nicholas Birns (eds.). 2010. *Mario Vargas Llosa and Latin American politics.* New York: Palgrave Macmillan.
de la Cadena, Marisol. 2004. *Indígenas Mestizos: Raza y cultura en el Cusco.* Lima: Instituto de Estudios Peruanos.

de la Cadena, Marisol. 2008. La producción de otros conocimientos y sus tensiones: ¿de la antropología andinista a la interculturalidad? In *Saberes periféricos. Ensayos sobre la antropología en América Latina*, ed. Iván Degregori and Pablo Sandoval, 107–152. Lima: IFEA-IEP.

de la Cadena, Marisol. ¿Son los mestizos híbridos? Las políticas conceptuales de las identidades andinas. http://www.cholonautas.edu.pe/modulo/upload/Formaciones%20de%20Indianidad%20-%20cap%203.pdf. Accessed 15 Oct 2012.

de Llano, Aymará. 2004. *Pasión y agonía: la escritura de José María Arguedas*. Catamarca: Editorial Martin.

Degregori, Carlos Iván, y Pablo Sandoval, comps. 1989. *Qué difícil es ser Dios: ideología y violencia política en Sendero Luminoso*. Lima: El Zorro de Abajo Ediciones.

Degregori, Carlos Iván, y Pablo Sandoval, comps. 1991. El aprendiz de brujo y el curandero chino: etnicidad, modernidad y ciudadanía. In *Elecciones 1990, demonios y redentores en el nuevo Perú: una tragedia en dos vueltas*, ed. Carlos Iván Degregori and Romeo Grompone, 70–132. Lima: IEP.

Degregori, Carlos Iván, y Pablo Sandoval, comps. 2008. *Saberes periféricos. Ensayos sobre la antropología en América Latina*. Lima: IFEA/IEP.

Deleuze, Gilles, y Félix Guattari. 1977. *Anti-Oedipus: Capitalism and Schizophrenia*. Trans. Robert Hurley, Mark Seem, and Helen R. Lane. New York: Viking Press.

Deleuze, Gilles, y Félix Guattari. 1987. *A Thousand Plateaus: Capitalism and Schizophrenia*. Trans. Brian Massumi. Minneapolis: University of Minnesota Press.

Díaz Quiñones, Arcadio, y Tomás Eloy Martínez. 1993. "La modernidad a cualquier precio. Conversaciones con Mario Vargas Llosa" *Página 12*, "Primer Plano". *Suplemento cultural*. Buenos Aires: 9 May 1993. http://webiigg.sociales.uba.ar/grassi/textos/vargas_llosa.pdf. Accessed 10 Oct 2012.

Domínguez, César. 2012. World literature and cosmopolitanism. In *Routledge companion to world literature*, ed. Theo Dhaen et al., 242–252. London: Routledge.

Dorfman, Ariel. 1971. Mario Vargas Llosa y José María Arguedas: dos visiones de una sola América. *Casa de las Américas* 11(64): 6–19.

Dunkerley, James. 1987. Mario Vargas Llosa: Parables and deceits. *New Left Review* 162: 118–119.

Dussel, Enrique. 1972. *Teología de la liberación y ética. Caminos de liberación latinoamericana, II*. Buenos Aires: Latinoamérica Libros.

Escárzaga-Nicté, Fabiola. 2002. La utopía liberal de Vargas Llosa. *Política y Cultura* (Universidad Autónoma Metropolitana, Unidad Xochhimilco) 17 (Spring): 217–240.

Escobar, Alberto. 1984. *Arguedas o la utopía de la lengua*. Lima: Instituto de Estudios Peruanos.

Escobar, Alberto. Relectura de Arguedas: dos proposiciones. *Ciberayllu*. http://www.andes.missouri.edu/andes/Arguedas/AE_Relectura1.html. Accessed 7 Dec 2012.

Espezúa Salmón, Ruben Dorian. Científicos sociales versus críticos literarios (*Todas las sangres* en debate). S.e. S.f. http://www.cybertesis.edu.pe/sisbib/2007/espezua_sr/pdf/espezua_sr.pdf. Accessed 7 Dec 2012.

Faulkner, William. 1956. The art of fiction (Interview). *The Paris Review* 12 (Spring). http://www.theparisreview.org/interviews/4954/the-art-of-fiction-no-12-william-faulkner. Accessed 7 Dec 2012.

Faveron Patriau, Gustavo. 2002. Comunidades imaginables (Benedict Anderson, Mario Vargas Llosa, la novela y America Latina. *Lexis* 26(2): 441–467.

Flores Galindo, Alberto. 1992. *Dos ensayos sobre José María Arguedas*. Lima: Casa de Estudios del Socialismo Sur.

Flores Galindo, Alberto. 1994. *Buscando un inca. Identidad y utopía en los Andes*. Lima: Editorial Horizonte.

Flores Galindo, Alberto. Reencontremos la dimensión utópica. Carta a los amigos. *Ciberayllu*. http://www.andes.missouri.edu/andes/Especiales/AFG_CartaAmigos.html. Accessed 16 Aug 2012.

Forgues, Roland (ed.). 1993. *José María Arguedas. La letra inmortal. Correspondencia con Manuel Moreno Jimeno*. Lima: Ediciones de Los Ríos Profundos.

Franco, Jean. 1991. ¿La historia de quién? La piratería posmoderna. *Revista de Crítica Literaria Latinoamericana* 33: 11–20.

Franco, Jean. 2002a. *The decline and fall of the lettered city. Latin America in the Cold War*. Cambridge: Harvard University Press.

Franco, Sergio R. 2002b. Reseña a Mario Vargas Llosa. *El lenguaje de la pasión*. *Revista de Crítica Literaria Latinoamericana* 28(56): 273–289.

Franco, Sergio R. (ed.). 2006. *José María Arguedas: hacia una poética migrante*. Pittsburgh: Instituto Internacional de Literatura Iberoamericana, Serie ACP.

Franco, Sergio R. 2010. Diez líneas de fuerza de la crítica arguediana. *Revista de Crítica Literaria Latinoamericana* 36(72): 341–358.

Franco, Sergio R. 2012. *In(ter)venciones del yo*. Madrid: Iberoamericana/Vervuert, Serie ETC.

Franco, Jean. 1999. Narrator, author, superstar. Latin American narrative in the age of mass culture. In *Critical passions: Selected essays*, 147–168. Durham: Duke University Press.

Franco, Jean. Pastiche in contemporary Latin American literature. In *Critical passions: Selected essays*, 393–404.

Franco, Jean. What's left of the *intelligentsia*? The uncertain future of the printed word. In *Critical passions: Selected essays*, 196–207.

Franco, Jean. 1999. *Critical passions: Selected essays*, ed. Mary Louise Pratt and Kathleen Newman. Durham: Duke University Press.

Franco, Sergio R. 2005. Tecnologías de la representación en *El hablador* de Mario Vargas Llosa. *Espéculo. Revista de estudios literarios.* http://www.ucm.es/info/especulo/numero30/hablador.html Accessed 18 Apr 2012.

Franco, Jean. 2006. Alien to modernity: The rationalization of discrimination. *A contracorriente* 3, 3 (Spring): 1–16.

Franco, Sergio R. 2010. The recovered childhood: Utopian liberalism and mercantilism of skin in *A fish in the water*. In *Vargas Llosa and Latin American politics*, ed. Juan E. de Castro, 125–136. New York: Palgrave Macmillan.

Fuentes, Carlos. 1980. *La nueva novela hispanoamericana*. México: Cuadernos de Joaquín Mortiz.

Furtado, Celso. 1964. *Desarrollo y subdesarrollo*. Buenos Aires: Eudeba.

Geertz, Clifford. *Works and lives: The anthropologist as author*. Stanford: Stanford University Press, 198.

Gómez Mango, Edmundo. 1990. Todas las lenguas. Vida y muerte de la escritura en '*Los Zorros*' de J. M. Arguedas. In *El zorro de arriba y el zorro de abajo*, ed. Eve-Marie Fell, 360–368. Madrid: Editorial Archivos.

González Casanova, Pablo. 2009. *De la sociología del poder a la sociología de la explotación. Pensar América Latina en el siglo XXI*. Bogotá: CLACSO/Siglo del Hombre Ediciones.

González Casanova, Pablo. Colonialismo interno (Una redefinición). http://bibliotecavirtual.clacso.org.ar/ar/libros/campus/marxis/P4C2Casanova.pdf. Accessed 29 Junio 2012.

González Vigil, Ricardo. 1995. Introducción. In *Los ríos profundos*, ed. José María Arguedas, 11–67. Madrid: Editorial Cátedra.

Guattari, Félix. 1995. *Chaosmosis: An Ethico-Aesthetic Paradigm*. Trans. Paul Bains and Julian Pefanis. Bloomington: Indiana University Press.

Gutiérrez, Gustavo. 1971. *Teología de la Liberación. Perspectivas*. Salamanca: Ediciones Sígueme.

Gutiérrez, Gustavo. 1988. *A Theology of Liberation: History, Politics, and Salvation*. Trans. Caridad Inda and John Eagleson. Maryknoll: Orbis Books.

Gutiérrez, Gustavo. 1990. *Entre las calandrias Un ensayo sobre José María Arguedas*. Lima: CEP.

Gutiérrez, Miguel. 2008. *La generación del 50: un mundo dividido*. Lima: Arteidea.

Hare, Cecilia. Arguedas y el mestizaje de la lengua: *Yawar fiesta*. Actas XIII Congreso AIH. (Tomo III). http://cvc.cervantes.es/literatura/aih/pdf/13/aih_13_3_022.pdf. Accessed 7 Jun 2012.

Herlinghaus, Hermann (ed.). 2002. *Narraciones anacrónicas de la modernidad. Melodrama e intermedialidad en América Latina*. Santiago de Chile: Editorial Cuarto Propio.

Housková, Anna, Jana Hermuthová, and Klára Schirová. 2004. *Arguedas en el corazón de Europa*. Prague: Instituto de Estudios Románicos.